TRADITIONAL EMBROIDERIES OF INDIA

TRADITIONAL EMBROIDERIES OF INDIA

DR. (MRS.) SHAILAJA D. NAIK

A.P.H. PUBLISHING CORPORATION
Ansari Road, Darya Ganj,
New Delhi-110002

Published by
S.B. Nangia
A.P.H. Publishing Corporation
4435–36/7, Ansari Road, Darya Ganj,
New Delhi-110002
Phone: 011–23274050
e-mail: aphbooks@gmail.com

2026

Rs. 1495/-

Typeset by
Ideal Publishing Solutions
C-90, J.D. Cambridge School,
West Vinod Nagar, Delhi-110092

Printed at
RD DIGITAL PRINTERS
Ansari road , Daryaganj, Delhi-110002

FOREWORD

Embroidery is a beautiful thread work on a variety of fabrics, which makes the fabric more attractive. Women are the pioneers in creating excellent delicate embroidered garments since ancient times. In India, it has been practiced since sixteenth century which is being traced from the wall paintings, figurines found in India's valley civilization and sculptures. Due to its wide diversity in people and customs, we find wide variety in embroidery decorating cotton, silk, wool and velvet cloth with various types of stitches, and customary colours making the garment look beautiful and attractive.

The craftsmanship from every State has its own excellency, attracting people from all parts of the world. In the present fashion world, embroidered garments are preferred both by Men and Women. The use of various motifs, both natural and geometrical, colours, threads, application of stitches on different textures of the fabric to create master-piece is the beauty of the Indian craftsmanship. The use of mirrors, beads, precious pearls and stones, golden and silver threads on delicate designs add to the luxury of the garment which can be valued in terms of crores of rupees.

The creative embroideries are done on articles of personal wear like the Kurtas, Dupattas, Veils, Sarees, Hand-kerchiefs and dress materials of all kinds of Turbans. The household decorative accessories like curtains, luncheon and dinner mats, napkins, tray, wall-hanging pieces, and table covers can also carry on them the delicate embroidery motifs and borders to enhance the pleasant look of the room with their delicacy and beauty. Above all the embroidered articles done by the devoted hands are an excellent gift to reveal the real sentiments of love and devotion.

The taste for embroidered garments in the modern society is in increasing demand due to the fast changing fashions and their gracious look. Some of the traditional embroideries need to be popularised and develop into an industrial craft in order to save the reminiscent beauty of the past and everlasting art.

Here is a book written by Dr. (Mrs.) Shilaja which deals with all the traditional embroideries of India, their origin and know-how of each and every type of embroidery from all the States of the Country in a simple, meaningful language. The beautiful motifs and patterns collected and presented in the book can make the reader to understand clearly about the traditional embroideries.

The devotion in compilation and constructing of this book is worth appreciating. I hope this book will be very useful for the Home Science students as well as for those who are undergoing job oriented courses. The book will also serve as a guide for those who want to start embroidery on a commercial basis and who are interested to know about all the traditional embroideries of India.

Place : Dharwad
Date : May 8, 1995

N.L. MAURYA
DEAN

Preface

India, the country has the rich heritage of culture, tradition, art, music, literature, sculpture and does exhibit 'Unity in Diversity' through variegated charms of festivals, rituals, art, music, costume and languages. Clothing play an important role in the life of every individual since it is symbolic. It is a symbol to identify the groups of people regionwise, culturewise and designates the rank, role, occupation, status, standard of living of community at large. Clothing, not only the article used by people to cover but also a part and parcel of decoration that encircles, includes, painting, dyeing, printing, embroidery, ornaments cosmetics tattoos, hair dress, foot wear and other accessories.

It is observed from the ancient time, even the primitive man did decorate himself through bodily decoration and ornamenting his attire. Primitive man worshipped 'Nature' and it was one of the sources of inspiration from which he picked up motifs of floral, bird and animal kingdom available geographically. Dyeing and printing of various motifs through simple techniques of natural dyeing was not an end but a start to establish many handicrafts.

Indians are world famous for their magnificent workmanship and produced the most beautiful handspun and handwoven textiles, yet preserved and exhibited in many of the known Indian as well as western museums. Many visitors, poets, travelers, tourists appreciated the textile and embroidery of India to the core.

Each state in the country is unique by itself as far as textiles and its variegated designs are concerned. The traditional embroidery of each state has influence of not only the foreign countries like Persia, China, Iran etc., but also the neighbouring states too. Though, this being the fact, the statewise embroideries are unique and not a duplication of others. This is mainly because of the difference in the mode of people, the availability of indigenously manufactured textile material, ground fabric, influence of ecology, custom, festival, diety, occupation, skill, likes and flare for various motifs, technique of stitchery, threads and so on. However, it can be said that, the local people are totally responsible and are the pioneers of their unique embroidery.

Fashion is vicious circle, keeps on changing its trend from time to time, place to place and people to people. However, this change has hardly tapped the beauty of the traditional embroidery of any state. Infact in today's world, the traditional motifs, colours and technique have occupied almost a permanent base in the field of textiles. It is true that many of the natural, stylized and geometrical designs (motifs) used in todays textile designing have been taken from the traditionally based motifs. It is but natural at this juncture that there arises an urge to study and learn about the traditional embroideries of India statewise.

Therefore, an attempt has been made to prepare the treatise which narrates all about the traditional embroideries of some of the states like Bihar, Bengal, Gujarat, Himachal Pradesh, Karnataka, Kashmir, Manipur, Orissa, Punjab, Rajasthan, Uttar Pradesh and Metal embroidery.

This book is specially useful for the Home Science students both at UG and PG levels who study the traditional embroideries of India. The Pupils of textile designing, Polytechnic, textile manufacturing, job oriented courses (Textiles and Clothing) and the public at large.

This book is written for the people who is approaching an interdisciplinary study of embroidery for the first-time. The beginner may beat any academic level from undergraduate to graduate and graduate to post graduate, may be from any curriculum like Home Science, Textiles and Clothing, Textile Designing, Polytechnic, Job Oriented Courses (JOC) who need an exposure and enhancement in the field. In most of the Home Science, Textile, Clothing, Textile designing programmes, a student would normally study these contents.

This book can act as guide to the tutor who undertakes the teaching of Home Science, Textiles Designing, Polytechnic, Job Oriented Courses (JOC), to an embroiderer who works on commercial scale, to a batik painter as reference and other readers.

DR. (MRS.) SHAILAJA D. NAIK

Contents

CHAPTER 1
KANTHA OF BENGAL

The traditional folk art of Bengal is famous as Kantha which means 'Patched Cloth', and the special significance of kantha is quilting. The Dacca muslin saris of gray, black or white coloured, are one of the most artistic and beautiful specimens of Handloom textiles, were considered as very valuable by the women folk of Bengal. There are two types of embroideries. In the first type, the old and discarded cotton saris or dothis were piled up on the top of each other, quilted and embroidered. And the other type was quilted by using the discarded cotton bed spreads and the pictorial embroidery was done with Tussar silk threads.

Kantha stands as a model for skilled certainty. Because this fantastic embroidered piece is revived by utilising the wornout textiles, literally rags that would have been normally thrown away. It is a treasured art of every door where in, the Bengali ladies irrespective of their castes, classes and socio-economic groups, are expertised. The embroidery not only depicts the stitches employed but it also expresses the outflow of their creative, resourceful, imaginary, patient craftsmanship.

The size and thickness of Kantha varied according to its type. The layers of pieces are sewn together by simple darning stitch in white thread, drawn from the old sari borders. The design is first traced and the filling is done by coloured threads, taken from the coloured borders of saris.

Kanthas were produced in Hugli, Patna, Satagon, Jessore, Faridpur, Khulna and other parts of East and West Bengal. The Kantha of each individual is unique by itself. Because its always her own creation, idea, innovation, taste of fancies, and art of executing new fresh forms, designs, figures and motifs. It is the traditional art greatly encouraged by the family and therefore no scope for imitation. Though the ideas, themes, scenes and symbols are almost common as they come from similar ecological background, there is wide variation in the structural and decorative arrangement of the designs, composition of motifs combination of figures and colour scheme, technique and presentation varied from woman to woman. However, some basic traditional designs are commonly seen in each piece of their work.

The Needle work is done by original darning stitch along with satin and loop stitches. There are two modes of working. In the first style, the embroidery starts from the centre and ends by outlining the motif or vice versa. However, the embroidery gives rich textural effects by adding traditional colours like black, deep blue and red, which symbolise the nature, earth, sky and space respectively.

The motifs used in kantha embroidery has a great influence of Portuguese and European traditions. The first factory in India was started at Patna during the year 1920. Dr. Stella Karamrisch writes that kantha was first manufactured in 1875. The motifs are composed of heterogeneous objects like various types of lotus flowers, Mandala, Satadala padma, trees, creepers, foliages, floral scrolls, kalkas, animal figures, human figures, spirals, whirls, birds, fish, boats, submarine sceneries, ships, pitcher, mermaids, various sea monsters, comb, mirror, nut cracker, umbrella, chariot, palanquine etc.

The designs of kantha are taken from day to day life, depicting folk stories, epics, mythological background, ritualistic motifs, luxurious vegetation with roaming animals, deer running, dancing peacock, temples, hukkas, jewelleries, various types of costumes and so on, Some kanthas even represent the steeds of Gods like bull, swan lion, elephant, peacock, mouse, cat, eagle, owl, and swan.

The original kantha is double faced where the design appeared identical on either sides of the quilt. The great length of stitch is broken into tiny tackings which give almost a dotted appearance on either sides of the quilt like 'Do rukha'. Sometimes the embroidery is so finely done that it is very difficult to identify the wrong side.

Most of the Bengali women wear white saris and thus the background of the quilt material is often white. In order to break the monotony of this, and over come the dullness, a sort of open mesh of cut work effect is produced by drawing the threads, pulling the stitches or piercing the holes, specially in the corners. The main colours used are white, red, deep blue and black.

Bengal is also known for its applique art and is popular because of its very rarity. There are of two styles. The large and bold designs worked on wall hangings, canopies, bedspreads, tents, banners, flags where a lion or lotus motif is cut out in red material and appliqued against white background. The other style is of small patterns worked on personal items and household textiles like pillow covers. This is done by cutting the coloured cloth into narrow strips and stitched as outlines of the design. Applique on quilts earned a large market in the foreign trade during sixteenth century.

Lotus is the most common and important motif widely used in Kantha. An all over pattern of lotus may have the petals of red alternating with black petals. Black thread is used to give either outline for the design or sometimes filled with the stitches of the same colour. A couple of tantric motifs like 'Vajra', the thunder bolt, 'swastik' were used along with the spiral whirl, representing the eternal life cycle. Kalka is another important motif, a cone or mango shaped, embroidered in association with spiral whirls, broad band of circles, lotus or heart shaped foliages.

There are different kinds of kanthas named according to its utility. According to Jasleen Dhamija, there are seven types of kanthas used as wrappers in winter, for books, valuables, mirrors, combs, wallets, pillows and bed spreads.

Arshilata is used as cover or wrap for mirror, comb and other such toilet articles. It is a narrow rectangular piece of eight inch wide and twelve inch length. It has a wide border and the central motif is taken from the scenes of Krishna leela or Radha-Krishna raas. The lotus, trees, creepers, spirals, inverted triangles, zig-zag lines, scrolls are also some of the commonly used motifs.

Bayton, a three feet square piece serves as a wrap for books and other similar valuables. It has a central motif, usually the lotus with hundred petals called 'Satadala Padma'. This motif with hundred petals is simply a figure, which does not signify anything precisely. The traditional and folk design of oldest style in Bayton is the Mandala which symbolises the unity of all manifestations of life. The core has Satadala Padma with two or three borders on the sides. The other motifs commonly seen are water pots, conch shells, kalkas, trees, foliages, flowers, birds, elephants, chariot, human figures etc. Sometimes the figure of lord Ganesha and Goddess Saraswati with their steeds are also observed. Special motifs on Bayton are worked with swan, as a book wrapper. In other words the designs often are elaborate and this colourful embroidery is made with yellow, green blue and red coloured threads. This kantha is often carried while travelling and also presented as gift to their kith and kins.

Durjani (Durfani) is also known as Thalia. It is a square piece kantha, covers the wallet, has a central lotus motif with an elaborated border. The three corners of this piece are drawn together inward to make the tips to touch at the centre and are sewn together like an envelop. It will have another open flap to which a string, tussle or a decorated thread is either stitched or mechanically fixed, which can be wound and tied up when rolled. The other motifs used are various types of foliages, snakes and other objects taken from the natural surroundings.

Lep kantha is relatively a thick quilted wrap padder by more number of sari layers, placed on top of each other, to provide warmth during winter season. Lep is also popular as 'desired covering'. Simple geometrical designs are worked with running stitch using coloured threads. The entire Lep piece is been given a wavy rippled appearance by working simple embroideries.

Oar (ooar), the katha serves as a pillow cover. It is a rectangular piece whose size is about two feet by one and a half feet. Usually simple designs like trees, foliages, creepers, birds or a liner design with longitudinal border constitutes the ground base and decorative border is stitched around its four sides.

The most popular and striking kantha is the Sujani (Sujni), generally large rectangular piece of three feet by six feet, used as a spread during ceremonial occasion. Its size has provided full scope for the workers to express and exhibit her imaginary, self created designs. The rectangular piece is divided into nine equal parts and the motifs are distributed in these equal sized rectangular block. The lotus motif with a whirl in the center is the commonly used motif in Sujani. The other motifs observed are the scenes from Ramayana, Mahabharat, folk tales dancing gal. men riding, birds pecking the fruits, prancing movement of the animals, bees sucking the nectar, procession in motion etc. A moderately thick, light weighed Sujani has either two or more borders at the edge to strengthen the layers and to prevent further tearing. The border stitched at the edge of the rectangular piece has geometrical patterns in single colour, while the other is more ornamental and colourful. The cover sometimes has large kalka laid horizontally and separated by Vajra, the thunder bolt or a broad band of circles, lotus in each circle and heart shaped foliage between the circles. Sarfani is also a quilt used during ceremonies or functions as a cover or wrap.

Rumal is nothing but a hand kerchief and is the smallest among all the kanthas. A square piece having a size about one square foot. Lotus is the core and other motifs embroidered around it. Sometimes plant and animal motifs are also embroidered but invariably has a well decorated border.

The bed cover and wall hanging of kanthas were famous world wide. The women picked up the motifs from the epics and mythological scenes and the nature. It represents their traditional beliefs, individual skills, art and passions towards religion. It does depict the folk art. The ritual designs are worked only on festive occasion to fulfil their vows. The special characteristic of kanthas was, it never became a replica of other folk art but remained unique by itself. Kantha work is a model with inspired romance, philosophy, sentiment and holyness.

The simple running stitch was earlier used to join all the layers of cotton materials together. Later other stitches were used to enhance the surface enrichment. During the sixteenth and seventeenth century chain stitch was worked along with running stitch. Later few more stitches like, back stitch, satin and herring bone were introduced.

Kantha exists even today in the rural areas of West Bengal, exclusively a hand made work of women folk there at. It is now produced on commercial scale. At present few centers in Bengal have been set up to revive this folk art on commercial scale.

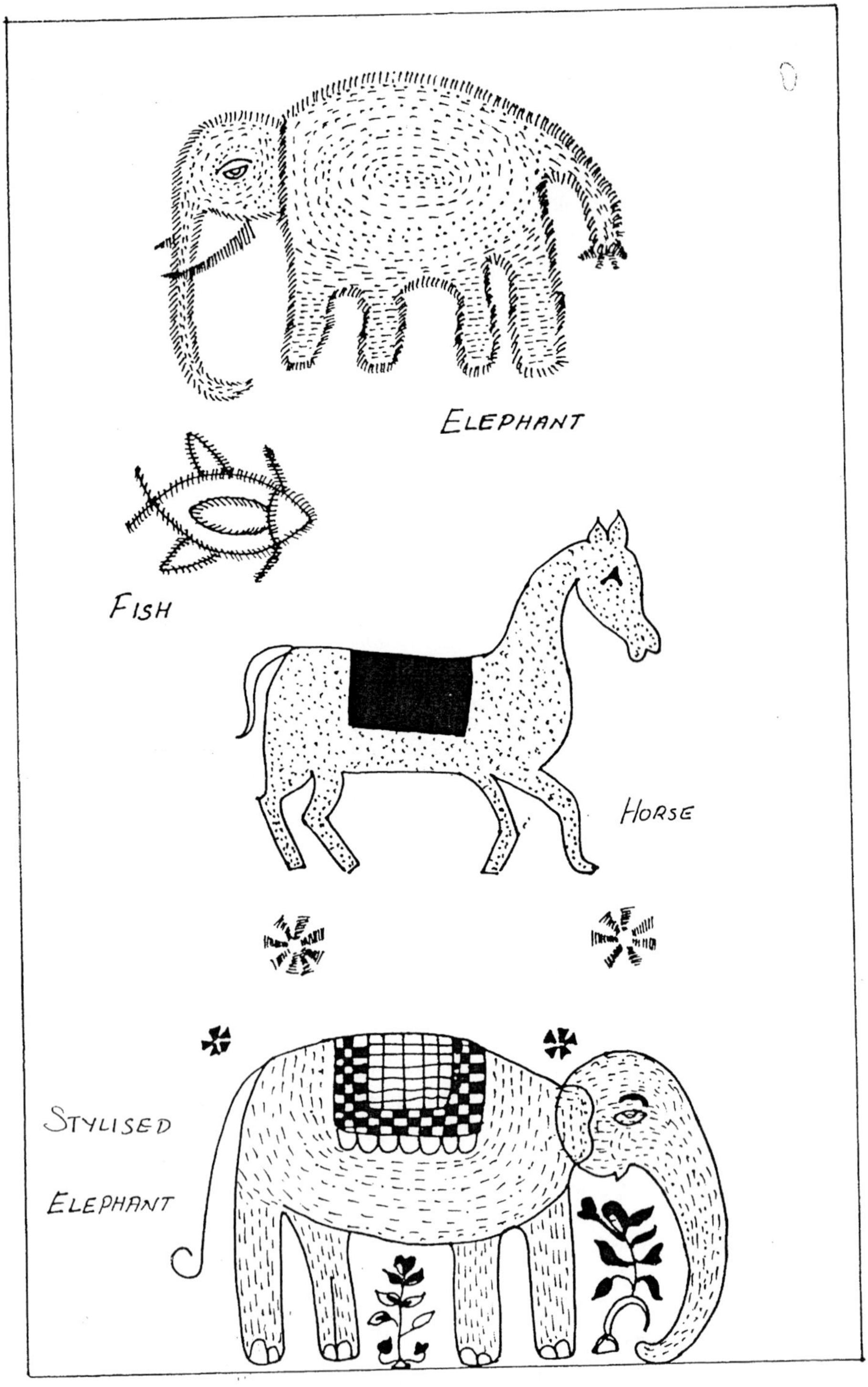
ELEPHANT
FISH
HORSE
STYLISED
ELEPHANT

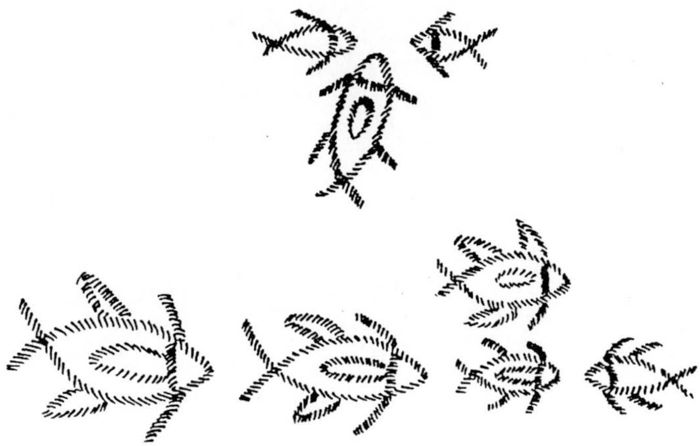

FISH

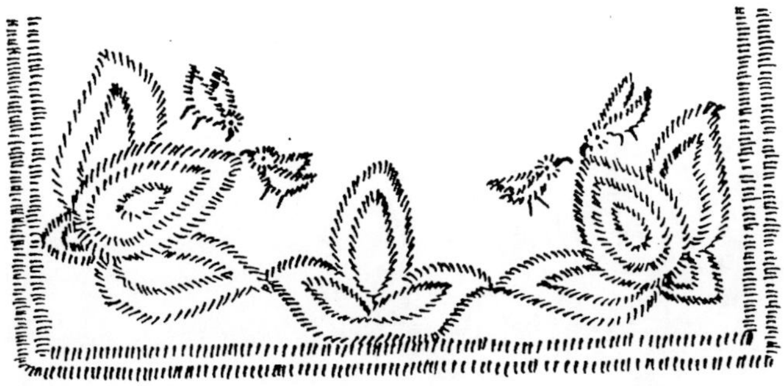

LOTUS

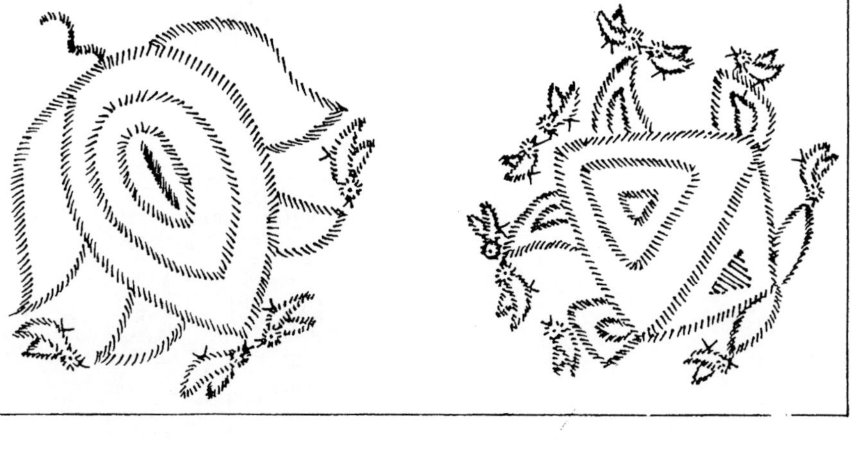

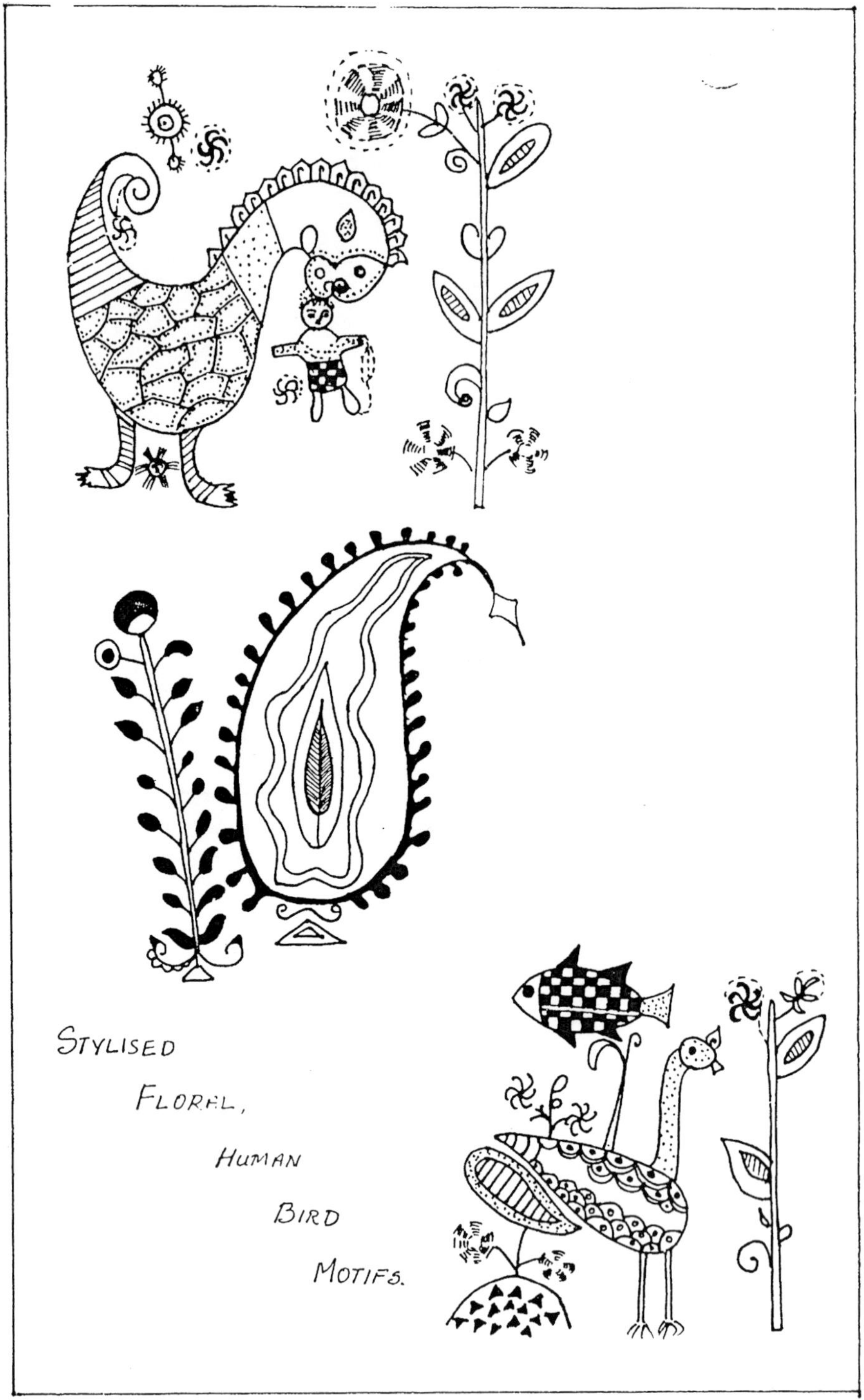

STYLISED FLORAL, HUMAN BIRD MOTIFS.

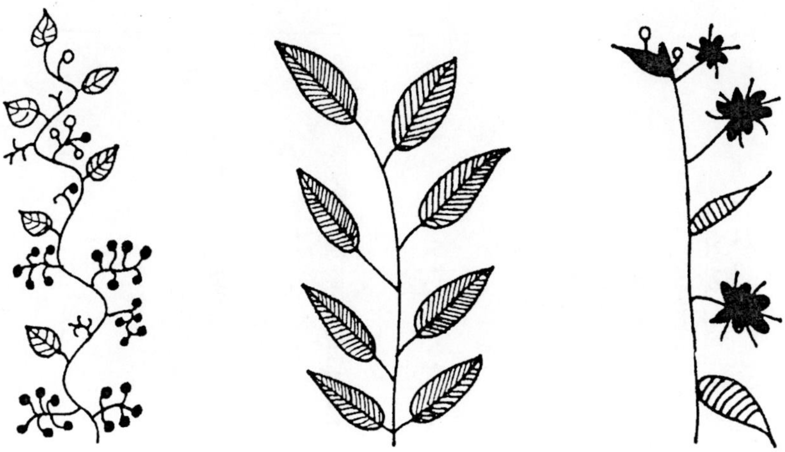

STYLISED FLORAL AND BIRD MOTIFS

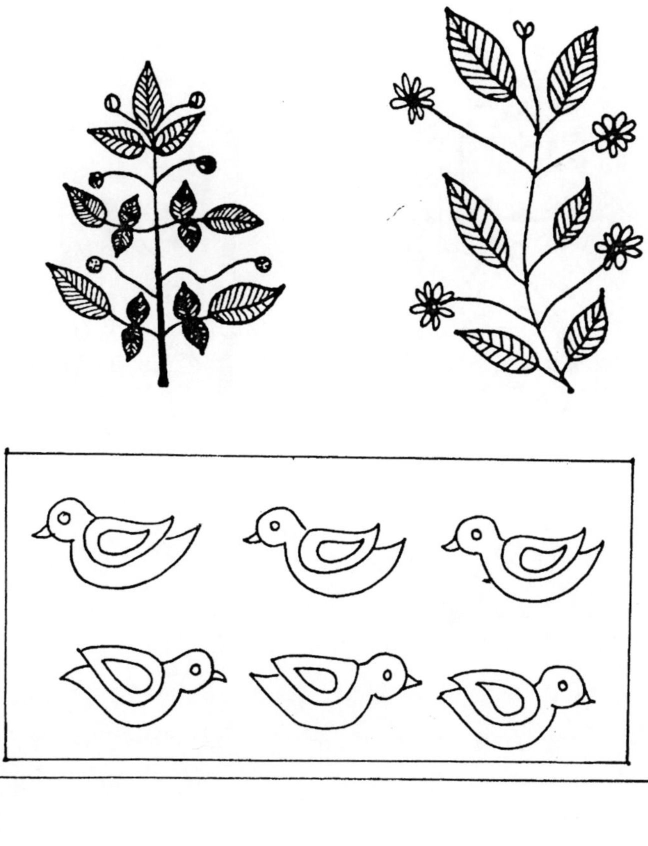

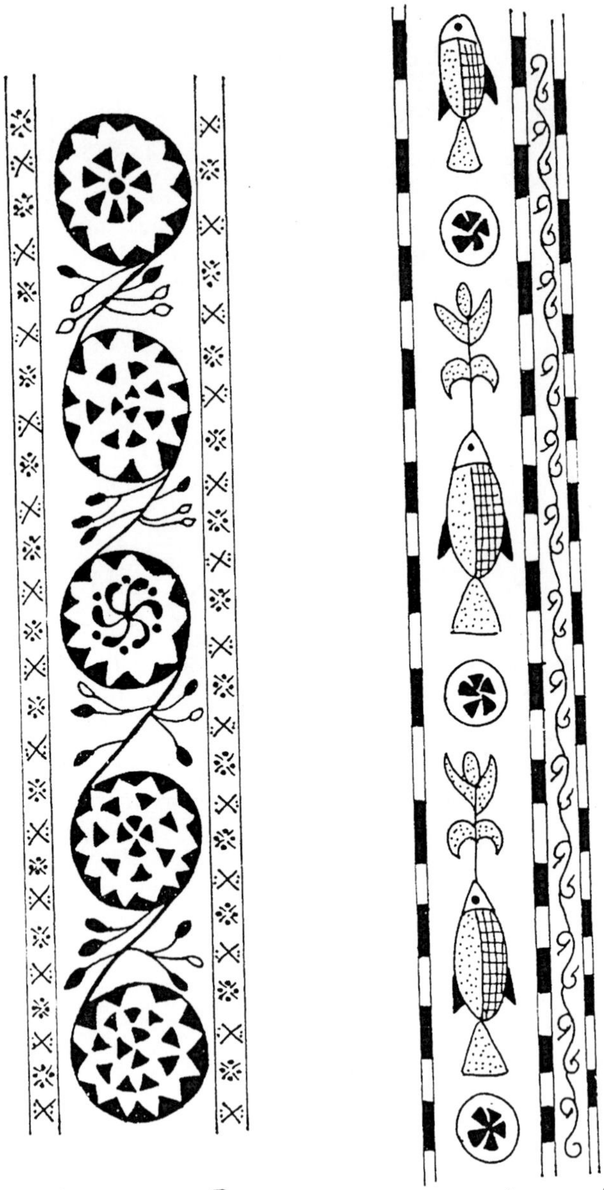

STYLISED FLORAL AND FISH MOTIFS IN BORDERS

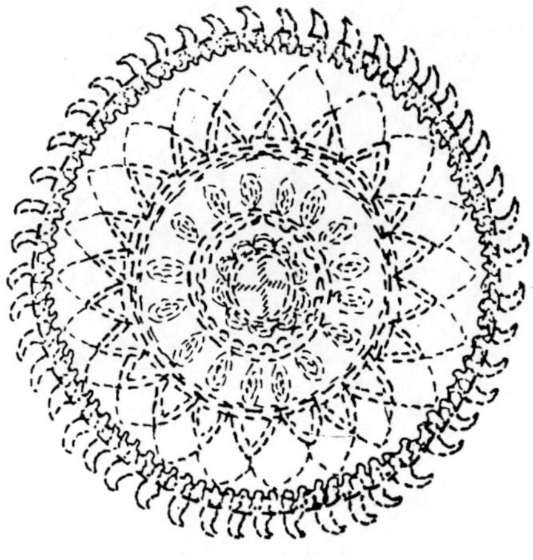

Lotus As Central Motif

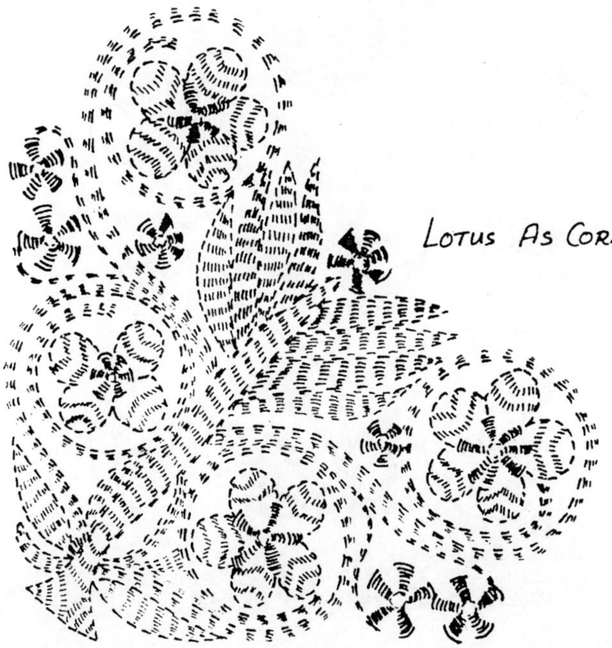

Lotus As Corner Motif

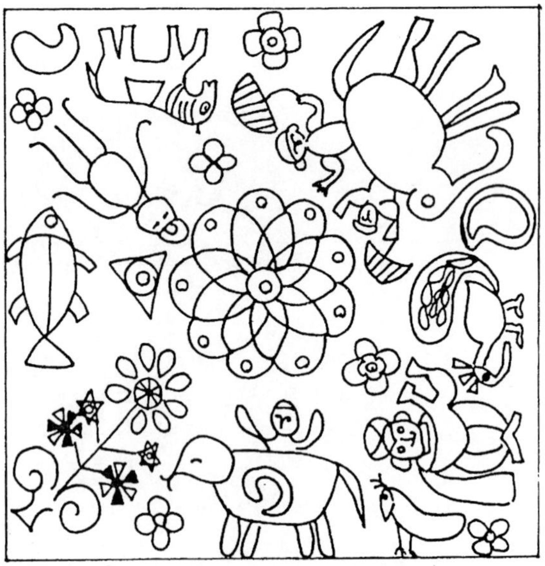

CENTRAL LOTUS SURROUNDED BY FLORAL, ANIMAL & HUMAN MOTIFS.

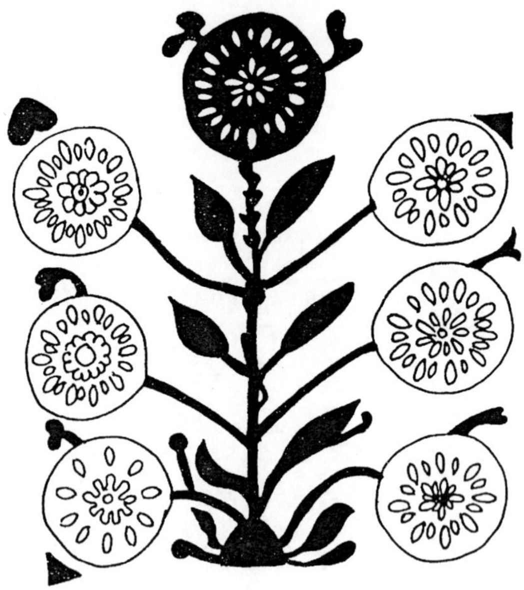

STYLISED FLOWERING TREE

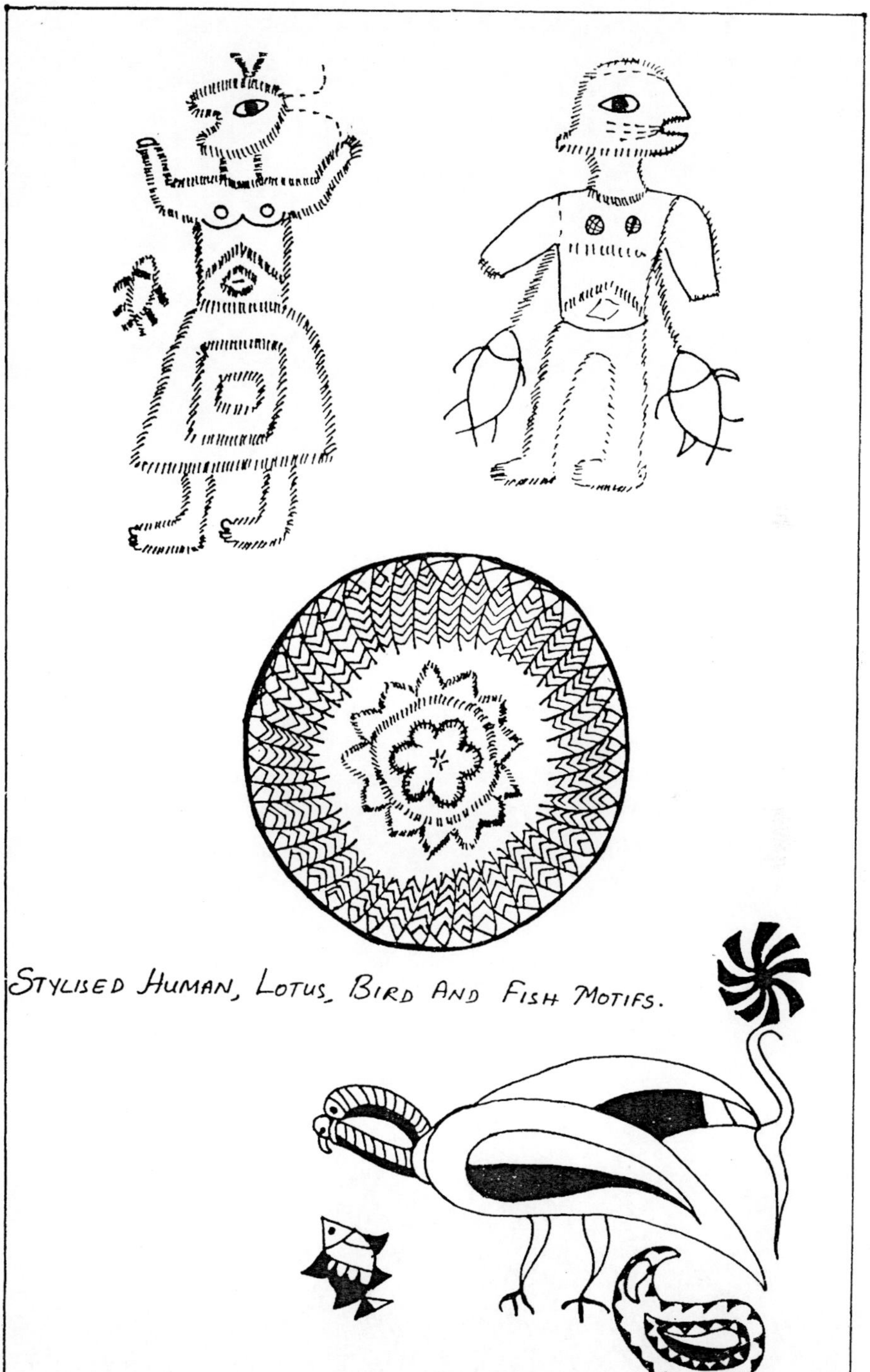

STYLISED HUMAN, LOTUS, BIRD AND FISH MOTIFS.

CHAPTER 2
KASHIDA OF BIHAR

Unlike Kashida of Kashmir, embroidery of Bihar is famous as Kashida of Bihar, more frequently done on garments of day to day use like, saris, blouses, caps, sashes, wraps, odhanis, baby bonnets and house hold textiles, like, table linens, pillow covers, cushion covers, quilts, bed spreads etc. However, the folk involved in Kashida work of Kashmir is men and that of Bihar is women.

Embroidery of Bihar is made in different styles, of these applique art is very common. This applique art is done on their own garments for personal use and sometimes produced for commercial purpose too. Since the former is for self, consists of motifs of imagination and are either abstract or highly stylized. Two techniques are employed in applique art, one in which the fabric is cut into different shapes, sizes and patterns, and the entire composition is attached. This work is famous as Khatwa, more complicated and laborious. In the other method the stripes are cutout according to the shape of the motifs and attached separately on to single piece of separate cloth to make a composition. However, applique for commercial purpose is usually confined to canopies (shamians), wall enclosures (kanats), and tents, which are used for ceremonial purposes. The motifs included are trees, flowers, foliages, birds and animals, depicting the traditional designs from Moghal empire. The background is usually either red or orange on which the applique in white or sometimes blue is worked.

The embroidery consisted of three distinct stitches namely the chain stitch, popularly known as Jhinkana (Jhinkhana), because of the slight light sound, that the needle makes when pulled through the cloth. The blouses are embroidered in chain stitch. The women have full freedom to express themselves because the designs were never copied from any books. The designs cover a wide range of items that intimate the innermost emotions of women and mostly their treasures like jewelleries such as a string with a pendant or a necklace with five or seven strands.

The other type of embroidery is 'Bharat' which resembles Bagh of Punjab. In Bharat work the stitches follow warp and weft directions, parallel to the weave. The background is usually red on which the embroidery in white, green or yellow is worked. Sometimes white background will have Bharat work in black, blue or steel blue colour. Motifs comprised of geometrical shapes, wavy lines, diamonds, simple flowers encased within the square, i.e. along with Bagh style, floral motifs were also employed.

Apart from Bharat, the geometrical patterns were embroidered with long and short stitches. And the design is outlined with running stitch either in single or double rows.

According to Jasleen Dhamija another type of stitch, a combination of chain stitch and applique work usually done on caps and blouses along with woven tapes and laces. Here, the main aim is to create variety of textures, using various types of fabrics. The combination is so unique that hardly any two caps or two blouses are alike. The most commonly found motifs are a green parrot flying with its wings wide open, a tree full of blossom exhibiting its wealth, fish swimming in a pond, a rider riding the elephant, etc. Some motifs of mythology included Durgamata on her steed, tiger, Sathi goddess and so on.

The women folk of Bihar express their views, ideas, taste and self sufficiency in producing limitless variety of quilts, popularly known as 'Sujanis'. The old cotton saris are cut into required size, piled up and sewn through all the layers with tiny darning stitches in white thread drawn from the saris itself. The central motif on quilt is bold and worked with coloured thread, drawn from the sari borders. The motifs include swan floating on the water, children playing with kites, bride in a palanquin, birds pecking fruits, Goddess Manasa Devi in multicolours, Krishna paying with Gopis etc. This art of Sujani resembles the technique of Kantha of Bengal, Sujani is usually used as a wrap or cover but sometimes used to cover the musical instruments, books and other similar valuables.

At present, among all the embroideries of Bihar, applique art is relatively popular and therefore commercialised. Embroidery work is undertaken and done on saris, dresses, cushion covers, curtains etc. A single cut out piece is stitched on the cloth supplied.

All the traditional designs are collected on a piece of cloth and made into a master chart called Awalkhana, with a view to continue this art highly attracted by the growing generation.

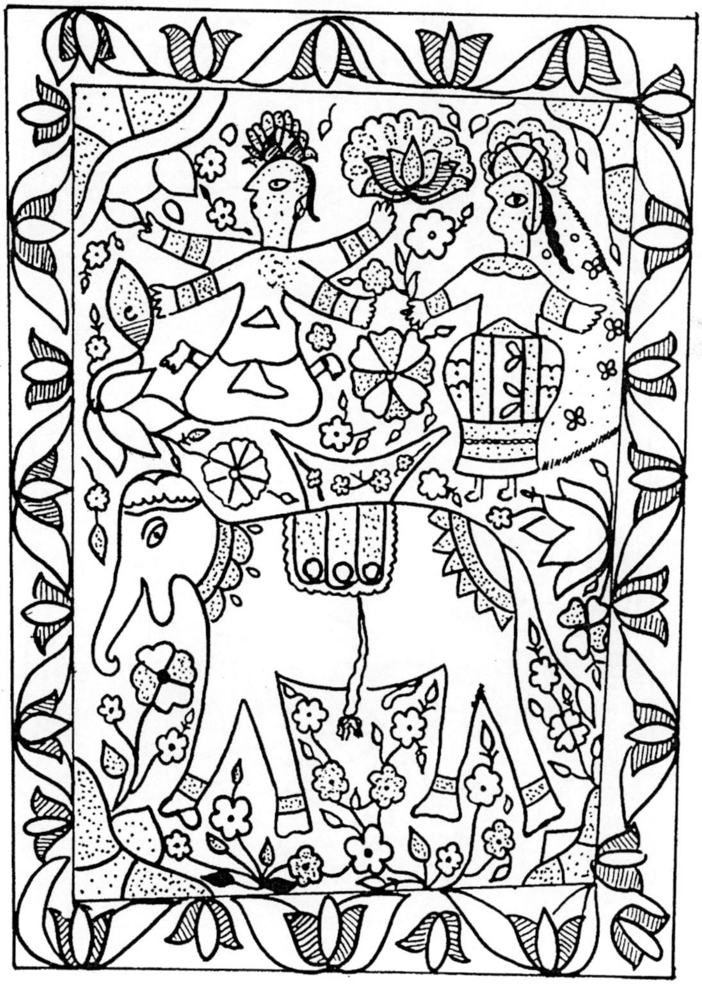

GOD INDRA & GODDESS INDRANI ON AN ELEPHANT

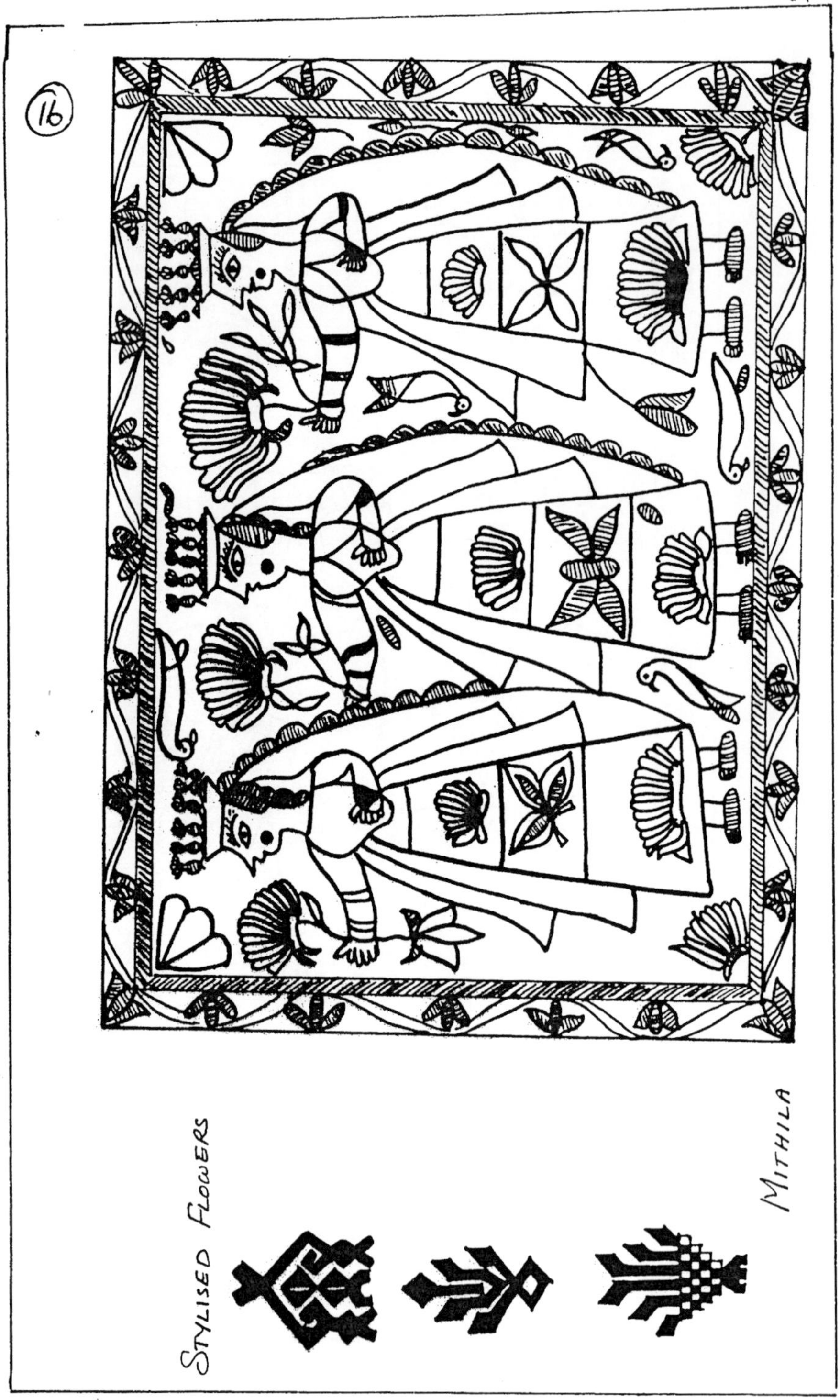
16
STYLISED FLOWERS
MITHILA

DANCING GIRLS

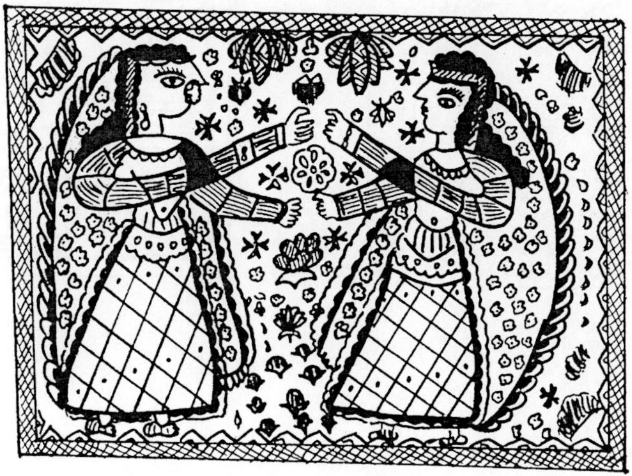

LORD KRISHNA AND RADHA DANCING

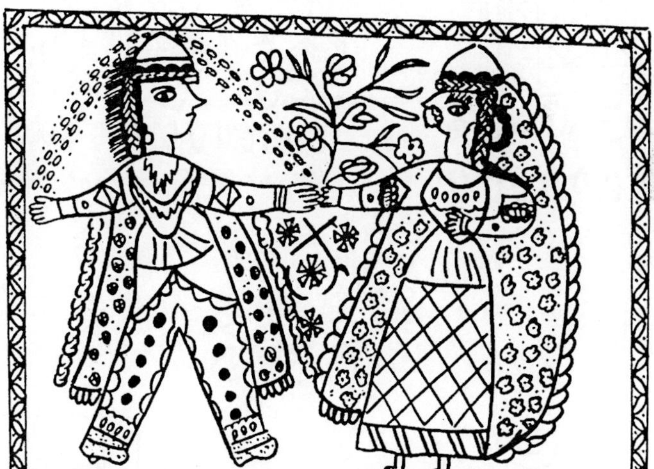

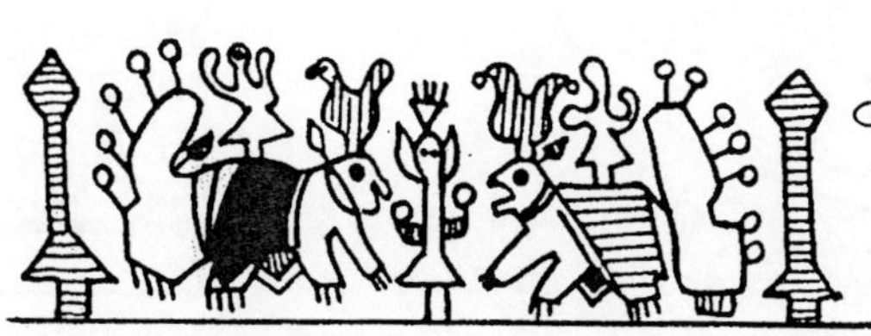

STYLISED SQUIRRELS

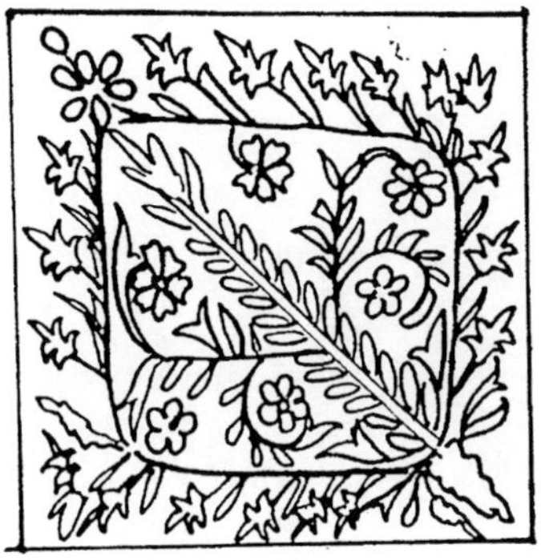

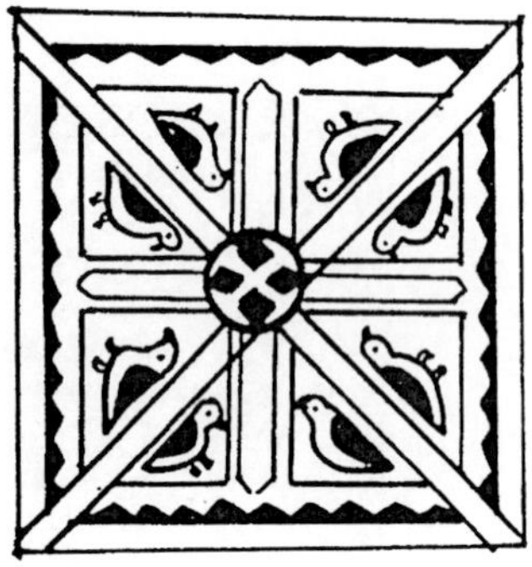

FLORAL SPRAY

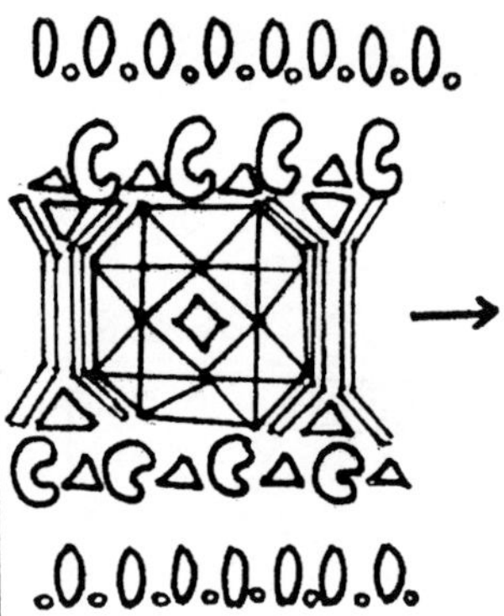

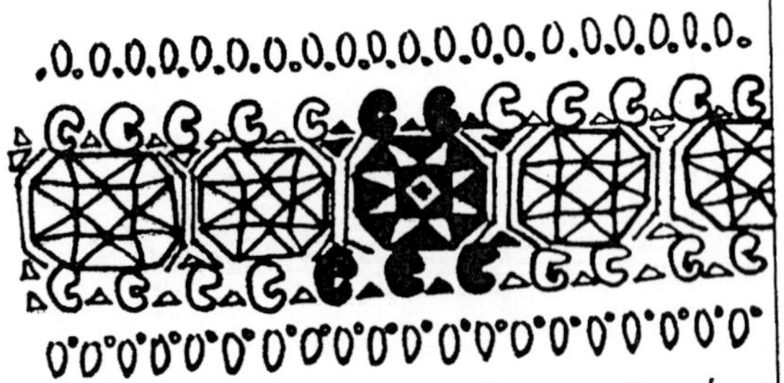

TRIANGLES & ZIG-ZAG LINE

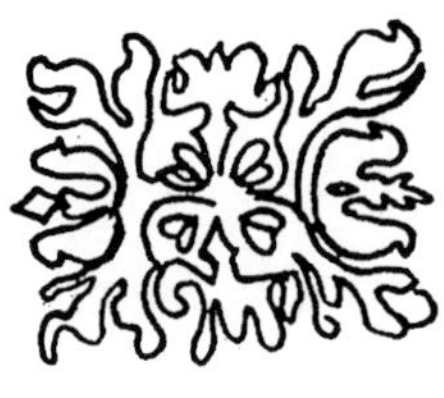

ABSTRACT MOTIF

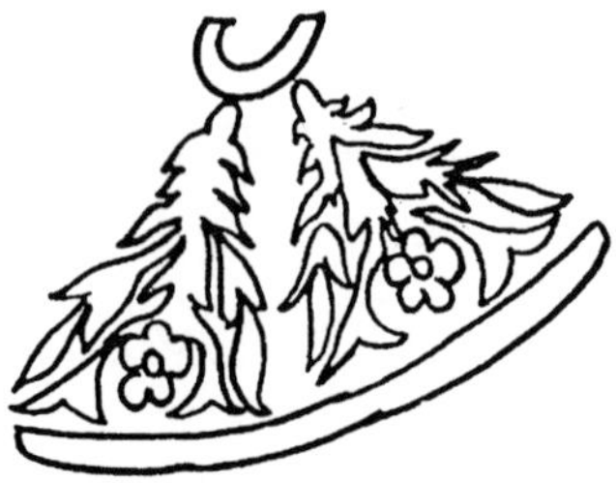

STYLISED FLOWER SPRAY

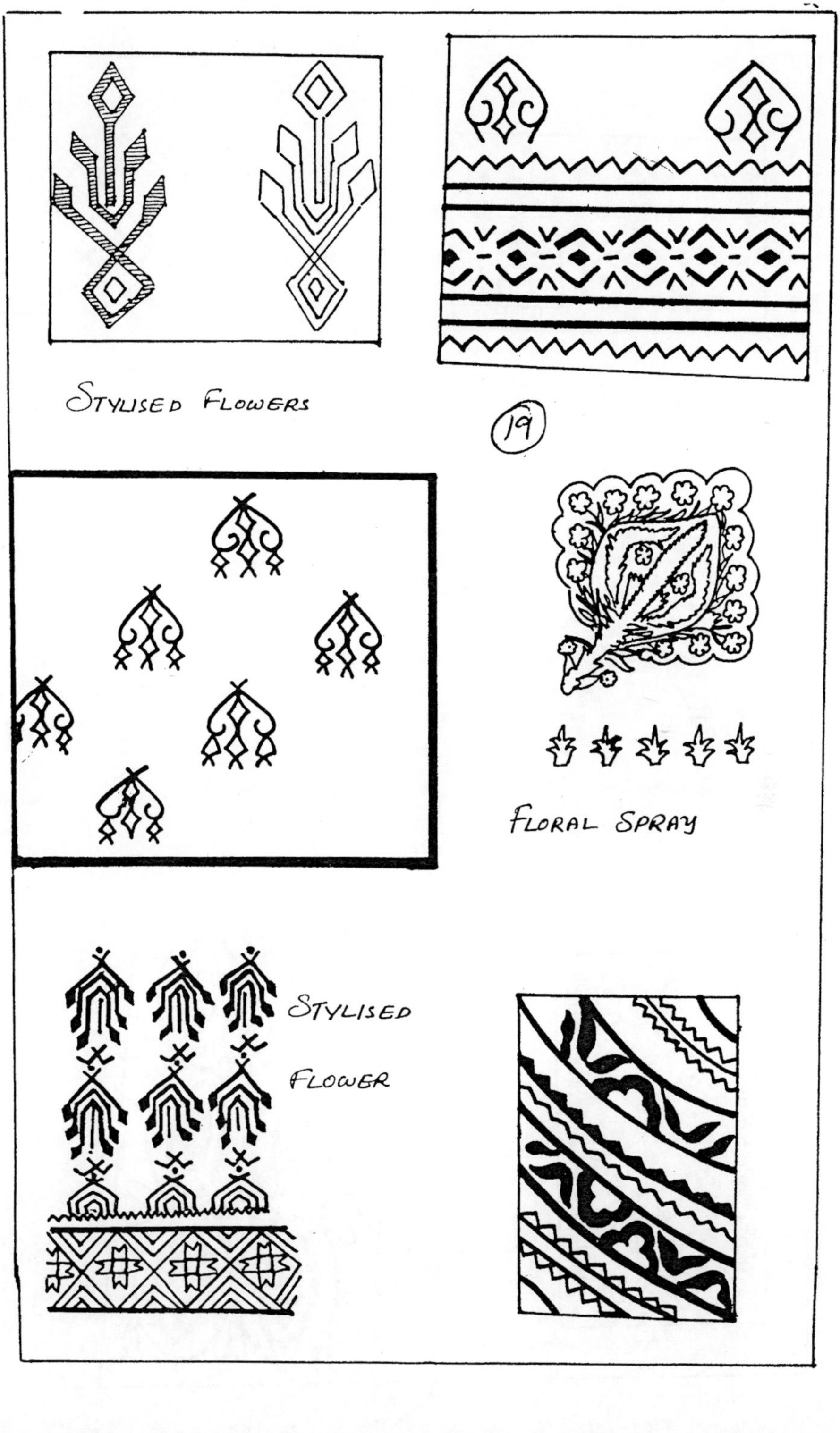
STYLISED FLOWERS
19
FLORAL SPRAY
STYLISED
FLOWER

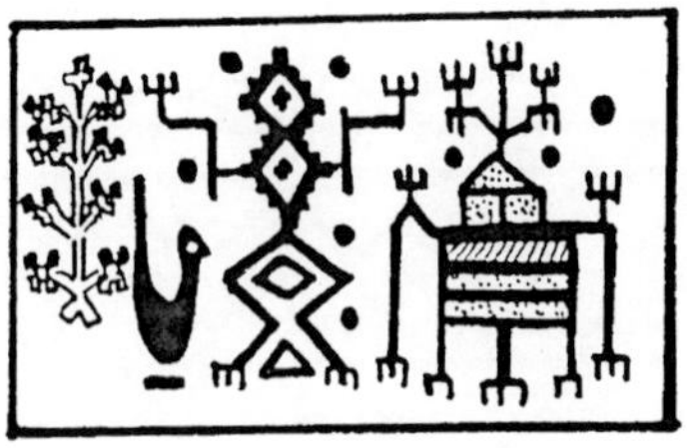

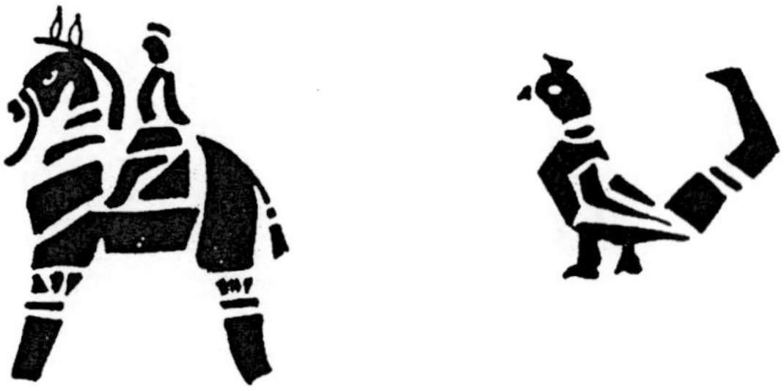

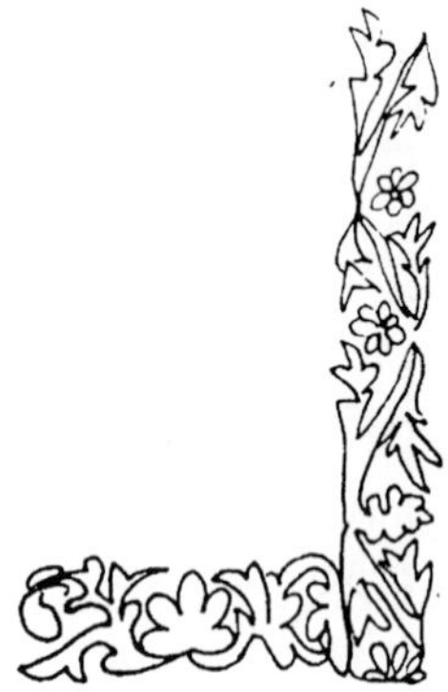

STYLISED HORSE AND PEA-COCK

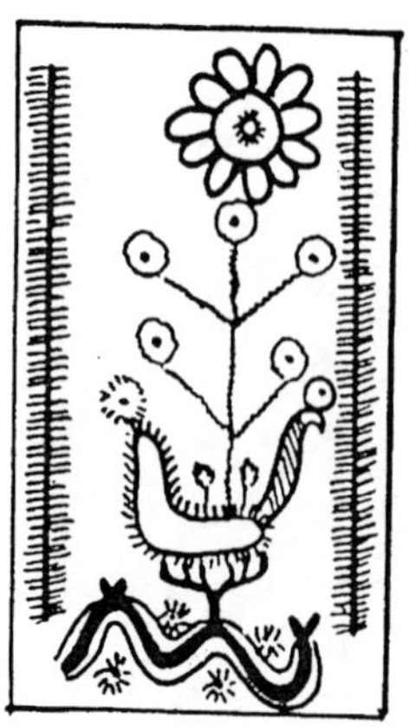

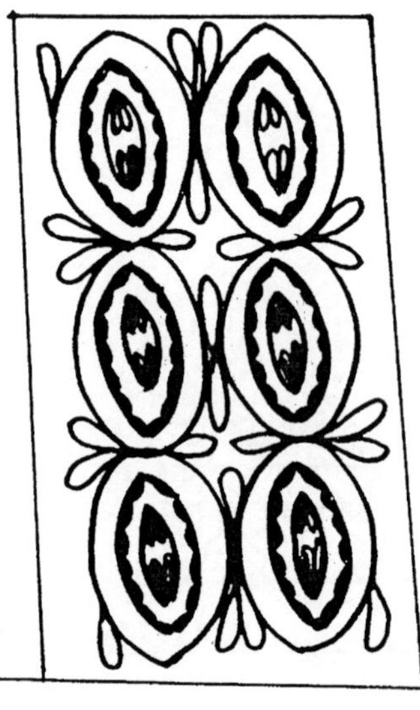

CHAPTER 3

EMBROIDERY OF GUJARAT

Gujarat, the state situated in the western part of India, is famous for the embroidery of Kutch and Kathiawar. The peasant, tribal and ladies of other community residing in the villages have maintained their tradition, culture and rich heritage through various styles of embroideries, i.e., it can be said here that greatest contribution to the Indian embroidery is from Gujarat state, precisely from Kutch and Kathiawar. However, the beauty lies in the rich designs, variety of motifs and stitches.

The village women, during their leisure time after harvesting, always engage in the needle craft and prepare beautifully embroidered costumes for their daughters each year. By the end of a decade probably the mothers can keep almost a dozen of such costumes ready to present the bride during her wedding as a part of dowry.

This embroidery was introduced by 'Kathi' the cattle breeders, who were basically wanderers and brought by Karna, the famous warrior of Mahabharat. These wonderers collected and gathered themselves in a place, and contributed variety, unique elements, patterns, designs, themes, moods and techniques of needle work, which became later an integral part of the embroidery of Gujarat. These wonderers worshipped Shiva and Ganesh and used to embroider the idols in the small squares called 'Sthapanas'.

A legend explains that, a notorious demon had enslaved thousands of women in a forest, who was killed by Lord Krishna and freed the women. Later, with passage of time, these women, turned out to be his gopikas, the playmates, who were brought to Dwarka. These women, hailing from various parts of the country were inherently talented in one or the other craft and stitchery, whose individual contribution nobled into a new form at Saurashtra.

The embroidery articles from Gujarat were world famous and exported to European countries during sixteenth and seventeenth century, said by J.M. Nanawati. However, there exists difference in the embroidery of Kutch and Kathiawar as a whole.

KUTCH EMBROIDERY

It is believed that the Kutch embroidery was taught to 'Mochis', the shoemakers around 300 years ago by a Muslim Phakeer of Sindh. However, Kutch embroidery has the foundation of various clans viz Ahirs, Kanbis, Mochis and Rabaris.

AHIRS BHARAT

The primitive peasants of Saurashtra are known regionally as Ahirs, expert in Mochi (cobbler) Bharat, usually prepared decorative articles and surface enrichment of their attires. It was totally a home craft, never attempted as commercial trade. The ladies of Ahir families, embroidered their traditional costumes during their off seasons. Ahir, is the hooked needle, with the help of which the embroidery was executed, appeared exactly like chain stitch. The embroidery is not only skillful in stitchery but talented in developing designs, preparing pattern, drawing and tracing the same on the fabric. The Ahirs from Surath and Gonagad area are well informed about the 'Khant School' embroidery, who exhibit intelligent selection in colour application of mirrors along with splendour needle work.

Kamala Dongerkery expresses that the Ahirs are a pastoral tribe which is believed to have migrated from Mathura along with Lord Krishna to Girhar in Kathiwar and thereafter might have settled in Kutch. The word Ahir may be derived from 'Ab ḥira' the Sanskrit word, means milkman.

The base material used was hand spun and hand woven coarse Khaddar on which a series of loops leading to chain stitch using Arhi along with abundant application of mirrors were observed. At present the embroidery is done on silk, or the locally manufactured satin fabric, the gajji silk, or a silky satin fabric, the Atlash

The hand work was done with colourful cotton thread on dark coloured Khaddar in olden days but now use the silky untwisted floss (heer) or the twisted silken thread, on choli, pajamas, jackets, bonnets, caps and other children's garments. The craftsman later introduced various colour schemes in the basic chain stitch to denote the stem, veins and other subtler parts of the motifs, a chief characteristic of the embroidery. Birds, flowers, creepers, foliages are some of the motifs, of them parrots, peacock, bulbul, human figure, dancing doll, karanphool, the flower shaped ear-ring, are the main.

KANBI BHARAT

Kanbis are basically the cultivators, migrated from Saurashtra, the women community engage themselves in the beautiful art of Bharat and are known for their patient work. It was cent percent home scale art where the Kanbi women got together in small groups and continue their work on household articles. The embroidery thread is cotton of yellow, orange, green, white and purple colours. The basic stitches employed are darning for out lining and herring bone for filling. The designs in Kanbi Bharat are distinct and have the influence of Persian art. They use the similar motifs as others but the specific ones are the sunflower, and kevada, the cactus flower. Kanbi folk are religious, orthodox and believe in worshipping the domestic animals like bullocks, the second lung of the cultivators. As a token of love and affection, Kanbi women prepare many beautiful articles for their domestic animals to decorate them during the festivals and while taking the procession. The articles more frequently prepared are the rectangular cover spread on the back of the bullock, conical covers, attractively tasselled to cover the horns, gorgeously embroidered veils to cover the forehead, face and muzzle. The other household articles like covers for wooden boxes, pataras, blankets and quilts, on which elaborate embroidery of parrots, peacocks, various shapes of foliages, climbers, creepers, tender twigs of mango are commonly observed. However, in Bhavnagar and Saurashtra, the lewa Kanbi take up the craft, predominant in white chain stitch for filling and running stitch for outlining.

MOCHI BHARAT

Mochi is the community belonged to the artisan, cobbler or shoemaker, who used a unique technique of preparing chappales and shoes, whose basic stitch has entered as a popular Kutchi Bharat. This craft was patronised by the local rulers and the craftsmen were engaged in Mochi work permanently. It is similar to Arhi Bharat, where the thread is pulled from the bottom to the top with the help of Arhi, creating loops and the successive repetition leads to a continuous line of chain stitch. Kamaladevi Chattopadhyay explains that, 'on garments most common buttis (polka dots), rounding off with a big size is known as Nadir Shah butti'. On larger surface areas like household textiles, many highly stylized flowers bushes, dancing doll, peacock, human figures are seen. Mochi Bharat, though appears simple, needs thorough, continuous practice to achieve efficiency. It is an elaborate embroidery usually incorporated for filling work, thus time consuming. The ground fabric in satin and articles embroidered are choli, ghagra, toran (door decoration), chaklas (square wall hangings), borders and so on.

RABARI WORK

Rabaris belong to a tribe of Giri region, usually migrating from place to place. Their style and technique of embroidery is entirely different from that of other community. Their embroidery is relatively effective, impressive, and attractive, usually done on a hand-spun, hand-woven Khaddar or Khadi material of maroon colour. The colours used are subtle and thus accentuate the stitchery. Rabaris used small piece of cloth of various size, shape, to produce bold effect against a plain background. This craft has no definite design, it appeared some what like applique work. Canopies, door curtain, partitions, wall decorations and other household articles were prepared. However, this craft was not implemented to decorate the main dresses and costumes may be because of its bold and elaborate effect, lacking delicacy, thus used only to emphasise the borders and these borders were completed with double cross stitch. The motifs comprised of beautiful birds, beasts, floura and fauna, human figures and so on.

The applique or Katab work existed in Kutch and Saurashtra where Kathis and Mahajans along with Rabaris have taken up the handicraft. They used geometrical designs done with bold and bright coloured fabric pieces of bandhani, patola brocades, satins and printed cottons, Mahajans, used white background for exception. More elaborate applique work included animal, human, bird, floral and land scapes produced by cutting and stitching in a definite all over design giving an impression of garden, water falls, valley, rainfall and so on. Their motifs expressed life, cheerfulness, action movement like horse galloping, lion roaring or springing, dog sleeping, deer hopping etc. Some composite animals like Gajasimha (half elephant and half lion), Kinnara (half human being and half horse), Mina vaji (half fish and half elephant), a golden swan with two heads, one each looking forward and backward, Kesari Simha, the king of thirty two kinds of Simhas has long hair, hump at the back, body like horse with along tail. Sun and Moon are being worshipped and used as motifs in their art. Moon symbolises the rabbit which narrates the story from Jataka tales.

These embroidery pieces now are sold on the pavements of few cities, of which most of them are used as decorative household articles like chaklas, torans, bhitiya (wall hanging), chandrawas (rectangular wall hangings), cushion cover, for divans and bolster.

KATHIAWAR EMBROIDERY

Gujarat is embedded in with Rajasthan, Maharashtra, Arabian sea and Pakistan. The embroidery of Kathiawar is similar to that of Sindh to some extent, unique in its own style. The craft is basically employed to decorate the traditional ladies costume of Gujarat, the Choli and Ghagra (chaniya). Kathiawar embroidery has a great influence of neighbouring states and places like Sindh, Punjab and Kutch. According to Jasleen Dhamija the Kathiawar women not only beautified their traditional costume by embroidering in vivid colours but also prepared household articles like toran, Chakla and Chandrawa. Displaying toran at the doorway is a symbol of welcoming the guests, as believed by the folk. It was also believed that the beautifully carved and decorated entrance doorways are the symbol of welcoming the people entered and the poorest of the poor, in absence of such carved doors, prepared the torans at her own labour. Brij Bushan explains, 'toran is a long embroidered flap or bits of patterned cloth decorating the lower edge of the valance'. During the wedding time, all the new costumes stitched for the bride are tied into a bundle by toran and latter is used as a decorate for doorways as symbol of welcome.

The main feature of Kathiawar embroidery is the lavish application of mirrors. However, the base stitches used are chain stitch, Heer Bharat, Abla Bharat and interlacing stitch or Sindhi taropa.

Chain stitch is similar to that of Kutch, but most of the times done with white colour and occasionally supplemented with other colours to give a bold impression. Chain stitch is accompanied by mirrors and used to emphasise face, eyes, hand, flower, sun, moon etc. The motifs also comprised of gal holding a flower, boy playing kite, man riding a horse and a palanquin. It is a distinct style of Bhavanagar embroidery.

Heer Bharat is the embroidery done with silk floss, the pat, highly lustrous, gorgeous that brings rich effect on the base. Though the stitch employed is darning, the name Heer Bharat is given for the thread that is being employed. The influence of phulkari of Punjab is evident at this juncture. Not only with respect to silk floss, the embroidery of Kathiawar tallies with stitchery and geometrical motifs of Phulkari. The composite units of square, triangles, rectangles and hexagonals cover the complete ground fabric. It resembles Bagh of Phulkari. The long stitches in each triangle run parallel to weft and perpendicular to warp producing shot coloured (light and dark) effect. According to Kamaladevi Chattopadhyay, 'Heer Bharat is carried on a bluish gray base with deep orange, dark blue and purple coloured floss, very rarely white. However, the most dominant colour is crimson red with little of cream and black, indigo, ivory, yellow and green in small places to touch up. At times to emphasise a pattern, design or motif, a small mirror is affixed in the center by buttonhole stitch. An interesting design was created by dividing a square into four equal triangles and a mirror in the center. Two each corresponding triangles are filled in by long stitches in vertical and horizontal direction. Gudari is a popular quilting where swirls and spirals are worked out with long stitches especially in black colour, building a background for the actual design. Over this background of black colour the motifs are embroidered in contrasting colours, however the emphasis is made by use of mirrors randomly.

Abhla Bharat is nothing but use of mirrors or a mirror inset embroidery. Though it is the traditional embroidery of Kathiawar, is now universally appreciated and thus used by all folk ways of India. The current trend is to inset the mirrors on a dark background to bring about a glittering effect specially at a candle light dinner or any evening functions. For fixing the mirrors especially the traditionally accepted round ones, the design is traced leaving a circle to attach them. The rest of the embroidery work is completed with stem or herringbone stitch by using silken floss. The traditional colours are blue, red, green and pink. The floral motifs with various shapes, types and colours of foliages, creepers, climbers, tendrils are the most common ones. Abhla Bharat is carried out on both family clothing and household textiles.

Sindhi Taropa commonly known as interlacing stitch practiced at Sindh, Kutch and Kathiawar. In Sindhi Taropa, the movement of the needle and thread is very important, does not bring any newness in the texture but can simply be said that an impression of the ingenuity of the women folk. Interlacing stitch involves two steps of embroidering, where in the first step, the long threads are stitched into the base of the cloth to form base structure or skeleton and in the second step, the thread is interloped through the basic structure or skeleton in reverse direction. The design is composed of small squares, lozenges, chevrons, discs, sometimes interspersed with flowers, birds, animals, etc. According to Jasleen Dhamija 'Sindhi Taropa was prevalent in Germany but it is really not known whether the Germans have introduced it into India or vice versa'.

Gujarat is also famous for Moti Bharat, the bead work. The main feature of this Bharat is, the beads are not stitched on a back ground but the beautiful rich coloured beads are stitched together with the help of needle and thread. The back ground is usually white beads, against which various motifs and pattern are stitched (woven) creating a solid surface with coloured beads. However, there exists no special set of motifs but are the same as that of other embroideries like elephant, camel, parrot, peacock, lady churning curds or pondering grain, calf drinking mothers milk and so on. The articles made of Moti Bharat were stiff nonpliable, hence used as torans for doors, bags, purses, wall hangings, play-toys, perch for the lady to balance the water pots on her head and other decorative, ornamental, show pieces to be exhibited in the house.

Though the craft of Kutch and Kathiawar fall under the traditional embroidery of Gujärat distinctively have many aspects in common like the stitches, motifs, use of Abhlas and so on. According to Mehta and Thakore who have studied these embroidery can be classified broadly into two groups on the basis of motifs geometrical, and figurative. Geometrical patterns are mainly employed in applique work where figurative like, rider on a house, king in procession seated on elephant, Ras leela, Gopi-Krishna, are picked up from few incidents of mythology.

Gujarat embroidery is not only rich by itself but depicts rich heritage of the state where several individuals express their ideas, views by making use of several colour schemes.

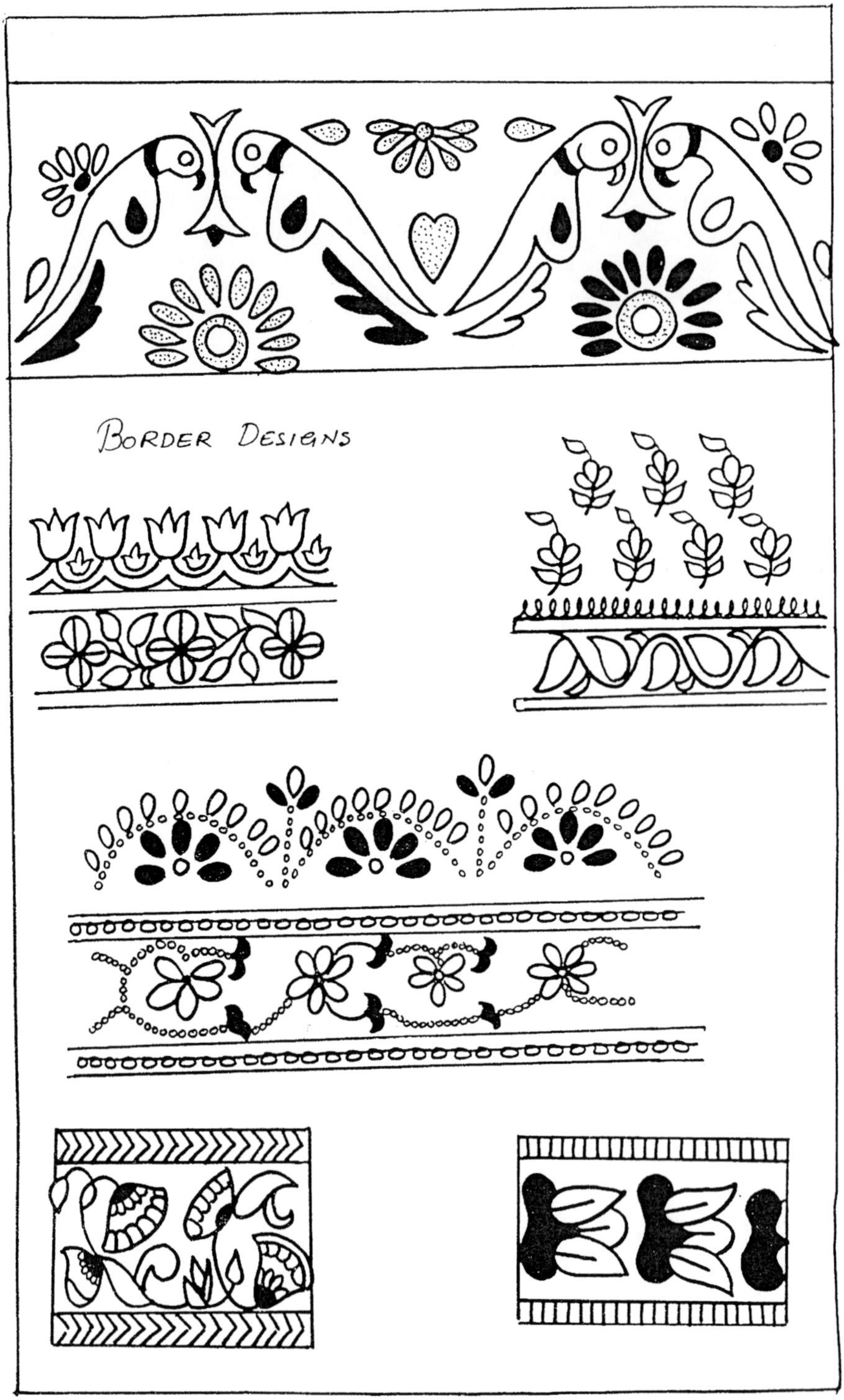
BORDER DESIGNS

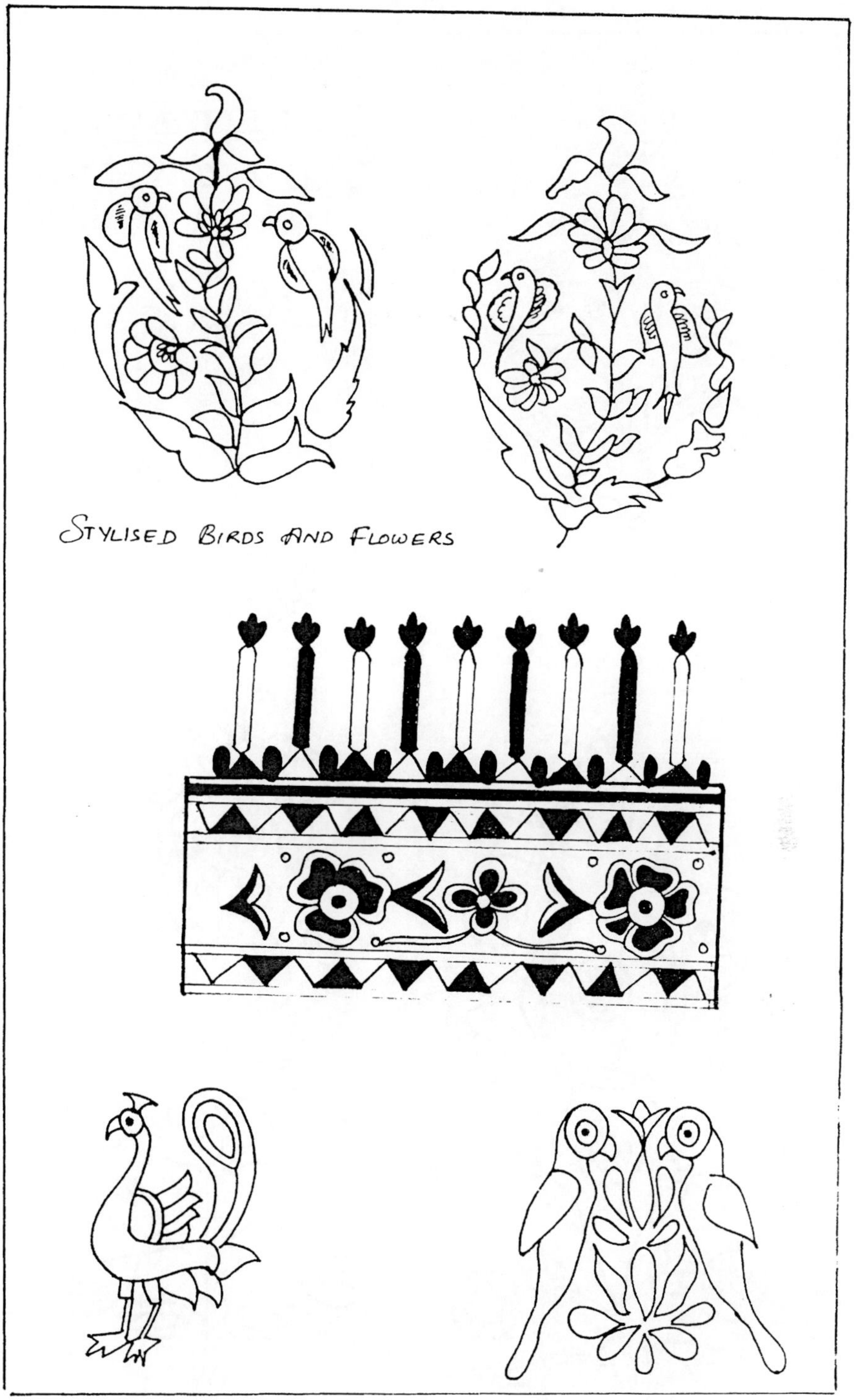
STYLISED BIRDS AND FLOWERS

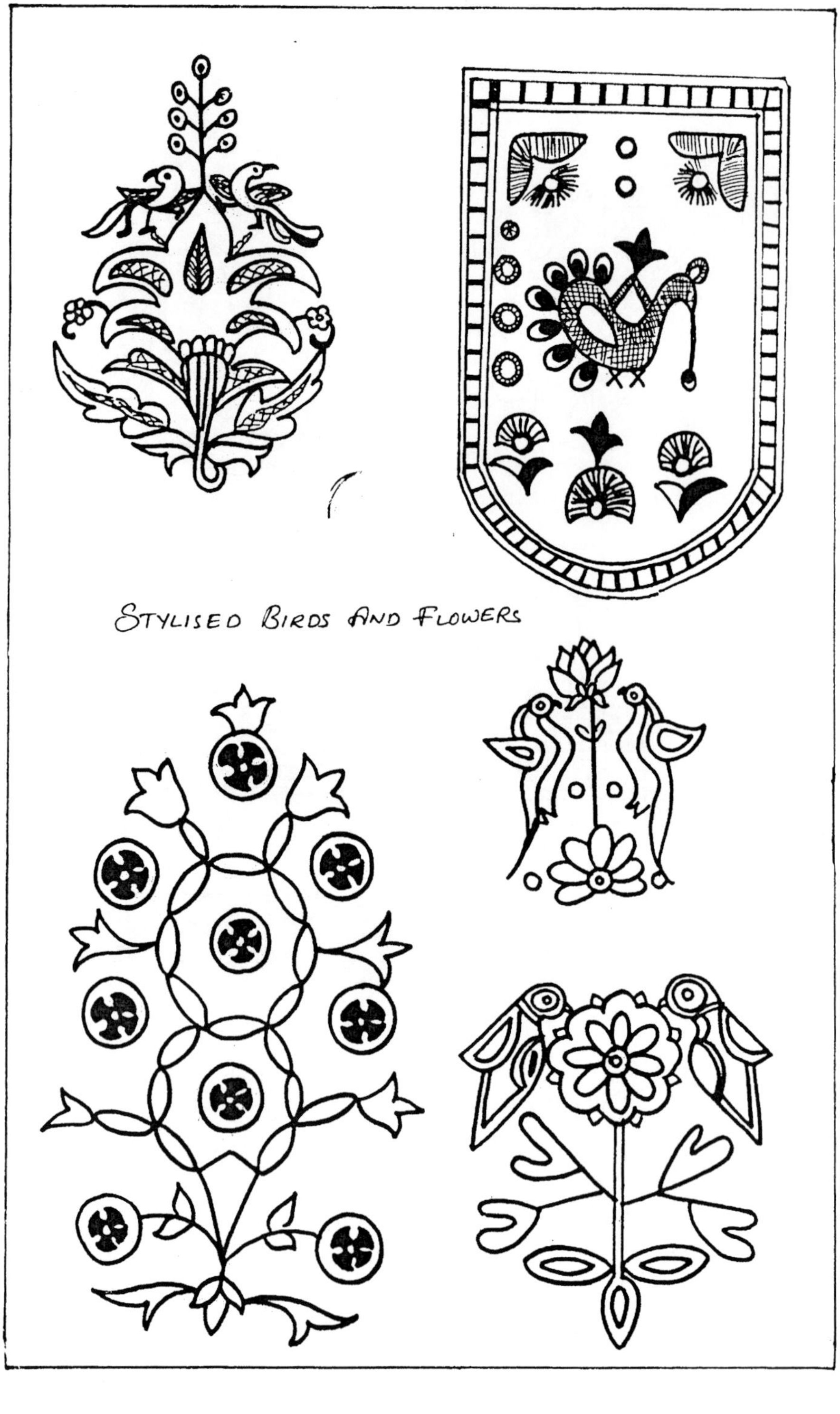

STYLISED BIRDS AND FLOWERS

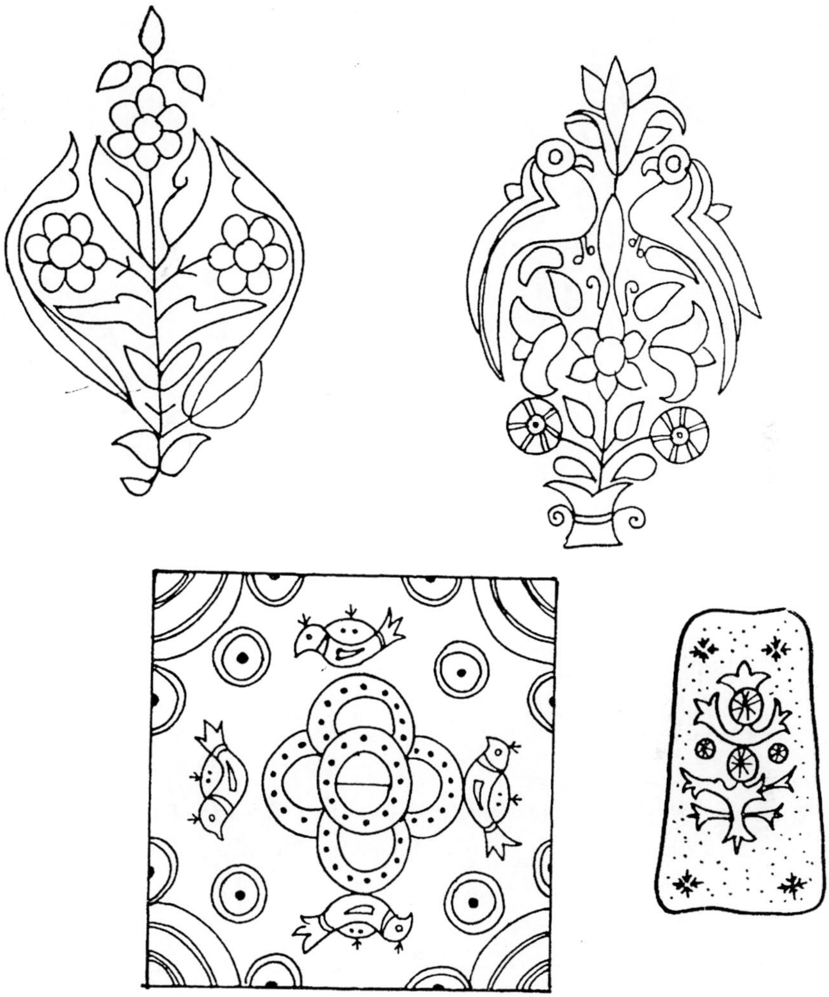

STYLISED BIRDS AND FLOWERS

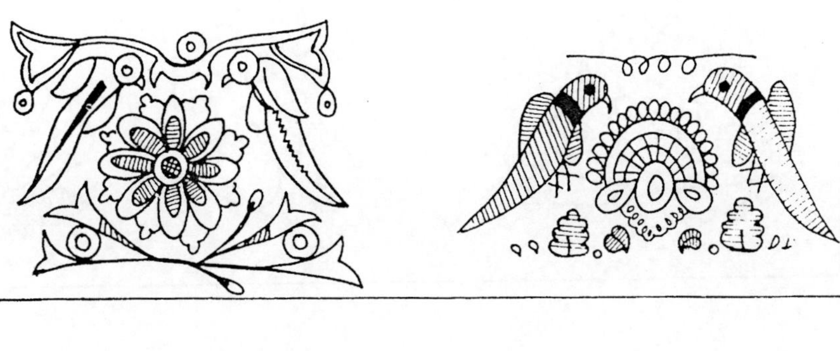

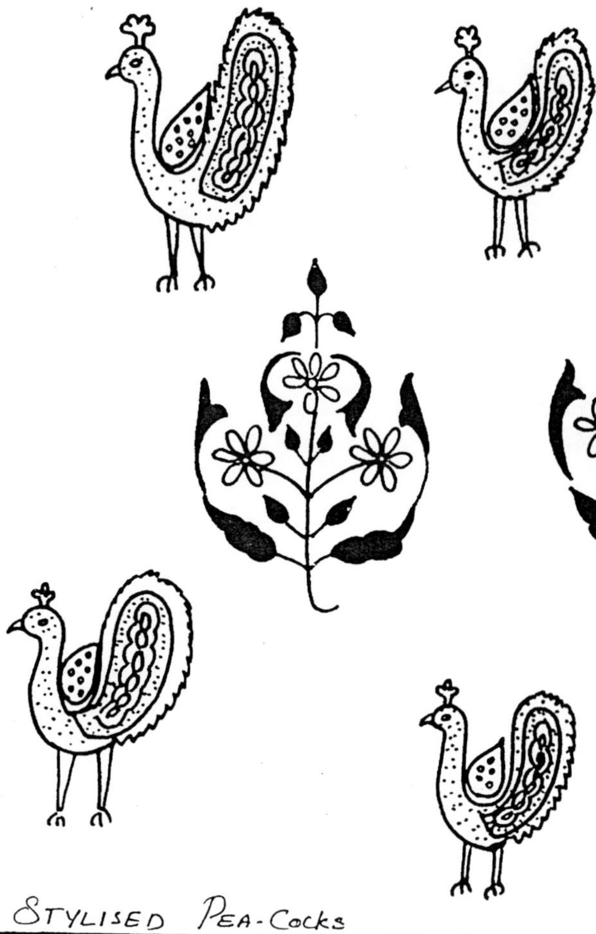

STYLISED PEA-COCKS

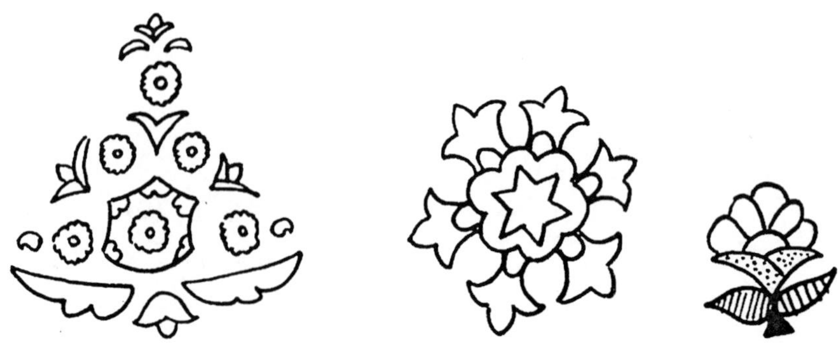

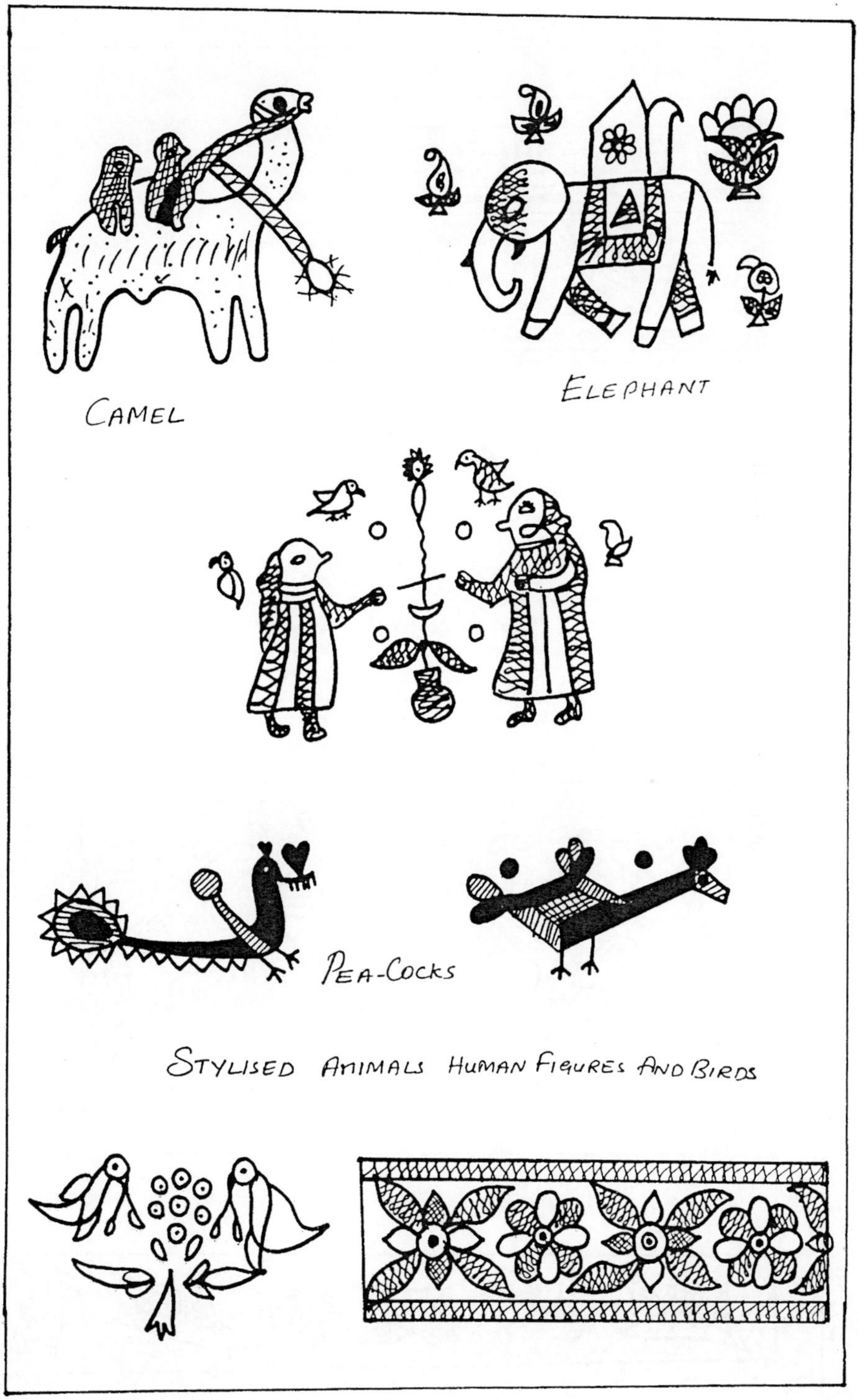

STYLISED ANIMALS HUMAN FIGURES AND BIRDS

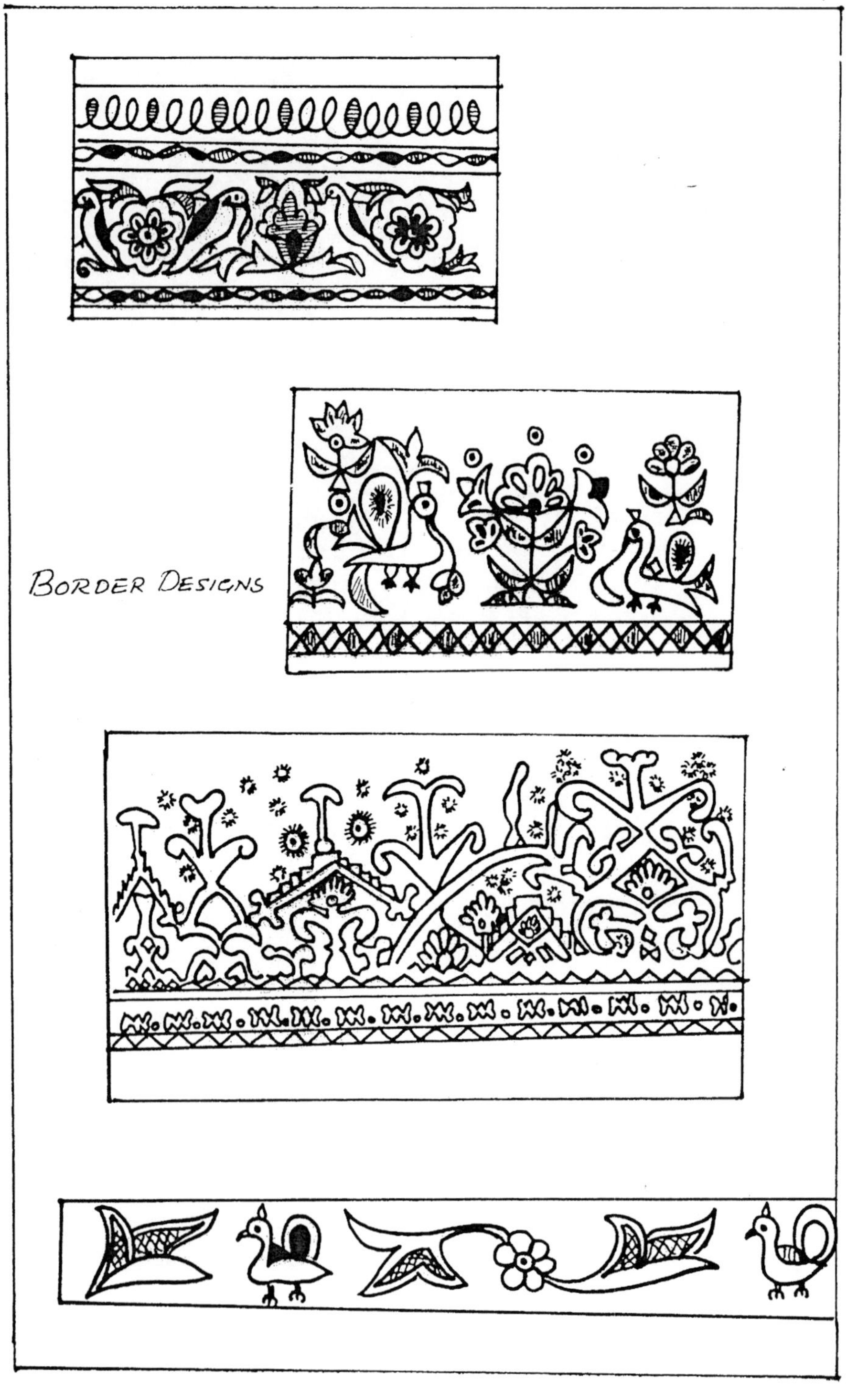
BORDER DESIGNS

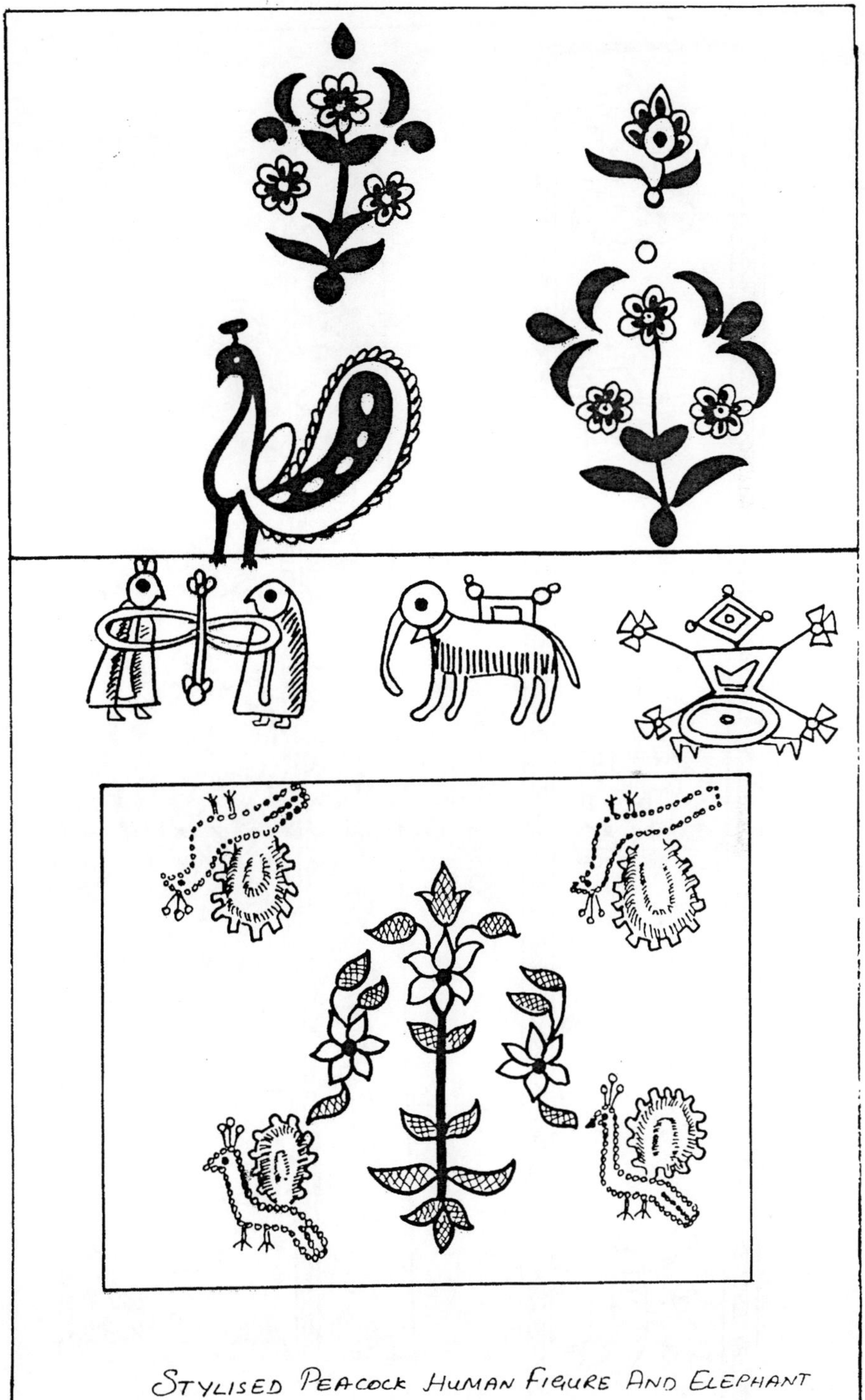

STYLISED PEACOCK HUMAN FIGURE AND ELEPHANT

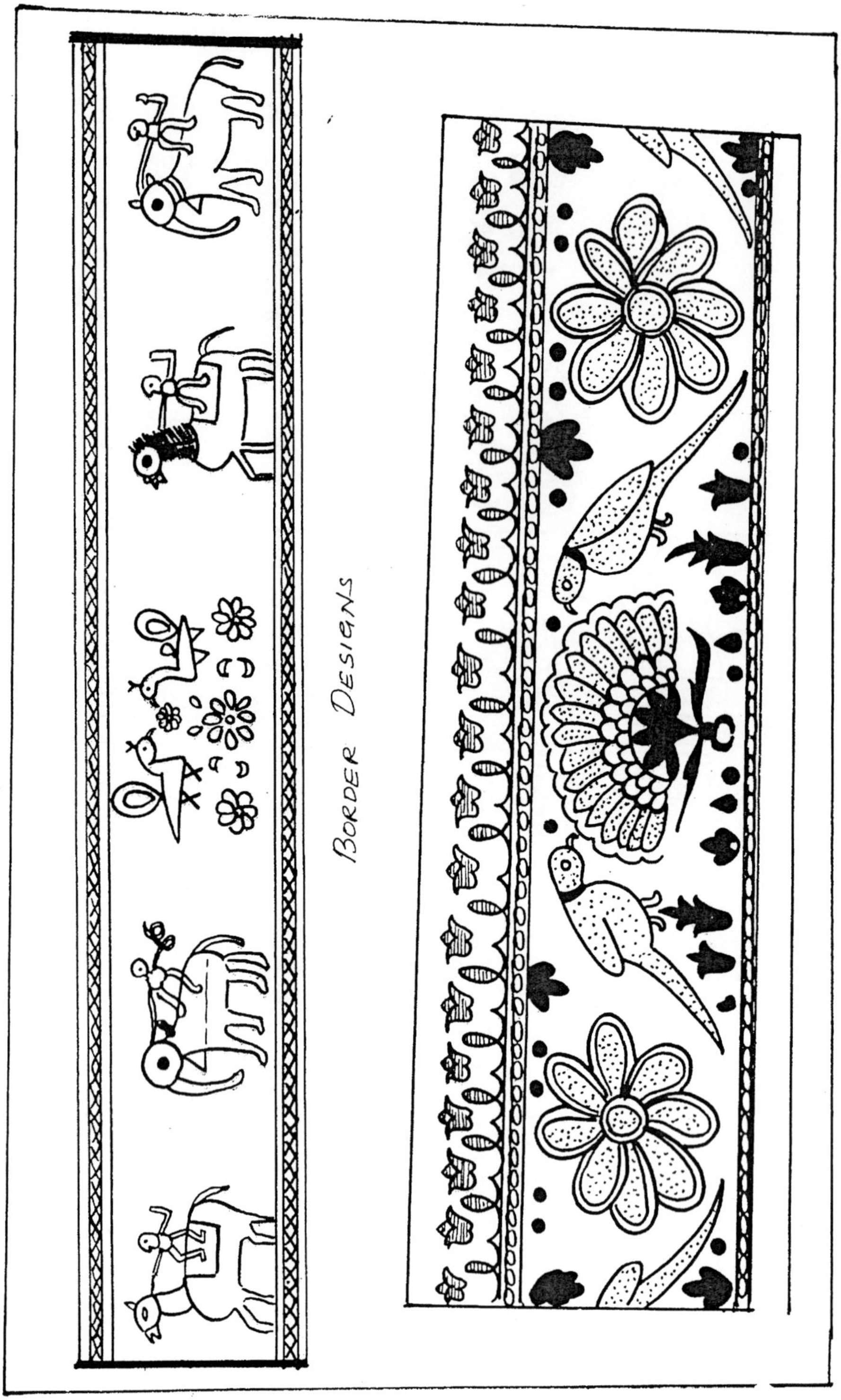

BORDER DESIGNS

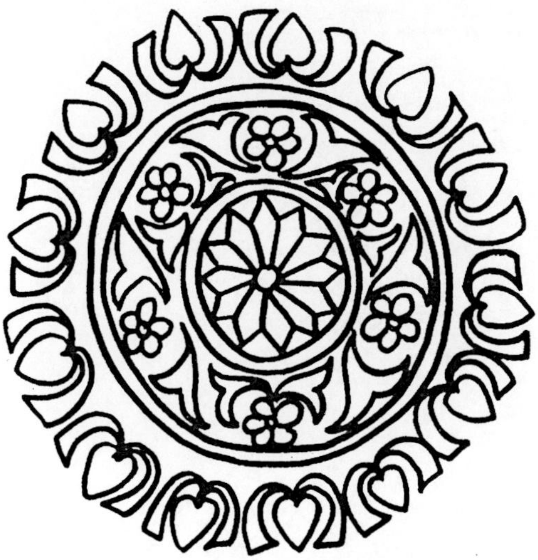

CENTRAL FLORAL DESIGN

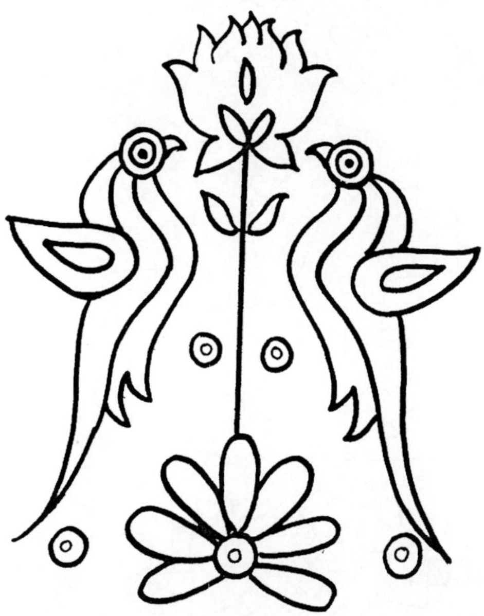

Sindhi Taropa [Interlacing Stitch]

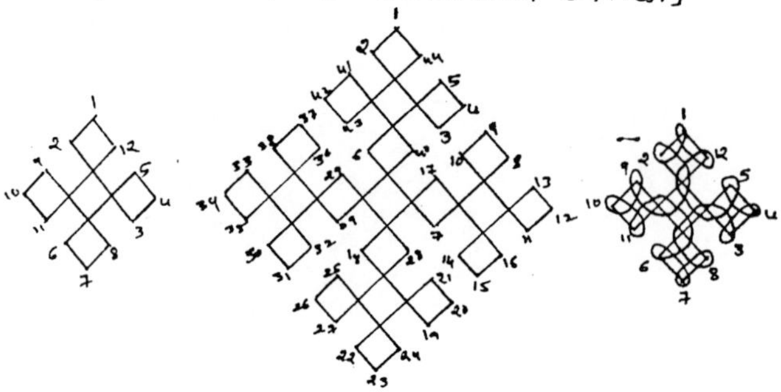

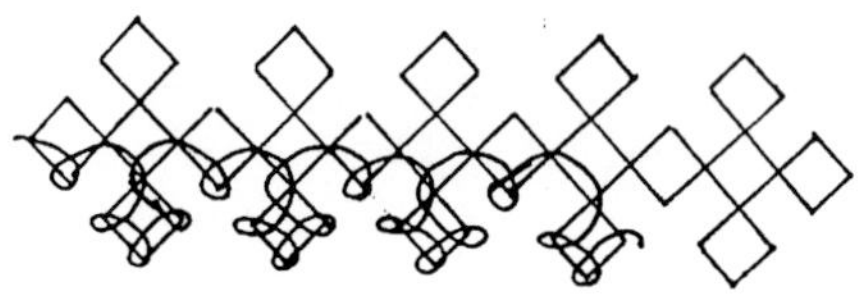

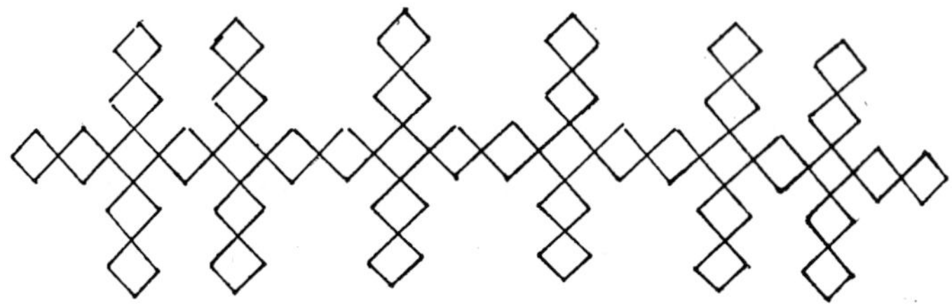

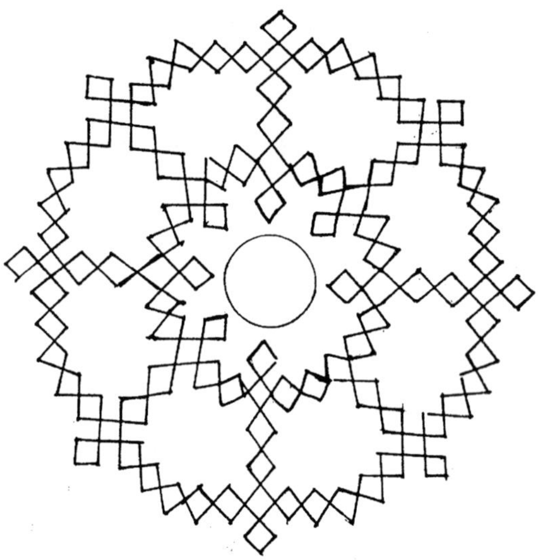

CHAPTER 4
CHAMBA RUMAL OF HIMACHAL

Himachal, the term is derived from Sanskrit where 'Him' means 'snow' and 'Achal' is 'lap' which depicts that the state has abundant snow fall during winter season. Himachal Pradesh is embedded with Himalayan mountains, Kashmir, Punjab, Uttar Pradesh and Tibet, in west, north-west, south, south-east and north-east respectively. History revels that, Himachal was ruled by brave, warriors and chivalrous Ranas and Thakurs. Geographically this state is been divided into three zones, lover foot hills, the Shivaliks, mid Himalayan zone, the Zaskar and the Himalayan zone, the Pirpanjal range. The state is full of beautiful hills, vallies and rich ever green forests. Hinduism, Buddhism and Jainism were the religions existed in the state, those days; but the great poems of, Sant Tulsidas, Sant Kabirdas, Jayadeva and Ramananda gave impetus to a new form of art, inspired by the Vaishnava doctrines. This Vaishnava cult gave emphasis on spiritual experience through loving his neighbours. This principle formed the basis of Kangra style of painting.

The evidences about existence of this embroidery pages back to fifteenth century, mentions in Buddhists literature that the embroidery was practiced in Pathankot, Chamba and other neighbouring remote villages. It is mentioned by Subhashini Aryan and O.C. Ohri that this Luxurious embroidery was done in Pahari areas like, Churah, Chamba Kangra, Salyali, Basohi, Nurpur, Jammu, Haripus, Guber, Kulu, Mandi and so on, during eleventh and twelfth century A.D. The embroidery depicted a fine, delicate, perfect manual work befittingly called as 'needle miniatures of Himachal' or 'Pahari Rumal'. The legend says that a 'rumal' (hand kerchief), was embroidered by Bebe Nanaki, sister of Guru Nanak Dev (1469-1539), and presented to him during his wedding in late fifteenth century which has been still preserved as a documentation in Gurudwara of Gurdaspur. This rumal had the base of creamy white colour, on which beautiful human figures, ever green trees with colourful blossoms, animals like goat and deers, saddled horse were embroidered. This art was prevalent in Punjab, because the lady Bebe Nanki was born and brought up at Talwandi Rai Bhoi, now in Pakistan and lived in Sultanpur Lodhi after her marriage, a small town in Kapurthala district of Punjab.

In Jataka tales, a mention was made about these beautiful embroidery done in Pathankot, Chamba and other surrounded places. During 1009 A.D. the Kanga fort was captured by Gazani Mohammed, the Mughal emperor, who looted all splendid textiles of Himachal Pradesh. Kanga school was known for its unique and exquisite style of painting and Chamba was the most picturesque needle work. Therefore, the Romans described the embroidery of Chamba as 'needle painting'. The facial expression of the figures are vivid and lively and the bodies are full of movement as it developed a style of its own.

It is believed that this embroidery is the influence of Pahari (Hill) miniature paintings and has fetched a definite shape. In Chamba it is said that during 1750s, Umed Singh and son were the great lovers of arts and this patronity continued with Raja Jit Singh, during 1800s. Probably it is during this era, the Pahari craft flourished in this tiny state. Since then Himachal embroidery is famous as 'Chamba'.

The primitive traditional Chamba has undergone gradual evolution with respect to motifs, colours, stitches, workmanship and aesthetic appearance. Reflecting back into the earlier Chamba embroidery, all most all the motifs namely, human figures, birds, flora and fauna were highly stylized and improportionately drawn. Colours employed were very bright, bold and brilliant. The Pahari style being aesthetically richer than earlier ones, evolved by the ladies of the court of Chamba and their attendants, and hence lead to the complete development in the image of miniature paintings. The folk style was replaced by subdued colours and become more popular during the eighteenth and nineteenth century.

People of this state have created things of immense beauty in their day to day life which is deliberately reflected in their fine arts of wood carvings, paintings, metal ware and of course traditional embroidery. This craft designated the traditions, customs, culture and ecology of their geographical area and the people among whom it has taken its birth.

Traditionally the ground fabric used was two types of unbleached cotton cloth, first being the light weight, fine, delicate, cambric like, semitransparent, manufactured at Sialkot (presently in Pakistan), Amritsar and Ludhiana, Second type being hand-spun, hand-woven coarser, relatively heavier khaddar. In later period the unbleached cotton material was replaced by mill made cotton cloth. However, cream or white coloured Tassar silk material was also commonly used for making rumals. Earlier, the white fabric was also commonly used for making rumals. Earlier, the white fabric was locally dyed by professional dyers using natural vegetable colours. Today, according to the taste, demand fashion trend and availability the ground fabric employed being terycot, organdie, linen, poplin and muslin of either white or light colours.

Hand drawing of free style was the mode of tracing or outlining the design or motif, carried out exclusively by ladies. These women drew the figures of their own creation and produced the images of their deity on the material as visualised by them. Of course it was the produce of self expression and were of highly stylized. Earlier charcoal was used for tracing the outlines but now oil method is being used. The artists 'chitra' used to prepare the designs for rumals, who had sufficient knowledge about Pahari Painting. The artists not only drew the designs but also guided the women about colour combination.

Unlike Punjabi girls being expertised in Phulkari in their early adolescencehood, girls of Himachal do start learning this art at an early teens and of course their skill in handicraft was one of the measuring sticks in selecting the bride and judging her ability as a housewife during matrimonial negotiations. Even now, it is a custom of Chamba girls to prepare a rumal, exhibiting her art and skill and a way of maintaining the tradional custom of Chamba families.

In Pahari embroidery the themes are taken from Purana, Ramayana and Mahabharata. However, common designs like Bagh and Rasmandala require a month to complete where as some of the intricate, elaborate and difficult themes like Battle of Kurukshetra takes around six months or so.

The threads used for embroidery were untwisted pat, which gave rich effect against dull rustic cotton ground. It produced an impression of smooth, glossy, gorgeous surface enrichment. However, the infinite shades and tints of bright, brilliant and contrasting colours were used. Most commonly used colours are red, yellow, green, blue, crimson and purple. Blue colour is always used for Krishna, whenever he is bear chested and crimson for feet. Red, blue and white colours are used for Brahma, Vishnu and Maheswara respectively. Gopis in vivid colours of yellow and green or dark pink or crimson combination. The outline of the motif is always worked with black.

At present the embroidery is done with twisted silk or chiffon threads. Pat has been mainly replaced because of its low strength and difficulty in handling.

Embroidery is done with double satin stitch done in both right and wrong side, where the effect is reversible. It is done so finely that not only the background is hardly visible but very difficult to identify the right side, since the work is never started with a knot but with a back stitch and the threads never been joined by knots. It was also observed that in some of the old wall hangings, chain stitch was used for both filling and outlining, in which case right and wrong side of the work was clearly identified. However, chain stitch was not practiced on rumals. Gujjar women used darning, sometimes even herringbone and satin stitches.

A greater population of Himachal Pradesh are Vishnawas, believers of Lord Krishna a reincarnation of Vishnu Bhagawan. The motifs collectively brought from the life history of Lord Krishna. There exists a compatibility between the movement of human and animal motifs in the needle craft.

Motifs, in Himachal embroidery consists of symbolic animals like, leaping tigers, running goats, cantering horses, fleeting rams, jumping deer, along with cows, calves, horses, elephants, snakes; bird motifs comprised of peacock, parrot, used may be as symbolic or purely as decorative. Sometimes these motifs are used in single to fill up the empty places. Single bird signified a sad, solitary one waiting for the male, a couple symbolised union of two souls.

Rumals comprised of elliptical frame work, having two to three inches of floral bodies on all the four sides. Center of the rumal has creeper motif and guldasta in the corners, pointing either towards the centre or towards the corner. Sometimes the complete rumal has the motifs of animals, birds, trees, creeper and foliages giving an impression of Bagh, moreover, the Cyprus tree is also widely used. It is also observed that many musical instruments such as, flute, Tambura, Drums (Dholaks), Veena, Sitar, Tabala are used in the art. Muslim Gujjar women used geometrical motifs, included triangle, squares, diamonds, rectangular, hexagonals and circles. However, most of the figures and motifs were simplified i.e., the body of human figure is cone shape with a face and the elephant appeared like a rectangular, box moving steadily with a lotus on the trunk.

MAIN THEMES IN THE EMBROIDERY

There is a great influence of Mythology on the themes of paintings and embroidery. Along with the themes of Bhagawat Purana, Krishna Leela and Mahabharat, it is observed that Raga Ragini and Baramasa are also used abundantly, which is an influence of Vaishanva cult. The dancing figures appeared so vivid that they are rarely in motion. It is to say that Krishna in all his various forms and charaeters occupied the central figure of much of Himachal embroidery.

The scene of Rasa Lila is another common theme where the blue bodied Krishna leads the gopies in circular dance posture. The Rumals display other folk styles like marriage of Krishna and Rukmini, Vishnu in a lotus, Ganesh, Vishnu-Laxmi, Pahari women playing musician instruments, men smoking hukka, the pipe and so on.

RASMANDALA

Here the centre of the theme depicts Lord Vishnu sitting in the Padma, the lotus has four arms, each holding a padma, a Gada (lotus bud), a Shankh (conch shell) and his weapon, the Sudarshan chakra. However, the figures were disproportionate and many times the human figures have bird like faces. The other empty part of the rumal is covered with floral and guldasta motifs, except the corners which had human figures (Gopies) playing Dholak.

KALIYA DAMANA

Krishna Killing the horrified kaliya kalinga sarpa (serpent), who lived in Jamuna river.

SAMUDRA MANTHANA

The ocean was churned by Devas (Gods) and Asuras (Demons) using a serpant, Vasuki as rope and mountain Meru as the churning rod. Both nectar and poison were the products of Samudra Manthana. However, many more things emerged out of the ocean due to the vigorous elaborate churning. And this scene of Samudra Manthan has been taken as a motif for embroidery of rumal and wall hanging. Since, this being an elaborate scene, the motif is divided into several panels embroidered individually and later joined all of them together. This miniature style has some what proportionate human figures, exhibiting delineated forms. A largest motif of Samudra Manthana was eight feet wide and two feet long.

RUKMINI HARANA

The elopement of Rukmini and her marriage is the zist of the theme. It is an elaborate theme, embroidered on rumal depicting the various ceremonial activities performed on one part and preparation of Rukmini's wedding on the other. The scene exhibits, Rukmini grooming and decking up for her wedding, women engaged in various activities, musicians playing music, Sahelis (friends) of Rukmini busy in carrying out various chores, Rukmini praying, Lord Krishna taking Rukmini in his chariot, couple sitting in front of the vedi, the place where marriage rites performed, Priest enchanting the mantras and performing marriage rites, Barat, the procession of marriage, involving royal animals like, saddled house, elephants, drum beaters, musicians playing Ransingha and so on. However, these scenes were more emphasised and beautified by use of various flowers, foliages, birds and fruits, may be in between to fill the empty gaps or as borders.

BATTLE OF KURUKSHETRA

Mahabharat is one of the great epics of India and many themes of this epic is chosen for the embroidery. However, the most commonly found ones are the battle of Kurukshetra and exile of the Pandavas. This battle is elaborately depicted on a five feet wide and one and a half feet long panel of base material. Pandavas occupy the left hand side of the panel along with Lord Krishna on his chariot, Kauravas on the right hand side and Abhimanyu is placed in centre of the panel, showing the picture of being caught in the Chakravihu.

RAGA RAGINI

Raga, the tune of song and Ragini, the mode of song expressing the base for songs sung in a minimum of six versions. The Pahari painters were greatly influenced by the Vaishnavas, the Kshina cult, during eighteenth and nineteenth centuries and adopted Ragmala (Sangeeta Mala) theme. The popular Raga Ragini themes are Raga megha, Raga hindola, Raga vasanta, Rago Todi, Raga bhairavi and so on. The themes expressed the mode, mood, time, day, season, month during which the particular Raga is being sung.

ASHTA NAYIKA

It expresses various moods and personality of Nayik and Naika, presented in panelled embroidery. 'Ashta' means eight, i.e. the composite theme represents around eight panels of Nayik and

Nayika, in their variegated moods. Keshav Das has grouped the personality, character and moods of the heroes and heroines into eight categories and hence the name. The followings are some of the moods–

Abhisandhita	-	A quarrelsome Nayika has been astranged by her hero, who is full of sorrow and regrets for her behaviour.
Abhisarika	-	A bold, brave and daring Nayika forgives her family for the sake of her beloved.
Khandita	-	A Nayika betrayed by her lover, who promises and never turns up on the said night but spents the night with another.
Proshitapreyasi	-	A Nayika, humbly waiting for the return of her husband, who is out for business and has not returned on time. Sakhis, her friends trying to console but Nayika never been consoled.
Swadninapatik	-	A Nayika, whose lover is loyal and obeys her, loves her and appreciated her beauty, admires, her qualities and ofcourse a perpetual companion.
Utkala	-	A Nayika, waiting anxiously for her lover.
Vasakasajja	-	A Nayika, deeply involved with her lover, have a desire to lead a life with him and wants to express the same to him.
Vipralbhda	-	A Nayika, depressed, neglected by Nayik, who promises her to meet but never turns up. She waits for, him the whole night but invain. She is very much distressed for his disregard.

MINJAR MELA JALUS

'Minjar' the tassels, 'Mela' the fair, and 'Jalus' the procession, depicts the procession during the Mela. Minjar Mela is a very famous festival of 'Chamba, where the people sacrifice Minja in the river Ravi; to drive away the evil spirits and pray for their prosperity.

THE GUJJAR THEME

The Muslim gujjar women usually carried out embroidery locally, taking all the motifs from nature except, human and bird figures. However, it has the resemblance of Phulkari of Punjab. An elaborate Gujjar work is divided into number of penels of either square of rectangular for convenience, treated as an important segment having geometrical motifs. However, the most important and common elliptical floral framework does not exist.

A large number of household textile articles are prepared of Chamba embroidery. And the most common is the rumal, almost synonymous with the work, whose size ranged from twenty to thirty five inches. Wall hanging with various themes from Mahabharat, Purana ranged from two to several feet rectangular shapes. Sometimes even cholis are embroidered.

Chamba rumals are versatile in their utility, used as a cover while offering gifts in the Mandir, the temple, either to deity or priest called 'Eathaparu'; an immensely decorated oval or circular rumal hung behind the statue of deity is 'Chhabru'; a rectangular or oblong wall hanging draped behind the idol in the temples is 'Chandoa', are now becoming rare. Though rumals are no longer used as covers, it is customary for the girl to possess at least a rumal in her trousseau. Rumals were also used to cover the gifts that were exchanged during weddings.

It is observed that, the quality of the embroidery deteriorating day by day in Chamba may be due to the reason that, the easy availability of the printed material and articles, an inexpensive substitute for elaborate labour consuming expensive hand work, migration, modernization and civilization of the Pahari people, awareness about the demand, choice, taste of the public, realisation about the existence of other labour, time and money saving embroideries and other such decorations.

Himachal embroidery has been rooted in the soil of their geographical region that enhances the glory of nature, the Almighty God. It is evident that this embroidery was practiced in early twentieth century and some of the exquisite pieces of workmanship were exhibited in the museums. However, there was a great fear that urbanisation may inhibit the skill and art of Pahari rumals. There was scare always arised that this traditional art and crafts with vivid colours, motifs, forms and sensations may be swept off from the souls of Himachal Pradesh. But this art of embroidery is yet surviving because a new competus has been given by the Indian Handicrafts Board, and the Chamba Embroidery Revival Centre has been started in Himachal Pradesh. The embroidery which was originally done on cotton and silk base have been replaced by organdie, synthetics, blended and spun materials. However, the invaluable heritage of Himachal Pradesh is kept alive through adoptions with base material, motifs, colours, stitches, themes, and articles made to suit the present day demands and needs.

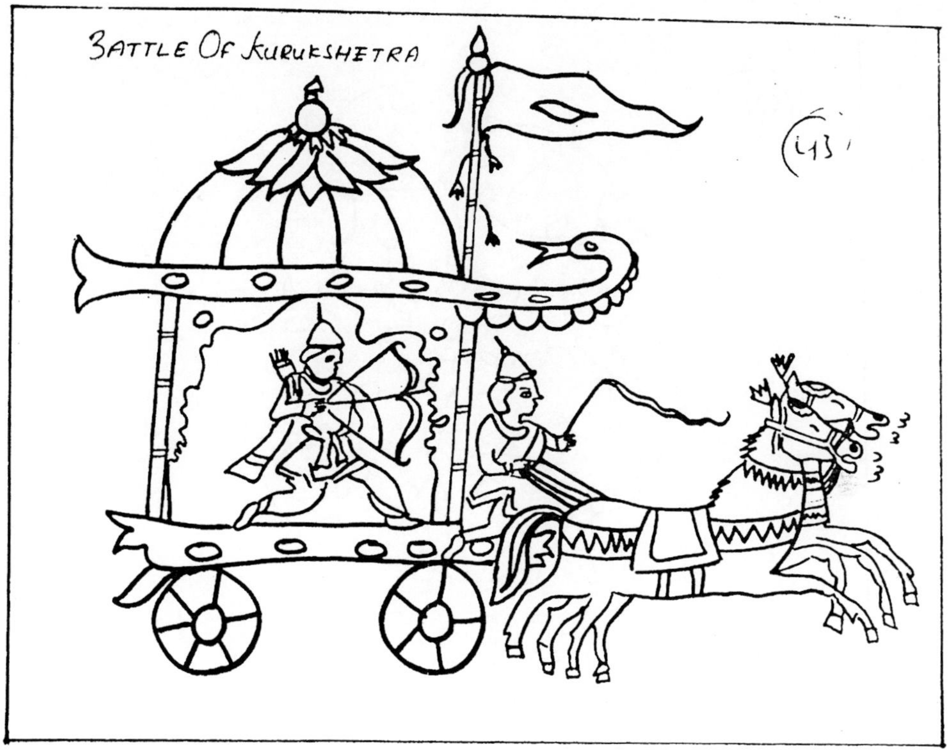
BATTLE OF KURUKSHETRA
43

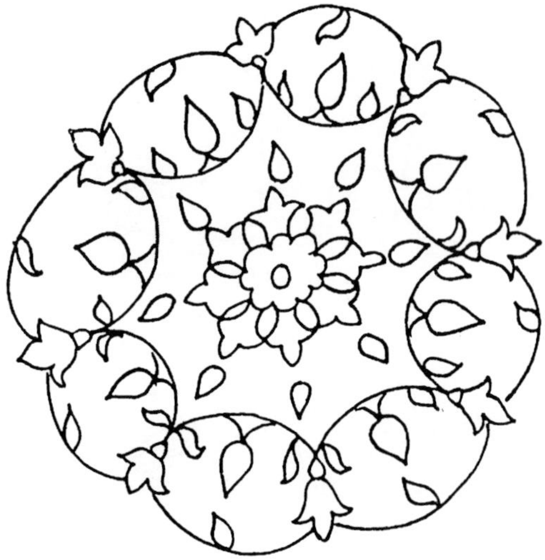

STYLISED LOTUS CENTRAL MOTIF

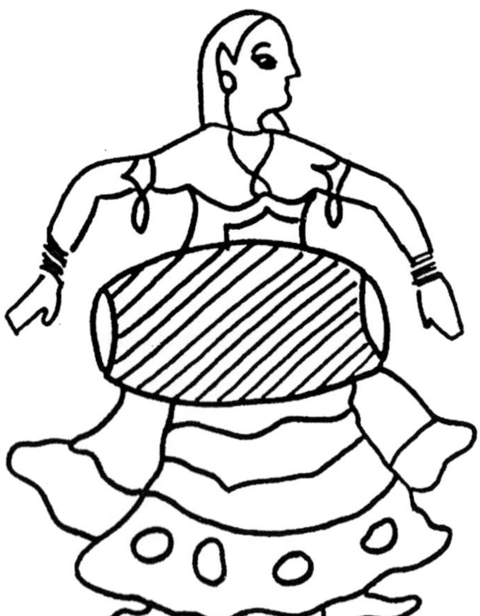

GOPI WITH DHOLAK

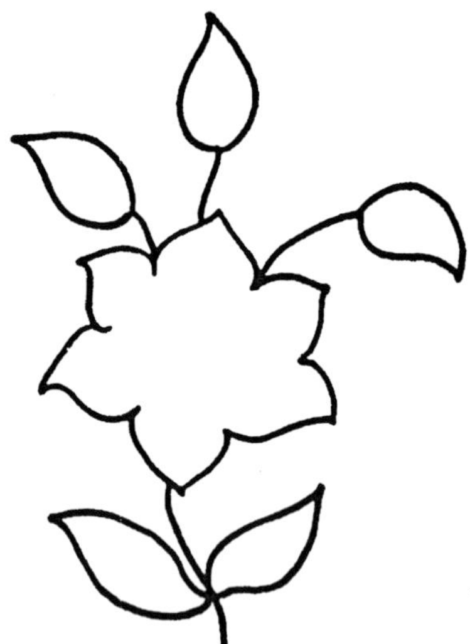

FLORAL MOTIF

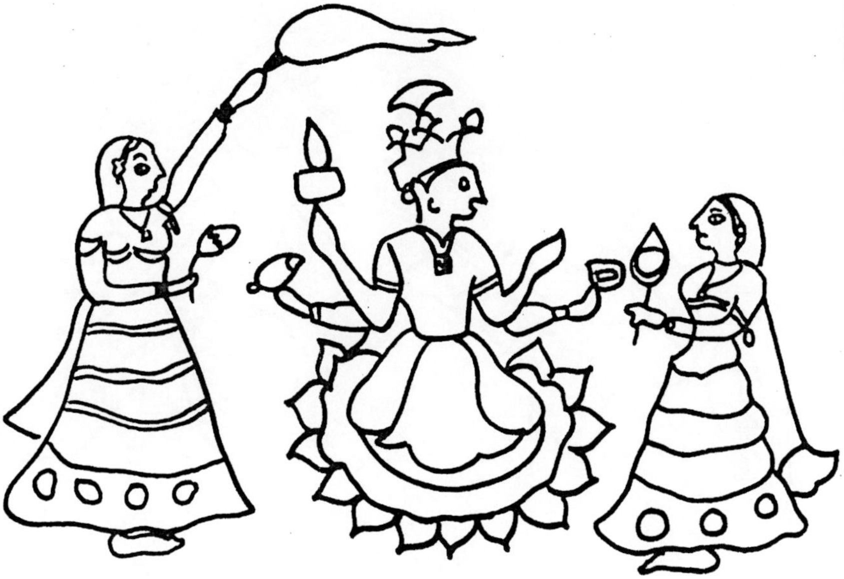

LORD VISHNU AS KRISHNA WITH GOPIS

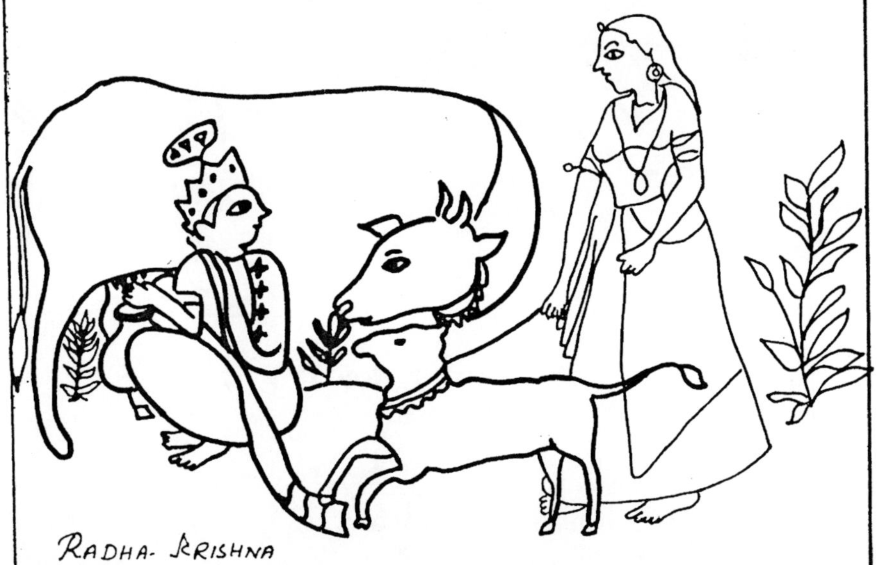

RADHA-KRISHNA

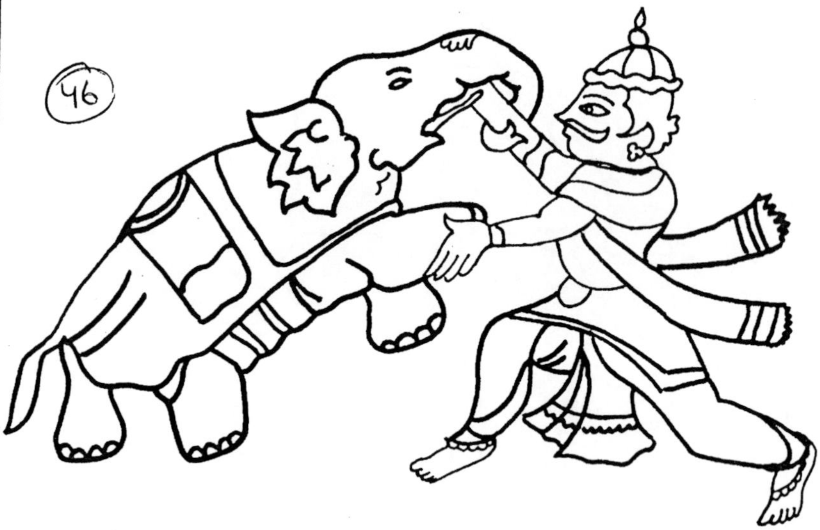

A WARRIOR FIGHTING WITH ELEPHANT

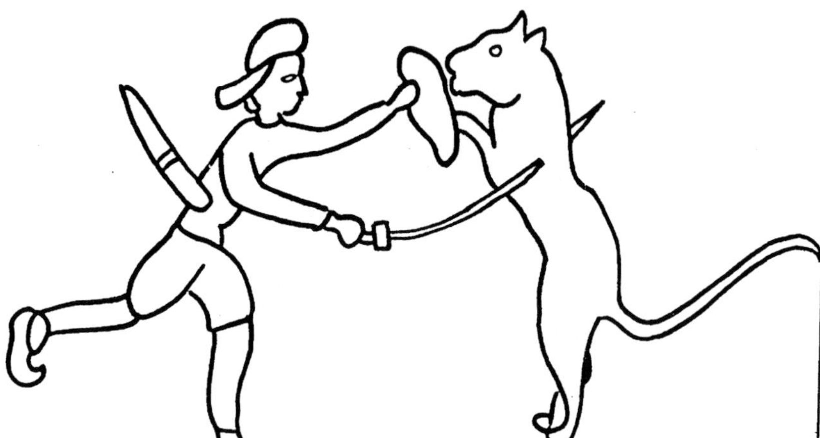

A HUNTER AND A LION

47

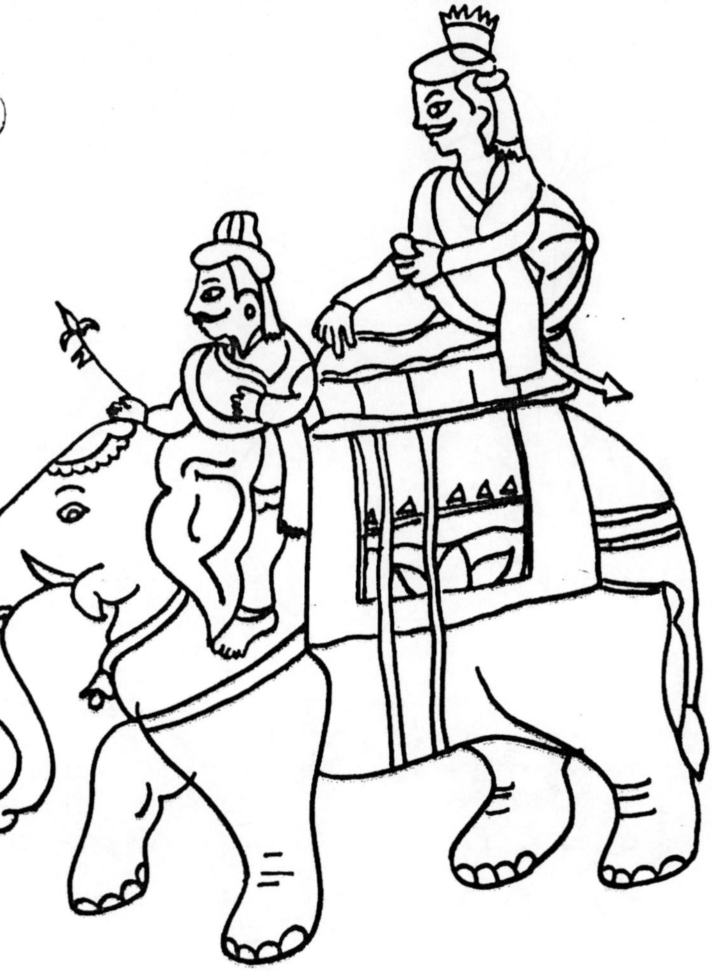

A NOBLEMAN IN A PROCESSION – MINJAR MELA JALUS

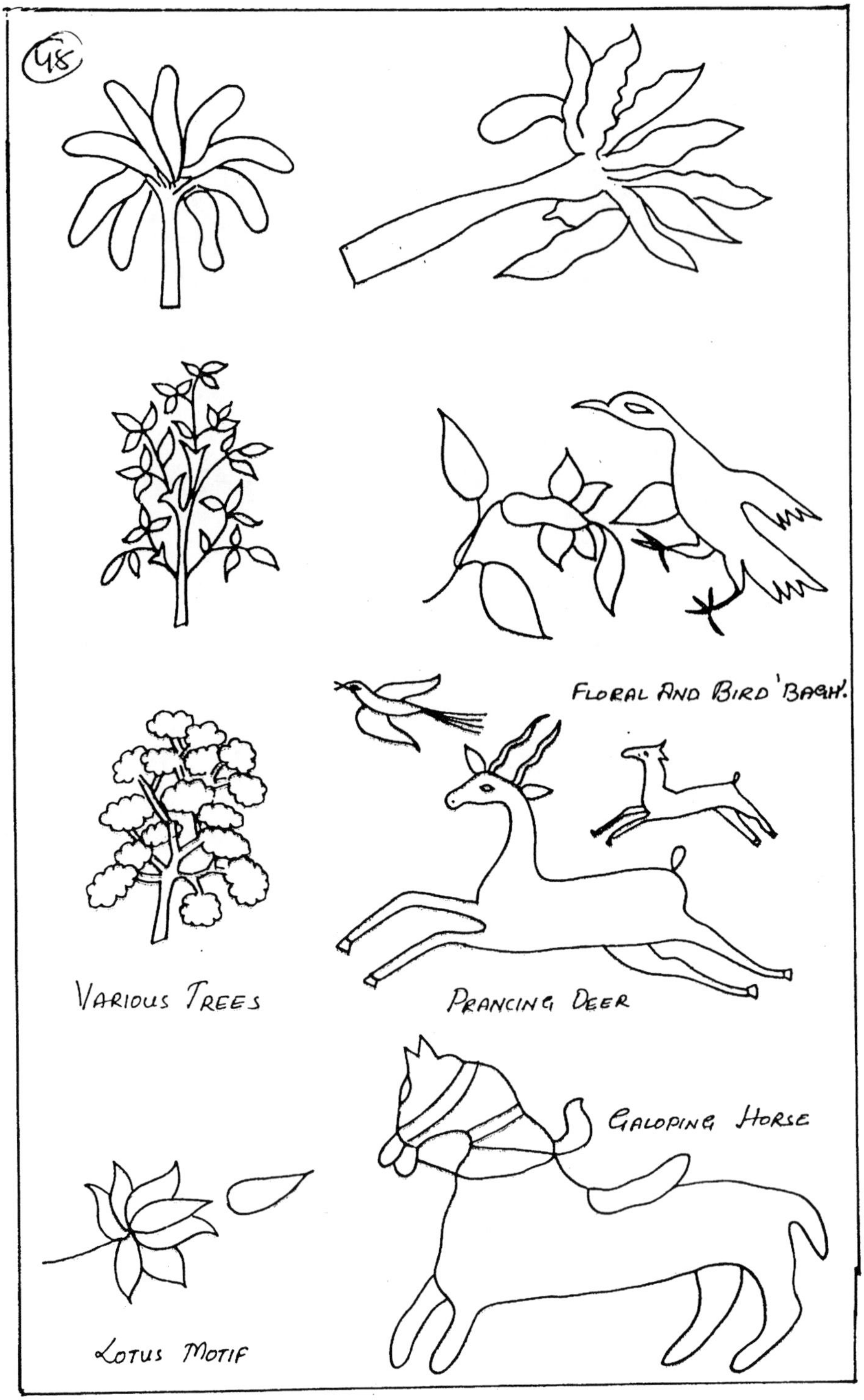
48
FLORAL AND BIRD 'BAGH'.
VARIOUS TREES
PRANCING DEER
GALOPING HORSE
LOTUS MOTIF

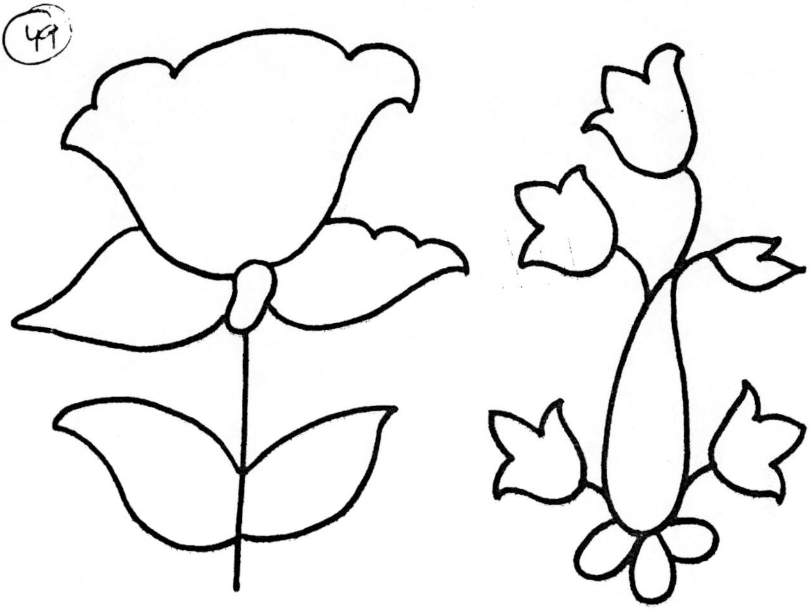

FLORAL MOTIFS USED ON CHOLIS, FANS CAPS ETC.

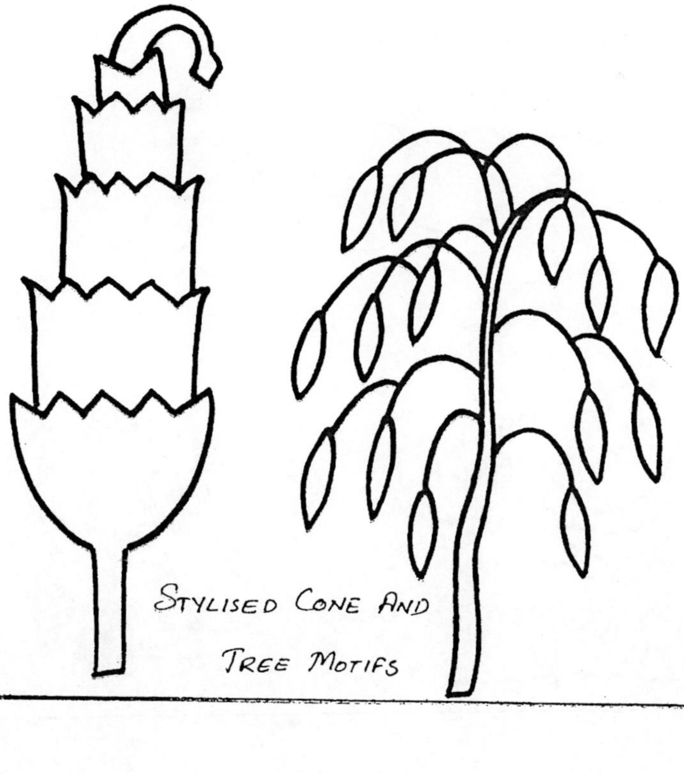

STYLISED CONE AND TREE MOTIFS

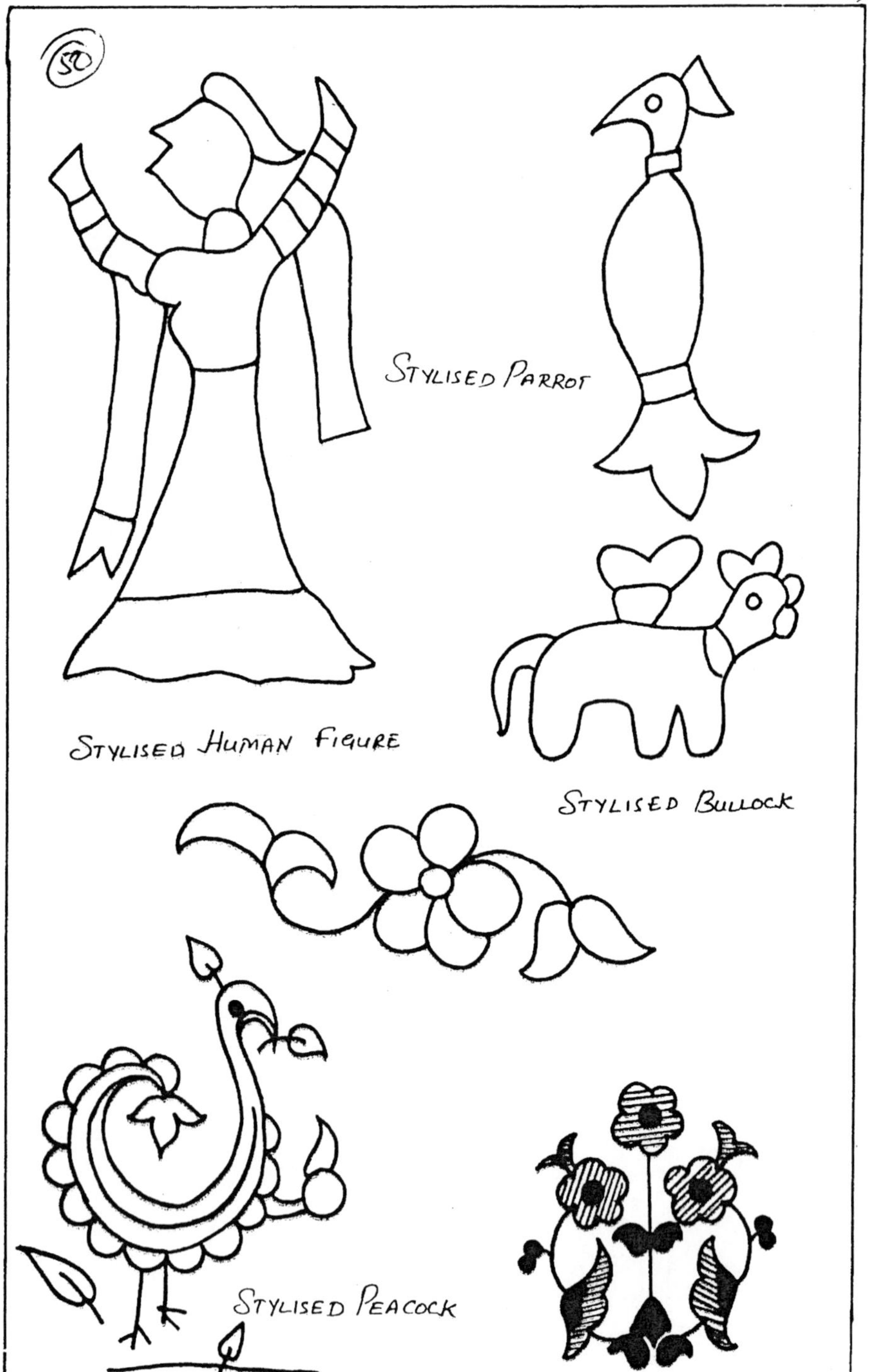
50
STYLISED PARROT
STYLISED HUMAN FIGURE
STYLISED BULLOCK
STYLISED PEACOCK

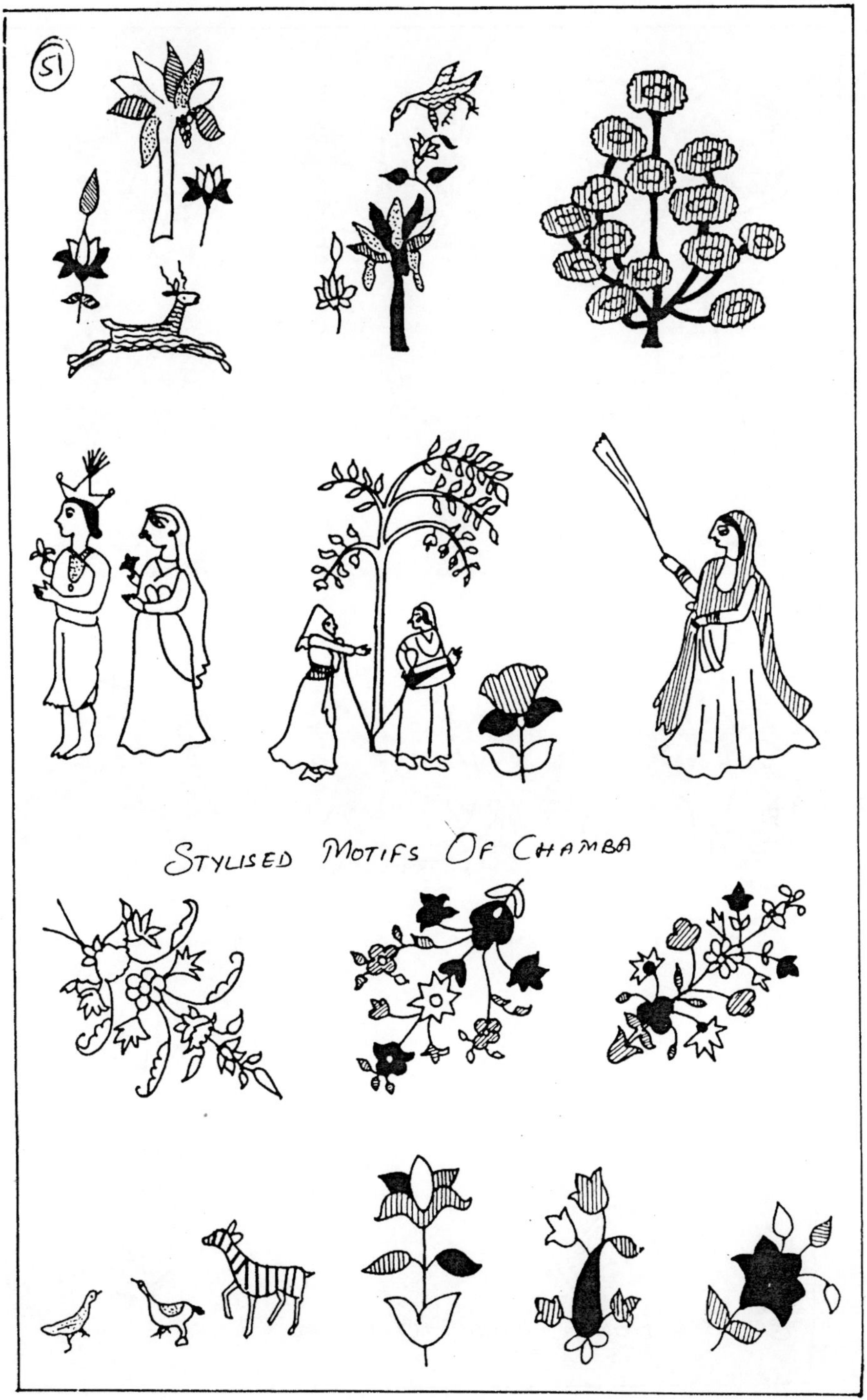
51
STYLISED MOTIFS OF CHAMBA

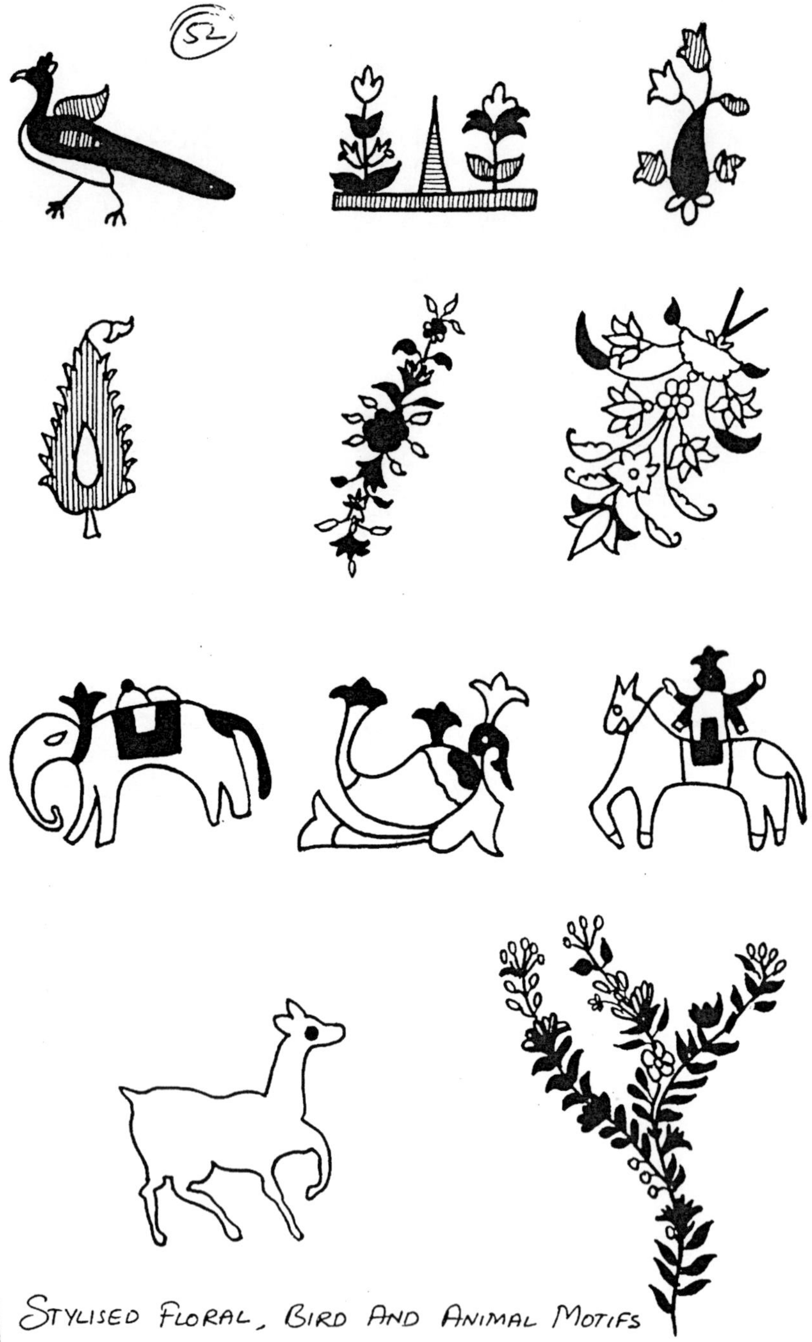

STYLISED FLORAL, BIRD AND ANIMAL MOTIFS

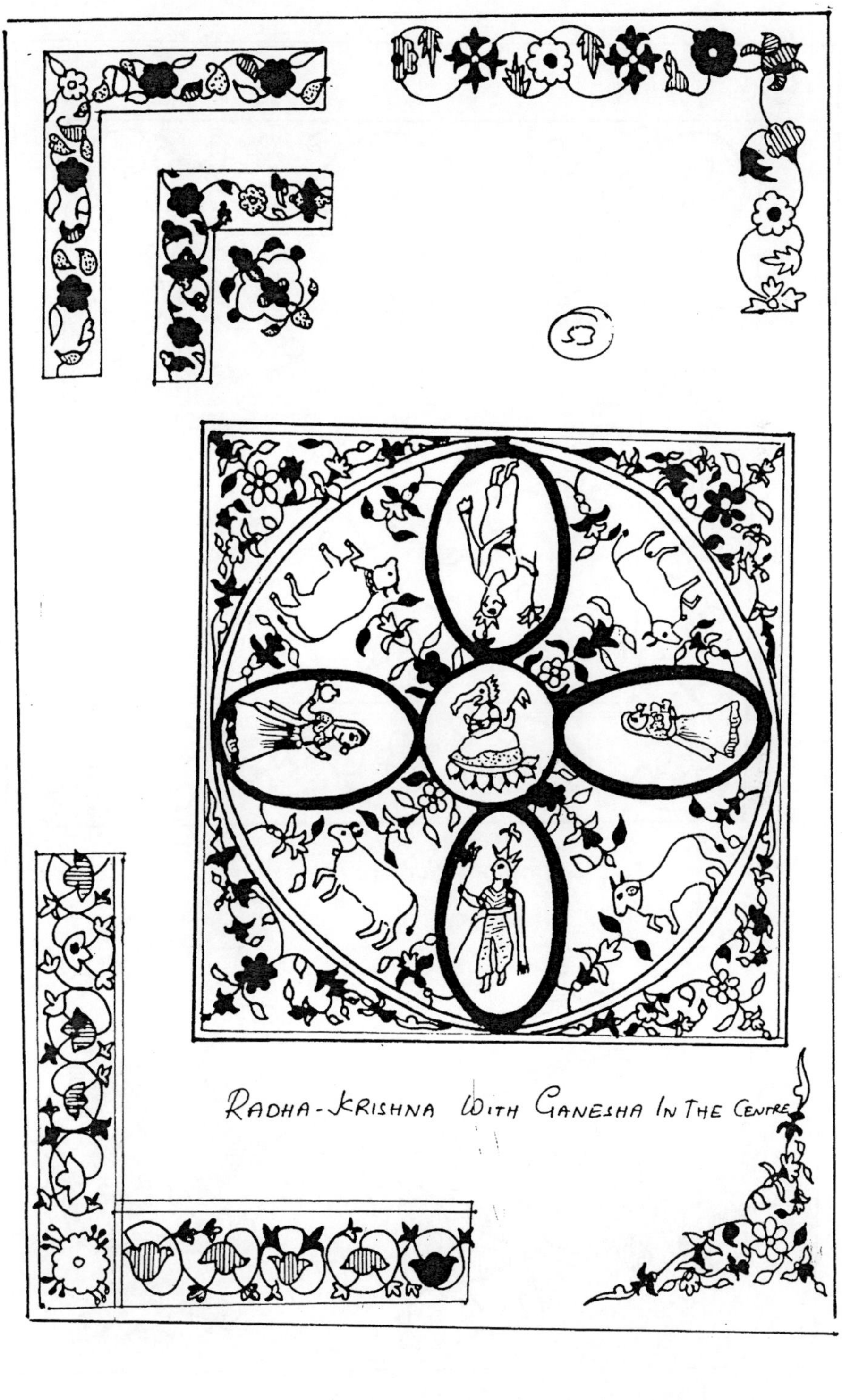

RADHA-KRISHNA WITH GANESHA IN THE CENTRE

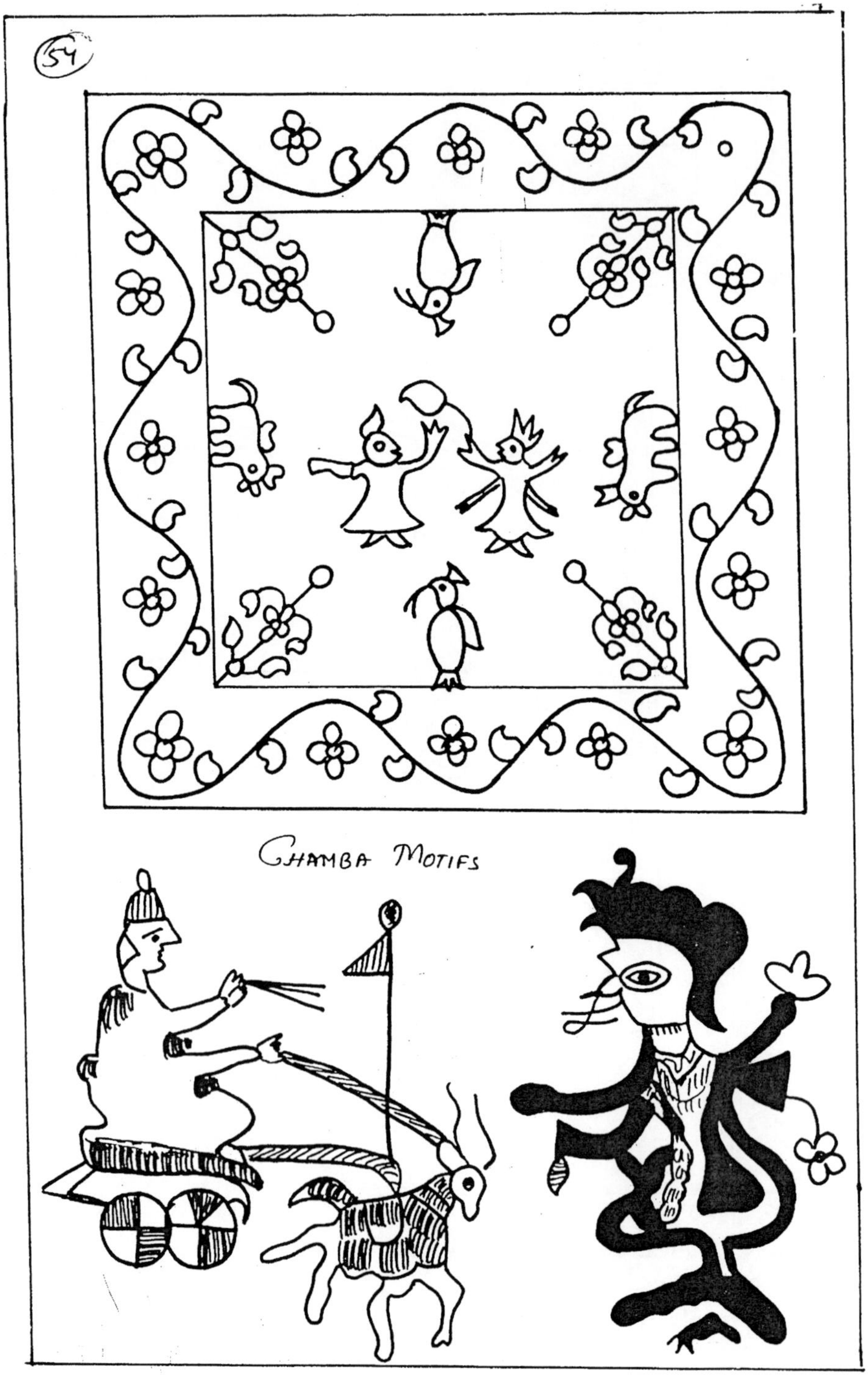
54
CHAMBA MOTIFS

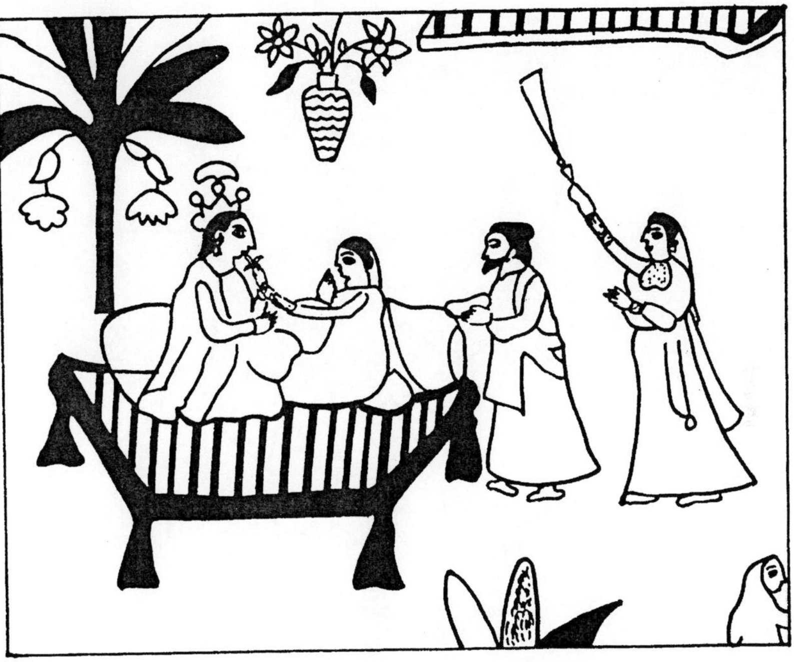

RADHA-KRISHNA AT LEISURE

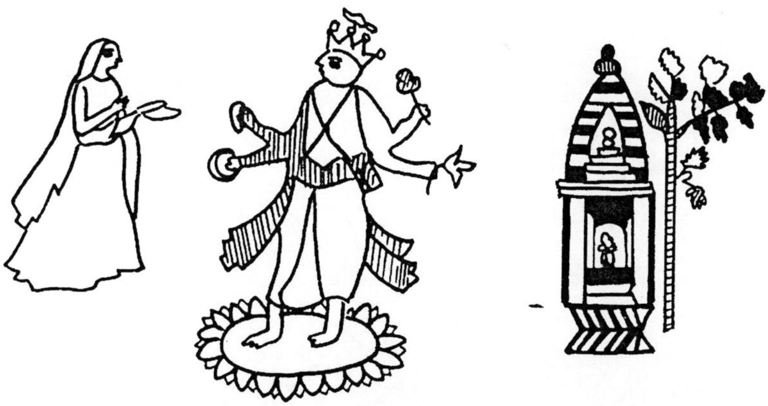

RADHA WORSHIPING LORD KRISHNA

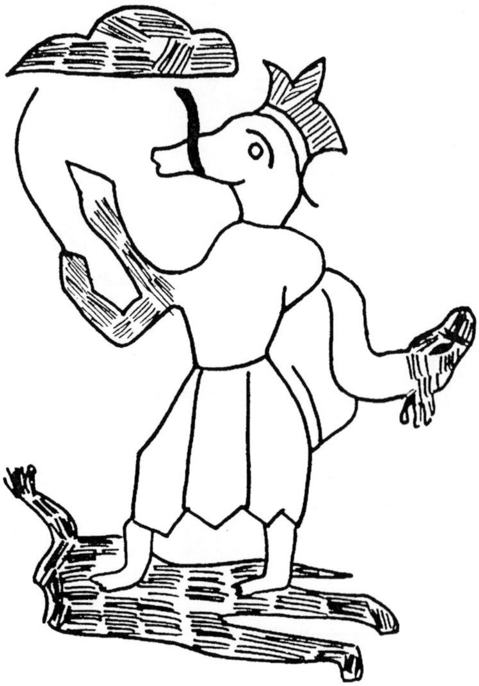

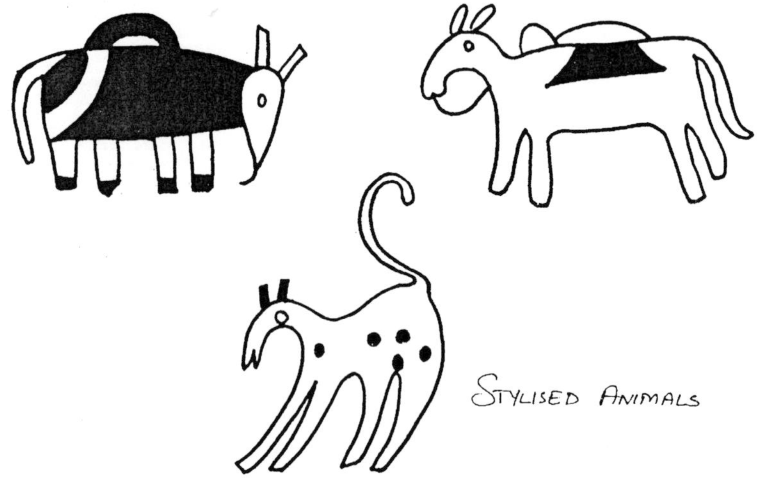

Stylised Animals

CHAPTER 5

KASUTI OF KARNATAKA

India has a rich heritage of art, music, dance, sculpture, architecture, carpentry, metal work, wire wörk, designing, painting, embroidery and so on. Among them Indian embroidery expresses unity in diversity because the art of embroidery exhibited by Indians who lived widely region wise.

'Kasuti' is a world famous embroidery of Karnataka state earlier was known as Mysore state, the motifs and art is a part of women's world. Kasuti embroidery speaks about the people of Karnataka their traditions, customs and professions. This is an outcome of the honest, zealous and innate desire of 'mankind' to practice the beautiful stitches on the articles of every day use. The urge of learning Kasuti was common to both royals, aristocrats and peasand women.

Karnataka Kasuti has a historic background, Smt. Indira Joshi explains that "there had a Second Golden Age from the sixth to tenth century in India after the decline of the Gupta Empire in North. Then the South was ruled by Satvahanas, Chalukyas, Rastryakutas, Pallavas, Pandyas, Cholas and others. Out of these emperors the Chalukyas who ruled Badami played an important role in the revival of art, culture and learning. Though there were wars among the emperors of various dynasties, they helped to re-establish the old vedic region and encouraged the cults of Shiva and Vishnu by installing numbers of temples to these deities. The most important world famous are the cave temples of Badami and the magnificent shrines of Aihole an Pattadakallu of Badami Taluk. It is said that Kasuti resembles the embroidery of Austria, Hungary and Spain. However, the origin of Kasuti is not known as, there are no evidences in the form of historical legends, exhibits, records, literature or any other sources of information. The word Kasuti can be analysed as 'Kai" means hand and 'Suti' is cotton thread, i.e. Kasuti is hand work of cotton thread, in Karnataka language.

During the seventeenth century when Mysore was being ruled by Maharajas, the women in the court were well versed in sixty four arts and one of them was the art of Kasuti embroidery. The women folk got inspiration of witnessing the various temples, caves, shrines, buildings beautifully sculptured with exquisite patterns, the traditional functions and the festivals and embraced these artistic activities in flourishing the art, culture and learning. The women expressed their artistic urge by embroidering delicate piece of colourful art, the Kasuti. There were no special classes arranged or books were made available for the folk to refer but this art was passed from person to person and generation to generation. The Lingayats, the followers of cult shiva, now also known as Veerasaivas, were of course expertised and leading in this art. During leisure time the grand mothers used to teach Kasuti to their grand children, daughter-in-laws and neighbours. In the olden days it was a custom that the bride had to possess a black silk sari, called 'chandrakali sari' with Kasuti work on it. As a matter of fact traditionally this embroidery is done on saris and blouses.

In Northern Karnataka, the main profession of the population is weaving and they produced traditionally world famous Ilkal and Ilkal type saris on fly shuttle pit looms in pure cotton, silk and rayon. On the other hand the khans (choli pieces) are also woven with extra warp figurines. Dharwad and Bijapur districts have hand loom weaving sectors, at present too.

Kasuti work is traditionally done all along the border and red coloured 'tope-teri seragu', the elaborate pallav and body of the sari. The motifs or butties in the body of the sari became smaller in size and the number gradually decreased towards the pleats of the sari. That is to say, each sari can have as many as sixty to seventy motifs, repeated in variety of colours, all over the body and pallav.

Kasuti started as a domestic art which kept pace with the sculpturing, architectural work of their men folk, who built the temples and buildings with elaborate designs and colour combinations. The artistic women picked up the designs like gopuram, deepamalas, tulsi vrindavans, chariot, palanquine, the steeds of various Gods etc. apart from many birds and animals.

Kasuti is famous in many places of Bijapur, Dharwad, Balgaum and Jamakhandi districts. Kasuti art has remained as home craft and not developed into a cottage industry as the embroidery was done on the articles of their personal use and perhaps these articles were not regarded as marketable commodities. The hand, work, skill art and embroidery were considered as a complement for the individual.

Each family used to try out various motifs on a piece of white cotton material, and preserved as a model or sample piece. The young girls in the family used to refer to this sample piece while learning the technique of Kasuti embroidery. Some families have even the motifs worked on the matty cloth, framed and preserved.

The motifs used in Kasuti embroider ranged from mythological and architectural to the beautiful flora and fauna, i.e., gopuras, palanquine, chariot, shiva-linga, bull (Nandi), tiger, lamp stand, crown of Shiva (Shivana Basinga), swastika, sun, surya mukhi, conchshell, asanas, Rama's cradle, snake (Naga devta), elephant, horse, tulsi vrundavan, Hanuman etc. Apart from steeds of Shiva and Laxmi, squirrel, parrot, sparrow, peacock, cock, duck pigeon, swan, deer, are also seen. Various types of foliages creepers, flowers are however, used in this embroidery. The main ones are lotus, chrysanthemum, jasmine, rui-phool (cotton flower), cashew nut (kalka), grapes, kevada, kalawar, diamond, badam, berseed, black bead, maggi hua, marigold, coconut flower, sparrows eye, rudraksha, tulsi leaf, brinjal seed, cardamum, chess square, flower pot, etc.

Many of these motifs are used as straight and corner borders ranging from half rich width to three to four inches size. All these motifs are embroidered in small, medium and large sizes.

Stitches in Kasuti are always vertical, horizontal and diagonal. The main speciality of this embroidery is that never the design is traced in the material to be embroidered and the embroidery starts without knotting thread but with a tiny back stitch. The stitches are simple, minute, intricate and pretty. Kasuti is done always by counting the threads. The four types of stitches are, Gavanti, Murgi, Negi and Menthi. Different patterns and motifs are worked in different stitches but some have mixed stitches. The number of threads on the material forms a unit, two to six threads for fine and coarse work respectively. However, the unit should remain constant till the design is completed.

'Gavanti' is the most simple and common stitch, derived from the Kannada word 'Gantu' means 'knot. It is a double running stitch, in which the first running stitch is filled in by the second running stitch on the same line. The second running stitch work exactly opposite to the first one. Gavanthi may be worked in horizontal, vertical or diagonal directions.

'Murgi' is a zigzag running stitch which appears like steps of a ladder or staircase. It is same as gavanthi stitch but works in a stepwise manner. The work in both gavanthi and murgi stitches is neat and tidy, where the design appears same on right and wrong side of the material. However, the stitches should be of uniform size. The distance between two stitches is nothing but the length of each stitch. Smallest motifs like square, triangle, hexagonal, ladders, flower are to be practiced so that the elaborate designs can be worked. A large geometric design is produced by grouping the tiny designs on regular intervals and sequences.

'Negi' is another stitch in Kasuti. 'Negi' in Kannada means 'to weave' i.e. the design with Negi design has an overall effect of a woven design. Negi is nothing but ordinary running or darning stitch. It is worked in long and short straight lines or floats and therefore the design does not appear identical on either sides of the cloth.

'Menthi' is the fourth type of stitch which means the ordinary cross stitch. In Karnataka 'Menthi' means fenugreek seed but however, people of Karnataka identify the cross stitch as 'menthi' only. This cross stitch is usually appears heavy as is used for filling purpose. This stitch requires more length of thread than the other three stitches. Similar to Negi, even this stitch does not give same appearance on either sides of the cloth.

In olden days Kasuti was done on Ilkal silk sari or Ilkal type village sari having broad pallav, called 'tope-teni' and simple border with plain body. In order to add colour and beauty to the sari, small Kasuti motifs were worked in the pallav region and many times the borders in negi and murgi stitches were also worked in. However, this simple handloom sari was made appear gorgeous by Kasuti embroidery. The choli worn along with the sari is known as 'khan', on which Kasuti was done with the matching colour, motifs and borders of the sari. The women folk used to decorate the Kunchagi kulai (bonnets), used for children and other women's regional costume was embroidered. But now Kasuti is also done on household linen like, kerchiefs, bed covers, sofa covers, cushion covers curtains, shopping bags carpets (Jute), plain saris of silk, cotton or synthetics, salwar suits, yokes, cuffs, collars, belts, pockets, dupattas, caps, and used as trimming for children's garments.

In olden days the thread used for Kasuti work was drawn from the tassels of pallav of Ilkal saris, to make the design appear flat, rich and gorgeous. In those days silk thread was available in Mysore. Now instead of silk yarns, mercerised cotton threads from D.M.C., Anchor, Kohinoor with guaranteed colour fastness is employed. A single strand is employed for fine and delicate work and for filling and coarse work two to four strands are taken. However, the number of strands varied according to the type of material, motif and stitch employed. Kasuti can be worked neatly in matty cloth, used for household linen articles. The canvas material can also be conveniently used for cross stitch work. As working Kasuti by counting threads is eye straining and hence people prefer to work on matty and canvas materials.

The colours most frequently used are red, orange, purple, green yellow, and blue. White is predominant on black background. The commonly used combinations are red-green, red-blue, red-yellow, red-white, orange-purple, pink-purple, blue-orange, green-yellow and yellow-white. In other words they used all bright and contrast colours to make the design appear more bold and clear.

The women folk in the village feel prestigious to possess a Kasuti Ilkal sari and express their love and affection towards this art by wearing it during various religious auspicious functions. Many expectant mothers receive the hand woven khans embroidered in Kasuti pattern as auspicious gifts.

Some of the young farm women in Karnataka, have taken up Kasuti work as their income generating business. The women are free from farm work by March till June in the year and this leisure time is utilised in earning their livelihood by Kasuti embroidering. In olden days the wages that the farm women received were in the form of roti, rice, paddy, jawar, green gram, Bengal gram, ground nut and other food grains; festival sweets and ofcourse cash sometimes. The cost of Kasuti work ranged between Rs. 2/-, 5/- and increased to Rs. 25/- slowly. However, the charges varied according to the labour.

Karnataka Government has identified 'Kasuti Embroidering' is a very good source of income generating activity for the farm women and Karnataka State Development Board is trying for the revival of Karnataka Kasuti. The Janata Shikshana Samithi and other Co-operative societies organise a training programme on 'Kasuti embroidery' for a period of ten months and the trainees get a stipend of Rs. 150/- P.M. The trained candidates take the orders and earn their bread. The 'Ilkal type Kasuti' which includes all traditional motifs embroidered in pallav costs about rupees six hundred. Maharashtra, especially Bombay is the main market for Karnataka Kasuti. The real appreciation for Kasuti comes from Northern India. The cost of Kasuti is usually double or triple the amount of the actual sari or dress.

Now in the world of computer, computer science and its technology, one can expect definitely that Kasuti can be computerised, which is ofcourse a sad fact. Because a tiny computer snatches away the source of livelihood of many young and innocent farm women and their family. Lets hope for its survival and revival.

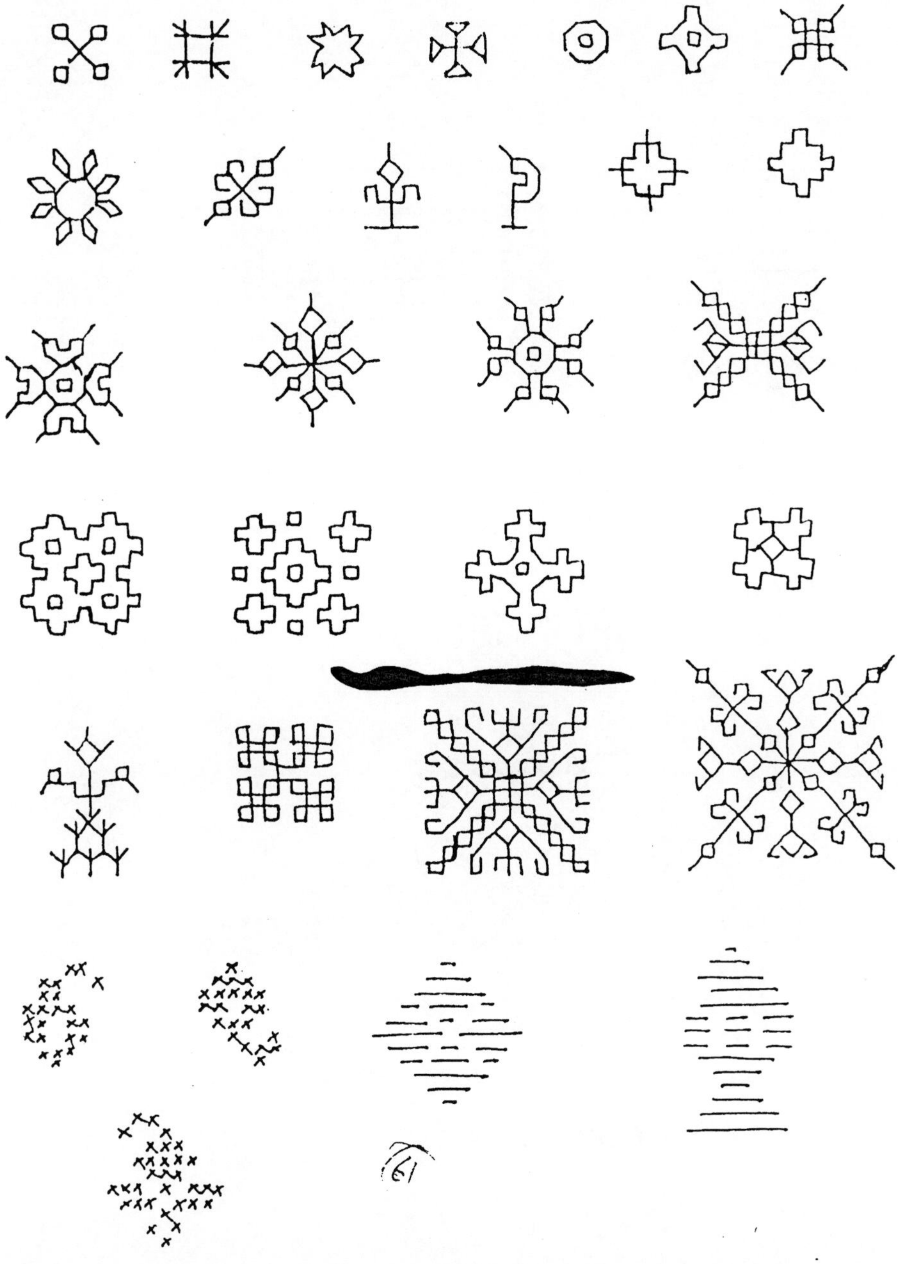

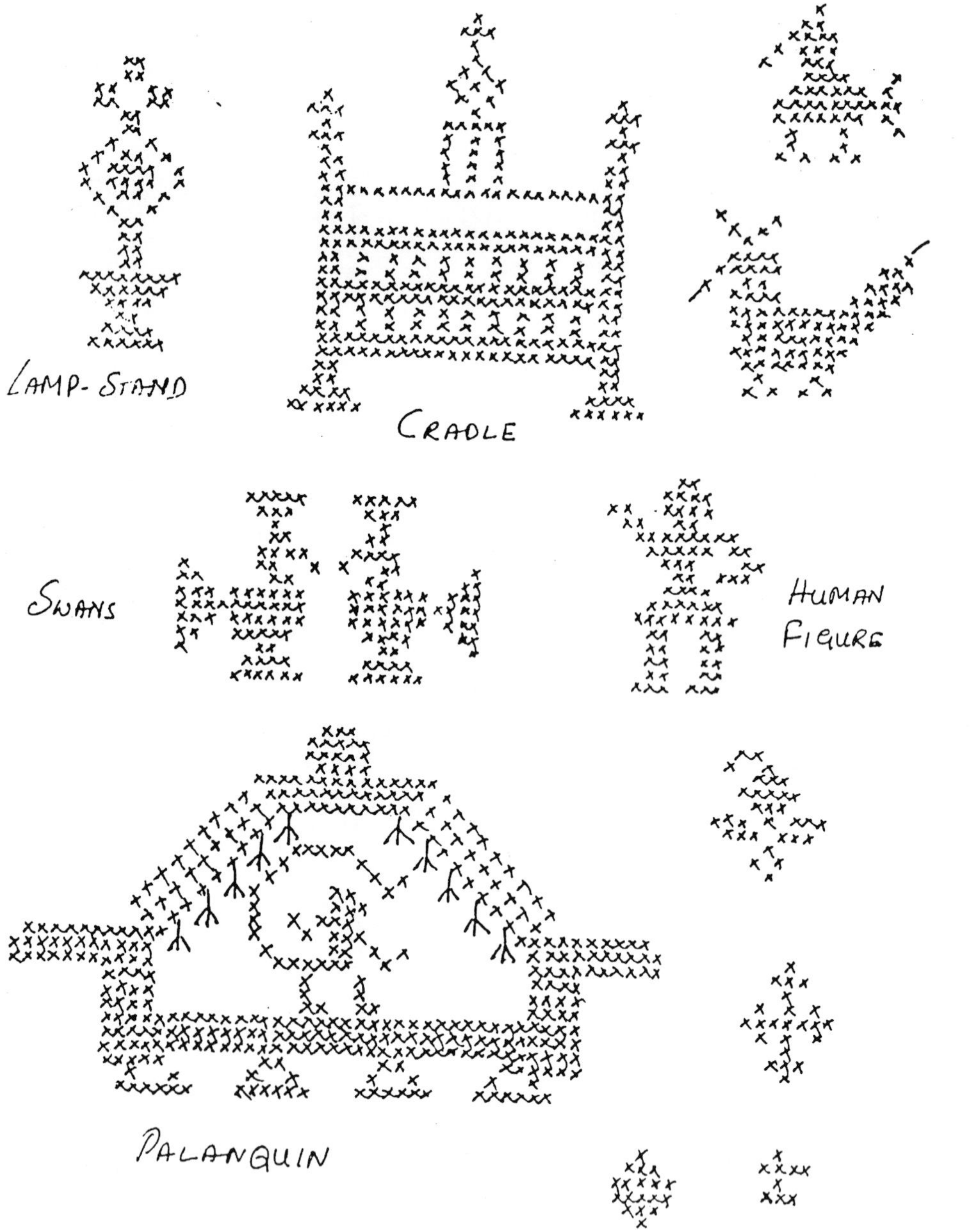
LAMP-STAND
CRADLE
SWANS
HUMAN FIGURE
PALANQUIN

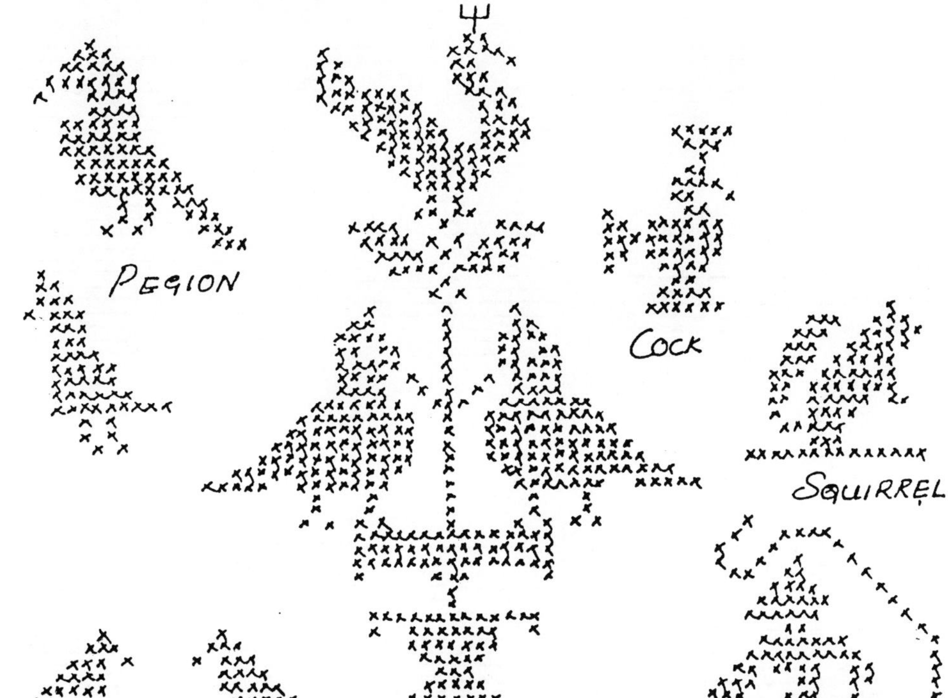
PEGION
COCK
SQUIRREL
SPARROW
LAMP
PEA-COCK
NANDI

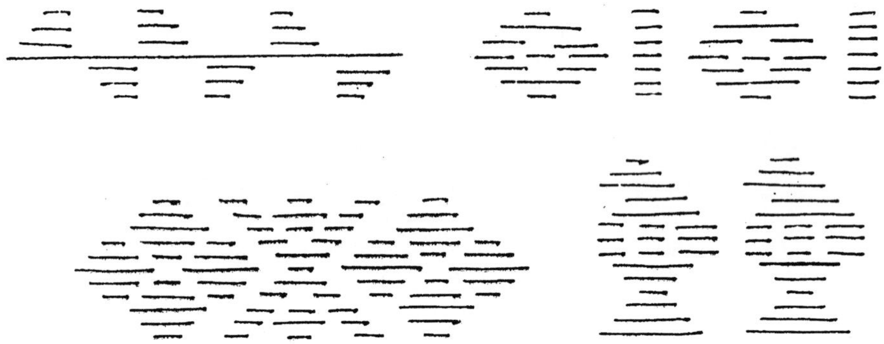

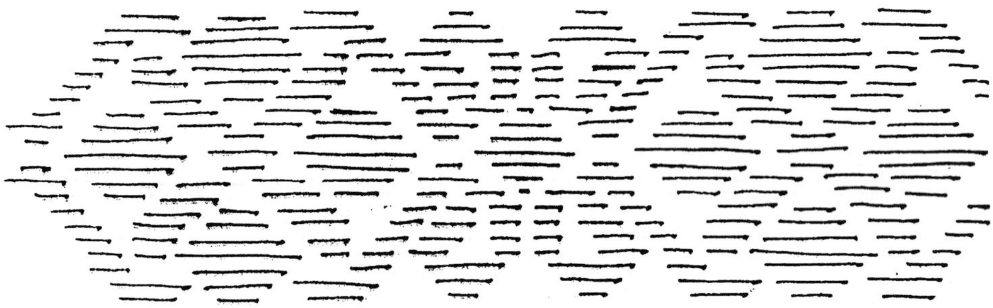

FLORAL BORDER

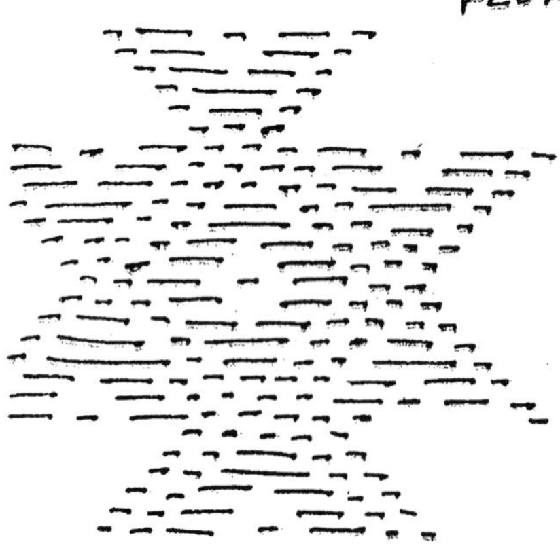

AASANA

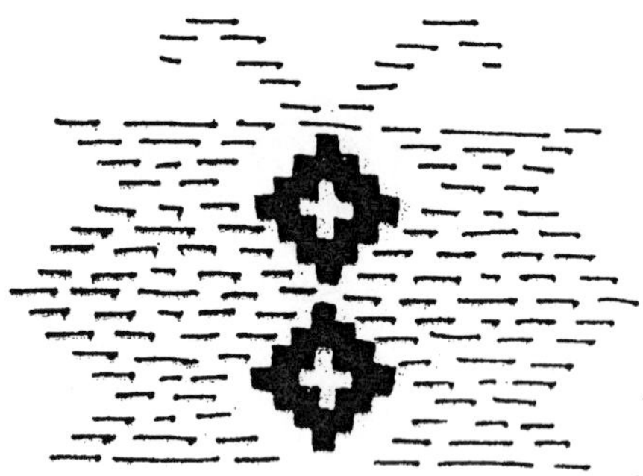

BUTTER FLY

A SERPENT

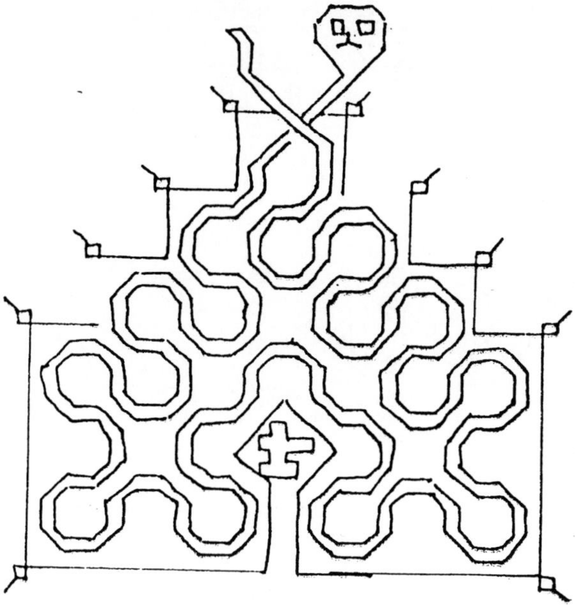

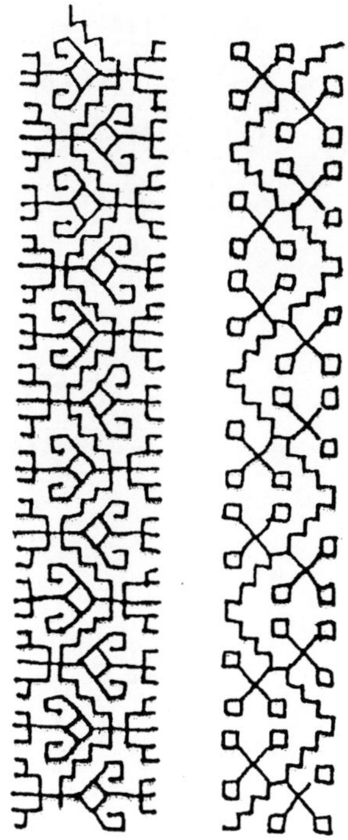

BORDERS

AN ASANA

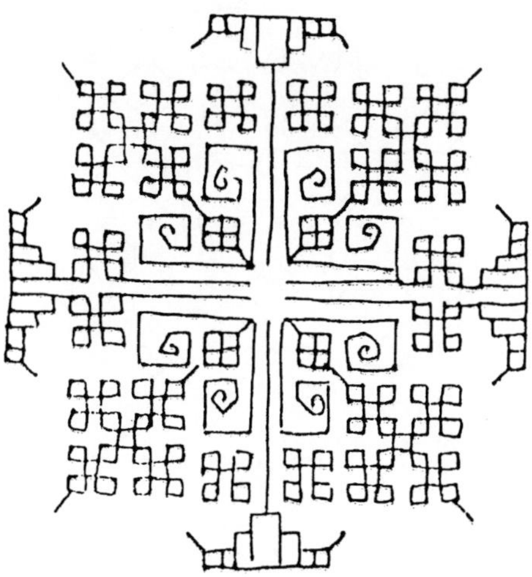

A GOPURUM

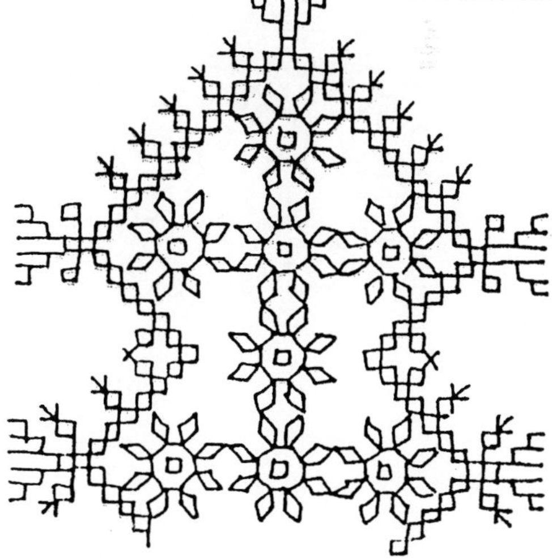

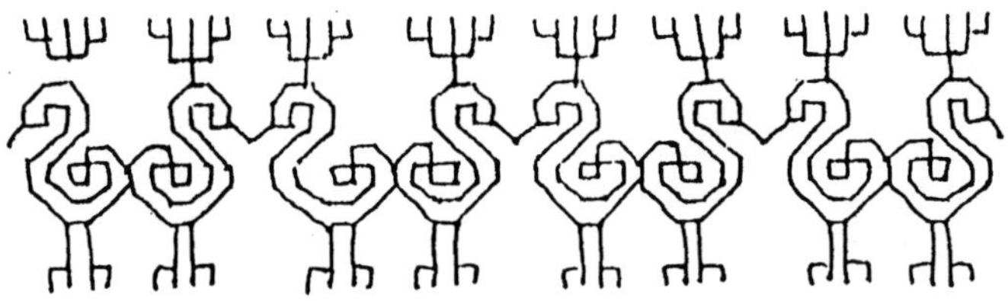

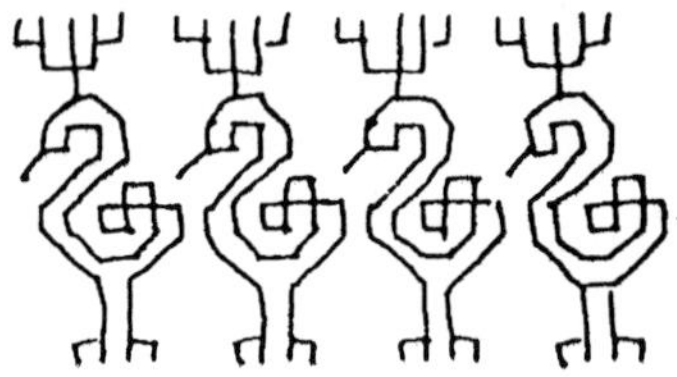

SWANS

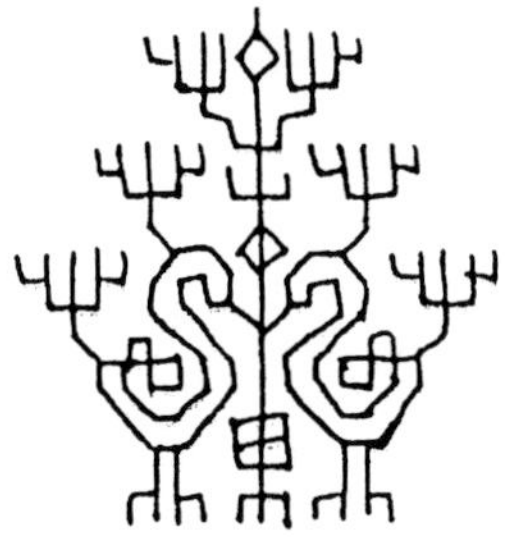

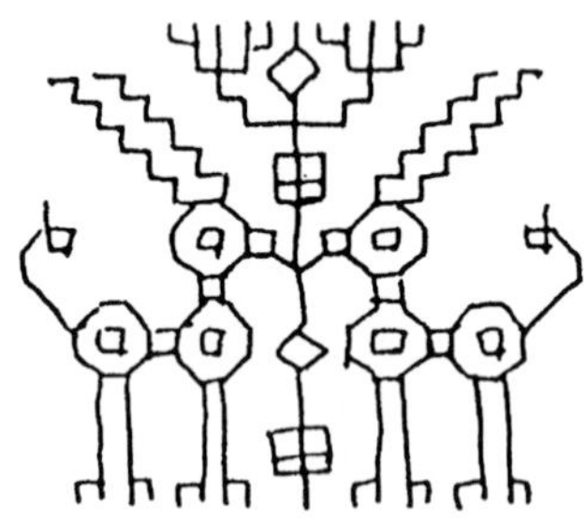

DEER

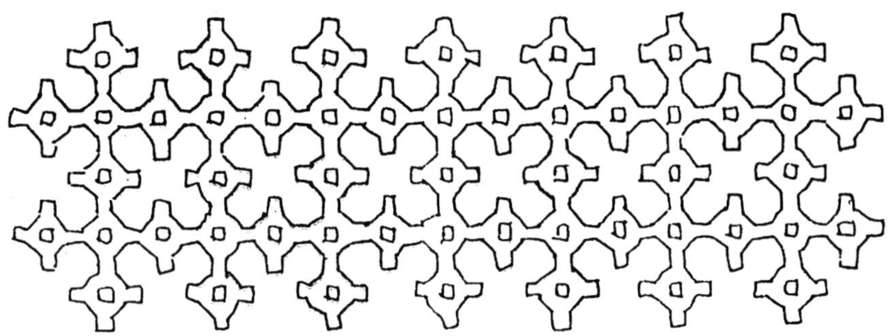

BORDER

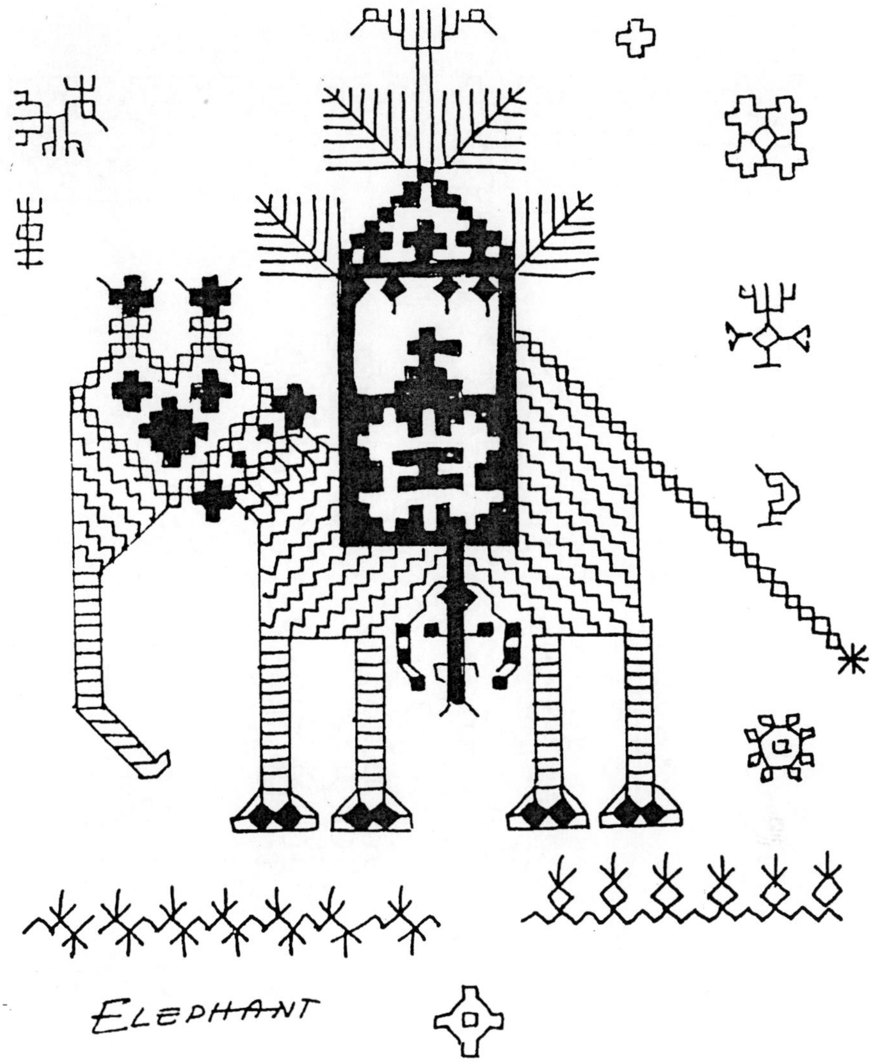
ELEPHANT

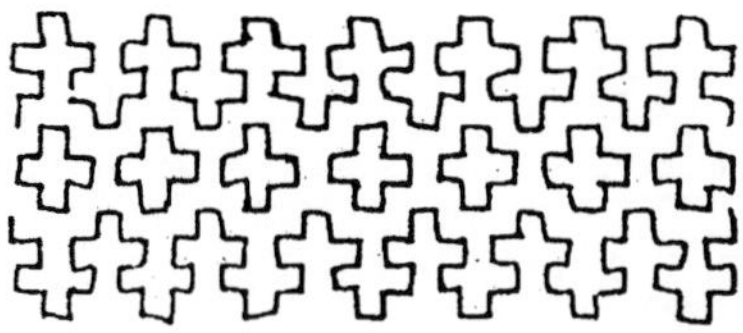

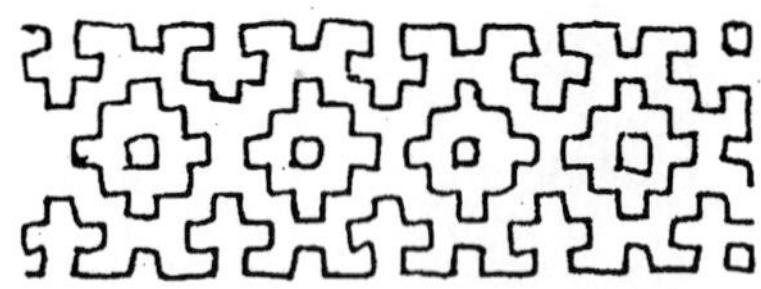

PEDESTAL

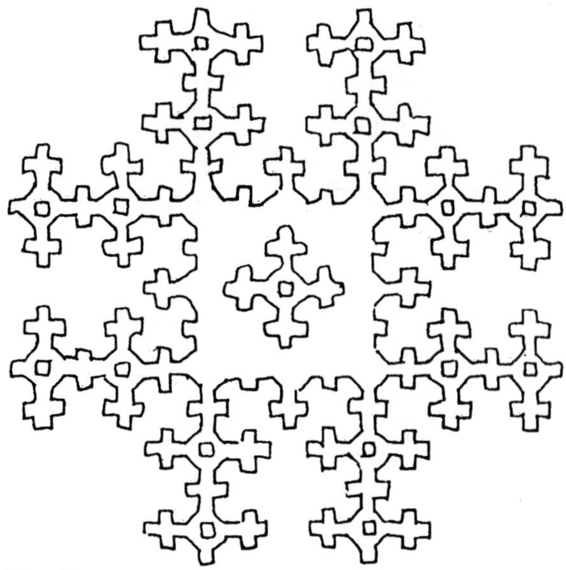

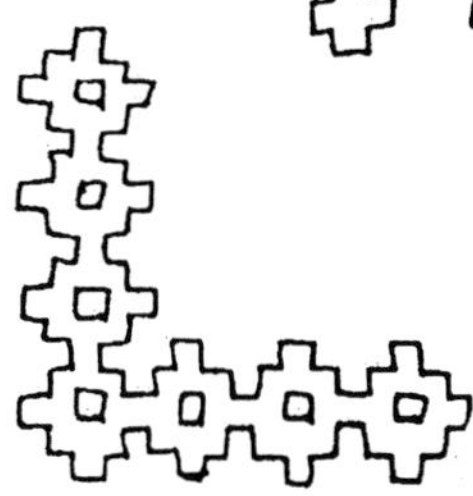

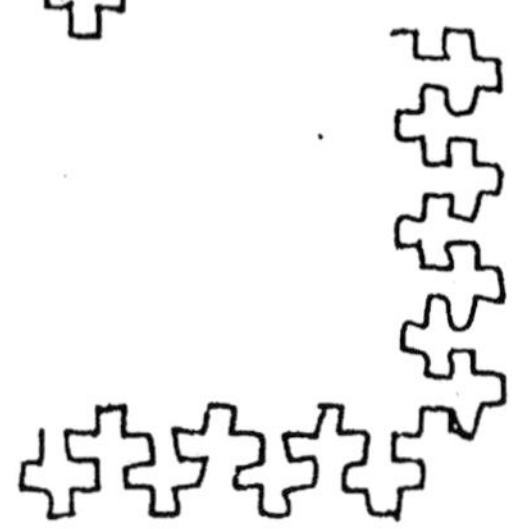

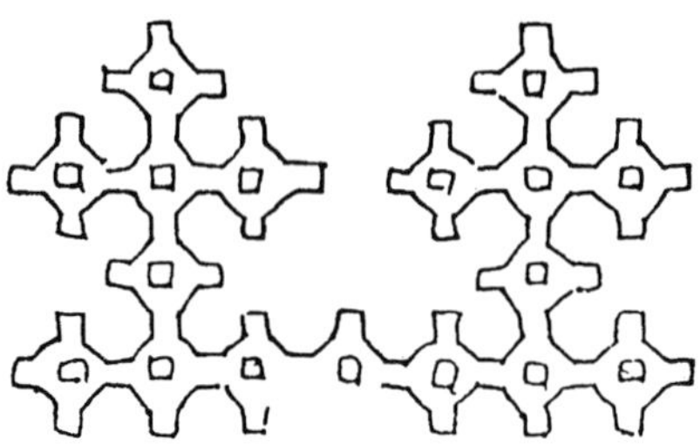

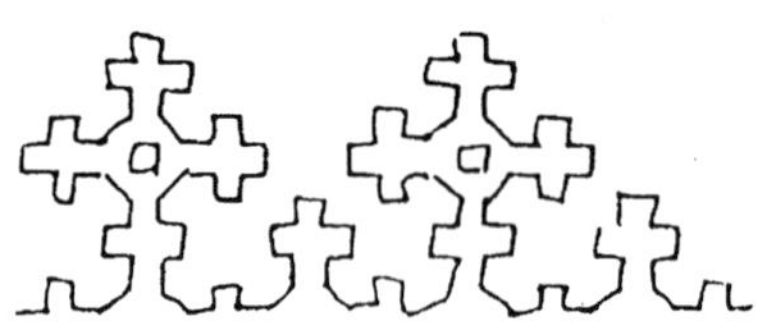

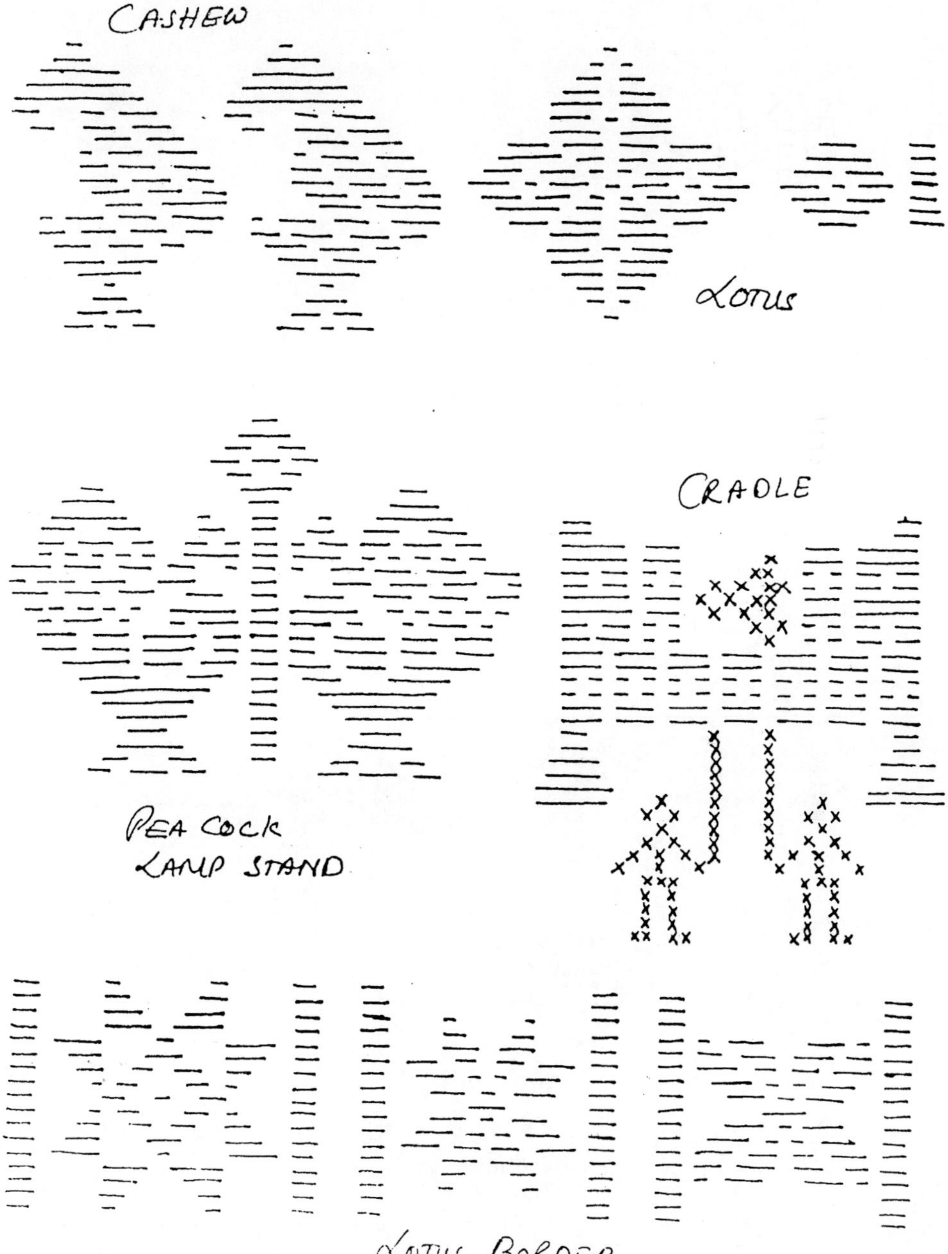
CASHEW
LOTUS
CRADLE
PEA COCK
LAMP STAND
LOTUS BORDER

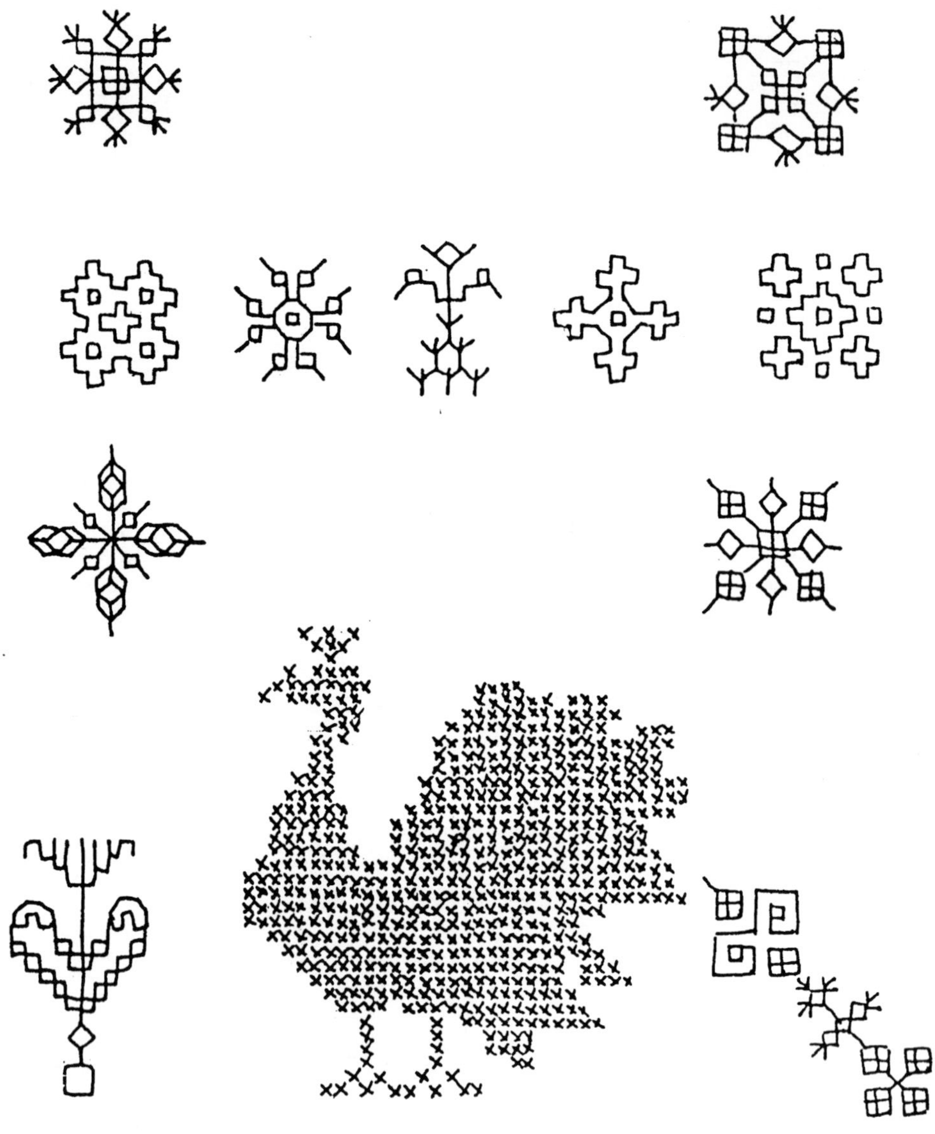

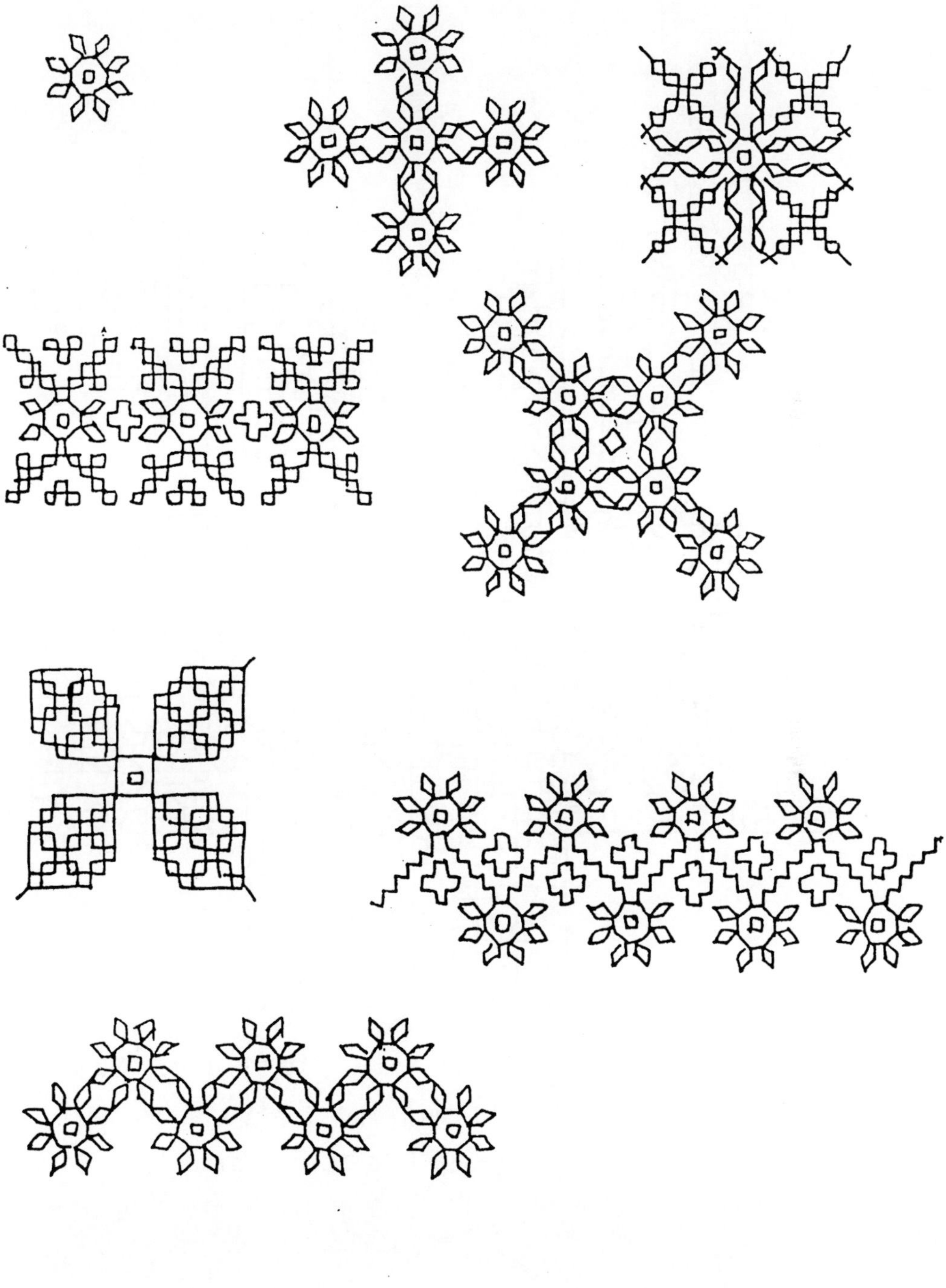

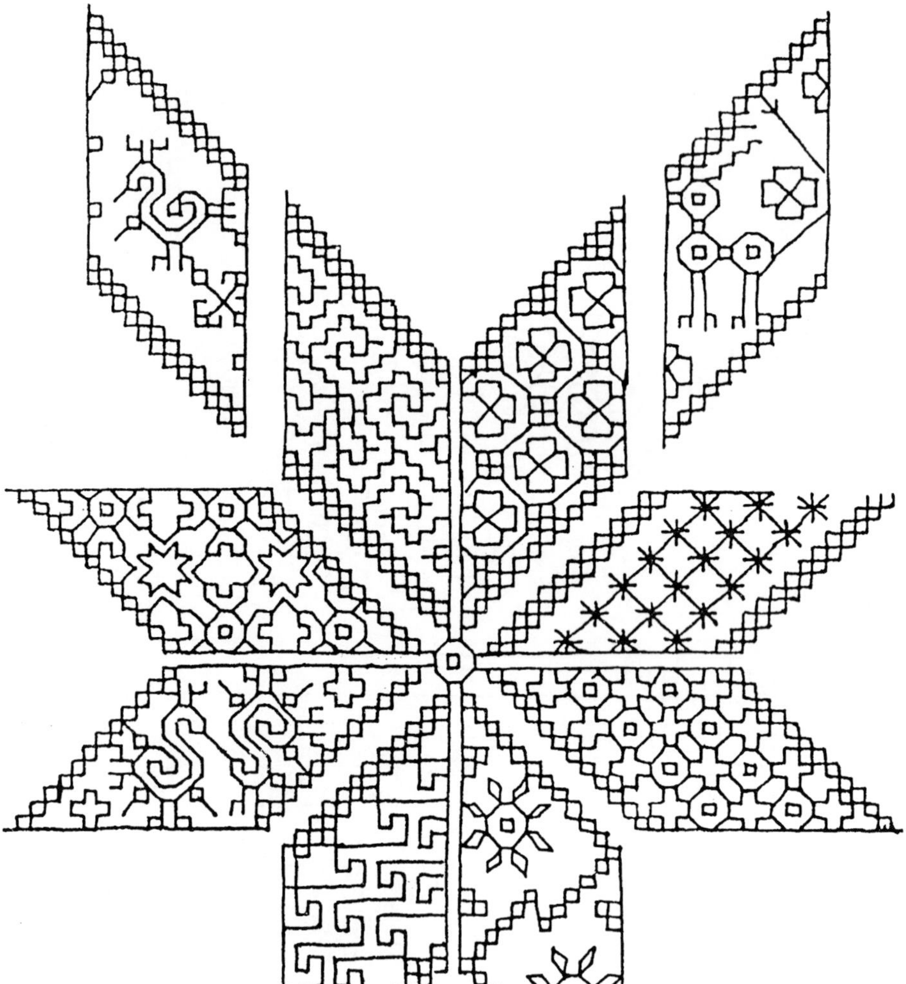

LOTUS
WITH DIFFERENT PETALS

KASUTI STITCHES

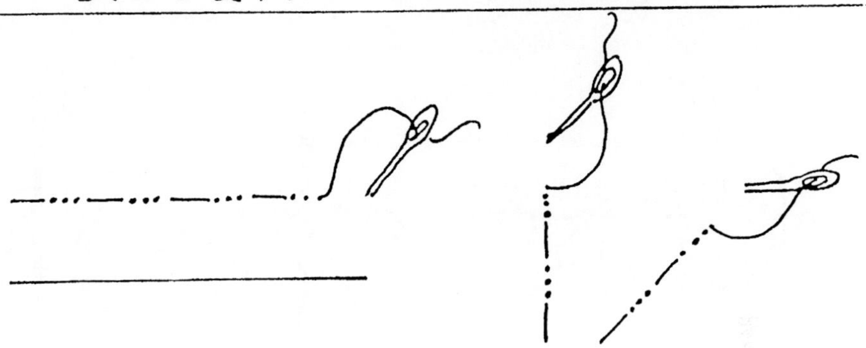

I GAVANTI STITCH

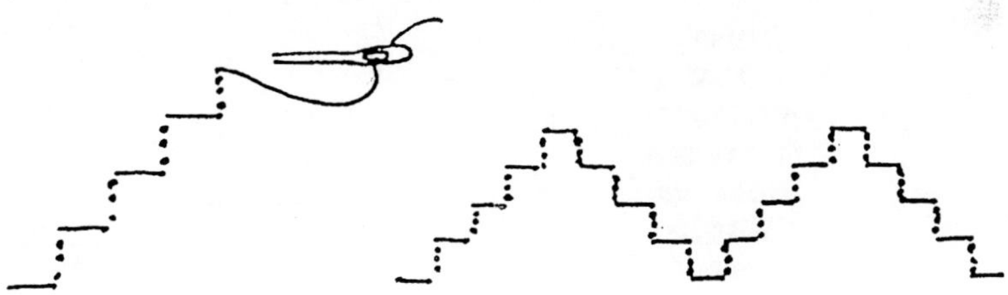

II MURGI STITCH

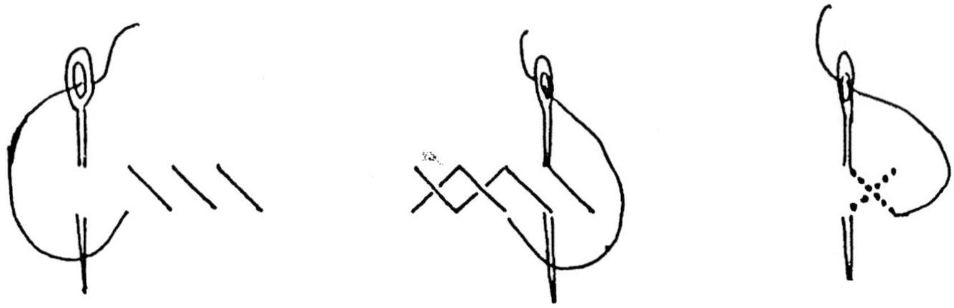

III METHI STITCH

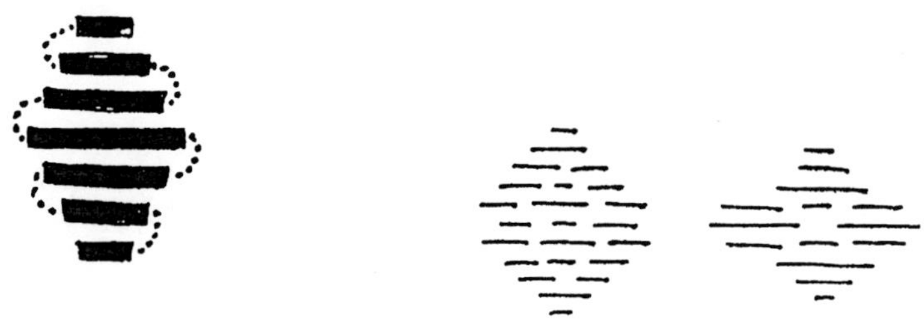

IV NEGI STITCH

CHAPTER 6
KASHIDA OF KASHMIR

The word Kashmir can be splitted as 'Kas' means 'water channel' and 'Mir' refers to 'mountain', however literally Kashmir means 'rock through' in the regional language. A legend reveals that a Semitic tribe 'kash', including Hebrew, Arabic and Jews, inhabited in Kashmir much before A.D. 541, might be one of the reasons for the title 'Kashmir'.

The Northern most state of India, Jammu and Kashmir is known for its beauty. The locality is embedded with enchanting beautiful and inexhaustible flora and fauna, transquil lakes, garden of perpetual spring, abundance of natural colour all around, which has inspired many writers, poets, artists and creative craftmen.

The best known of Indian embroidery is the Kashida of Kashmir and its carpet industry ofcourse world famous. Kashida on Kashmir shawls are recognised for their beauty, colour, motifs, artistic appearance and texture. Dr. Abdual Ahad, a historian from Srinagar, expressed that weaving in Kashmir was known as early as third century B.C. Twill tapestry weaving was popularly known during this period and shawls were sold as 'Kanikars'. According to Dr. Moti Chandra todays art historian, weaving brocade tapestry had commenced as early as eleventh century A.D. The industry however, reached its prosperity with the Mughal patronage.

The shawl industry flourished by Sultan Zain-ul-Abidin, during fifteenth century, who identified, selected and brought the most talented craftmen and weavers from Persia to revive the existing art. These craftmen brought new phase in the craftsmanship by introducing and moulding the whole composition, structure and style of shawl by employing new motifs and stitches with various colour combinations. However, this change brought close relationship and resemblance between Persian and Kashmir embroidery, specially with the motifs. Many of the Persian floral designs were artistically transformed to most naturalistic flowers of Mughal art, thus many Indo-Persian floral designs were evolved in the art of Kashida.

The demand for Kashmir shawls increased during Mughal rule. A mention was made about these shawls in Ain-i-Akbari during the reign of king Akbar. During the eighteenth century the shawls were exported to European countries and were gracefully draped by the European ladies over their outfit, ofcourses in an Indo-European style. By the end of eighteenth century the shawl industry was deprived because of high taxes and directly affected the cost of production. In order to bring down the prices and save the levy imposed, Khwaja Yusuf and Armenian agent played an instrumental role in producing the shawl with hand needle. He was the first person to exploit the skill to produce needle embroidered shawls.

However, the shawl industry declined by the end of nineteenth century probably because of increase in the cost, and change in the fashion trend, all over the world. Owing to the fall in demand, many weavers had to face economical crises. Some these weavers slowly shifted to carpet weaving, few concentrated on embroidering with hand needle and rest involved in producing inexpensive shawls with embroidered pattern.

There are various types of woven Kashmir shawls namely 'Pashmina Shawl', a superior quality shawl woven with pure wool. According to Rustom J. Mehta, 'these shawls are difficult to obtain as India has restricted its trade with Tibet'. Pashmina shawls are made from the fleece of Capra Hercus a species of wild Asian Goat. 'Do-shala' which means double shawl, sold always in pairs. Two identical shawls are stitched together, and are reversible, 'Do-Rookha' is another double sided shawl, which appears same on either sides, right and wrong. Sometimes a single design is reproduced in two different colours, giving double sided pattern like 'Dhoop-Chav'. The 'Jamewar Shawl' is a pure wool or cotsool a blend of cotton and wool used as background, on which a floral design and brocade is produced with silk and fine quality wool like Pashmina. There are shawls square in shape called 'Kasaba', specially produced on the demand of Europeans. They are generally in twill weave or basket patterns woven against plain background.

Basically Kashida is a cottage industry involves all most all the family members, residing near by Srinagar. Surprisingly this commercial art has been done by menfolk and has become a hereditary with the father to pass on the skill to his sons. The boys in the family of seven to eight years old, begin their work of Kashida with a very simple stem stitch on inexpensive shawls and continues to gain skill by repeating the motifs on small samples, beginning with outlining them. By the age of sixteen, he does attain the skill, hand, delicacy and profesy in the craft. After putting about twenty years of continuous practice he will be recognised to take up fine work on Pashmina and Shahtoosh shawls. Women folk do participate but amount of work attained by them will be relatively limited. The dealers place orders by providing the cloth and designs. However, the craftmen have their choice over threads and colour combination.

Before commencing the embroidery work the selected design is traced on the fabric. The tracing is done by the professional tracers called Naquashband (Nakshaband) who follow the traditional technique even today. For tracing, the fabric is spread on a flat surface and the perforated design sheet is placed over the fabric. Then the charcoal or chalk power is rubbed over it, which leaves the impression over the fabric. Sometimes gum arabic is added to the powder, to make the tracings durable. The design is outlined with 'Kalam' the pen. Greater percent of motifs are picked up from nature, which provides inspiration to Naquabandi, a hereditary profession carried from one generation to another. However, new designs have continuously been added depending upon the fashion trend and consumers demand.

All over the world in broad spectra, whenever hand work, embroidery, and intricate designing involved is always been considered as a women's craft. It is very interesting to note here that Kashmiri men are expertised in Kashida of Kashmir.

A large variety of flowers of tremendous colours, shapes, size namely lili, lotus, tulip, saffron, iris, bunches of grapes, apple, almond, cherries, plums; birds like Kingfisher, parrot, wood pecker, magpie, canary all appear in Kashida. The chinar leaf is the motif most abundantly used along with cyprus tree. Rustom J. Metha explains in his Masterpieces of Indian Textiles that "Primarily the flowers and foliages alone dominate, the delicate stems mendering all over, slender, Lanceolot leaves filling the interspaces, attempting to surpass even Nature's own profusion.

Many beautifully coloured butterflies found in the sanctuary and valley have occupied an important place in the Kashida. Animal and human figures are not found commonly, probably the influence of Muslims. But few old pieces depicted hunting scene popularly known as 'shikargah', available only in Museums of Srinagar. The borders of such motifs had bands of marching soldiers and horse riders embroidered on separate panels. The use of such motifs slowly declined and has given an impression that, such figures were never used in Kashida of Kashmir.

Several forms of cones existed in Indo-Persian art around seventeenth and eighteenth century. The cone shaped mango motif, the 'Kalka' or 'Badami Buta' or 'Buta', popularly known in regional language emerged into Kashmiri embroidery, which is now produced in infinite verities on naturalistic, geometrical and stylized grounds. This motif originates from Persian art, brought to Kashmir an exhibits influence of Indo-Persian art, during seventeenth and eighteenth century.

The ground fabric on which embroidery done is composed of various types of wool like Pashmina, Shahtoosh, Aslitus, varieties of silk, cotton, chinon and linen. Usually the embroidery is done on the undyed material of white or cream background. However, according to the demand of the consumers the mill made fabrics are dyed (except fine quality Pashmina and Shahtoosh) in darker shades such as black, navy blue, brown, bottle green, Maroon and so on.

The embroidery thread employed earlier was fine quality woollen yarns. Gradually woollen yarns were replaced by rich and lustrous silk threads. The bright, gorgeous in-expensive art silk (rayon) thread has entered the industry by replacing the expensive silk threads. Cotton threads of bright colours with good colour fastness are also used abundantly.

The embroidery is comprised of wide spectrum of colours of light and dark shades, such as crimson red, scarlet red, blue, yellow, green, purple, black and brown. Earlier, the yarns were locally dyed with indigenous natural colours. The dyers were expertised to produce as many as sixty four tints and shades in single colour, exhibited very good colour fastness. But now a days all the threads used in the industry are invariably mill dyed with synthetic dye stuffs.

The technique of Kashida originated with darn stitch, used as a finish to the shawl by the Rafugar. It is a simple running stitch gives a woven design effect on the shawls. Stem stitch usually in darker shade used to give shape to the motif by outlining it. Other stitches include Sozni (satin), zalakdozi (chain) and vata chikan (button hole). Occasionally herring bone, doria (openwork) and talaibar (gold work) are also employed. However, Kashida is the general term used to signify Kashmiri embroidery.

Kashida was mainly done on all types of shawls produced in Kashmir. But now this ornamentation has been widely produced on dress material, sari, coat, jacket, kurta, muffler, veil, dupatta, turban, table-linen, tea-cosy cover, cushion cover, bed spread, hand kerchiefs, curtain, quilt, table-mats, floor coverings like Namda and Gabba.

The embroidery on shawl is done at different parts like border, corner, centre, all over scattered and accordingly the names in regional language is given, says Moorcraft. The border design which runs all along the length of the shawl on either sides known as Hashia (Hashiya), could be in either single or double sometimes even triple. Phala is the embroidery done on both the ends of the article, popularly also known as pallu. Tanjir or zanjir is the border with chain stitch running either above or below the phala. Kunj Butta is a cluster of flowers in the corner. Butta is the generic name for the floral design, especially used for a cone or conical design, which is the main feature of Phala. Different names are given to the varied number of rows of Butta in the Phala i.e. when in two rows Dokad, up to five rows sehkad and more than five Tukadar. Alifdar is a Kunjabuta exclusively of green on white background. Matanbagh consists of floral sprays.

Applique art is another variety of Kashmir embroidery. The legend says that, Maharaja Ranjit Singh, rolled himself on the beautifully appliqued Gabba. It is a unique type of floor covering, inexpensive prepared from torn woollen blankets or shawls after being washed and dyed in various colours. There are three types of Gabbas viz. embroidered, appliqued and a combination of embroidery and applique. In applique type Gabba, the patches of various shape, size and colours were joined together. Bright colour combination consisted of yellow, green, black, red and white. The design comprised of mainly geometrical, an imitation of Persian design Gabba is centered around Anantnag.

Tapestry work is another kind of Kashmiri embroidery. This art was introduced by Major and Mrs. Handow to make household articles. Around 1935, tapestry work was done on the floor coverings for the first time. Dasuta, the canvas cloth on which embroidery is done with a blunt tapestry needle. The material is stretched on a wooden frame with the tracing kept along its side. Ear, the woollen thread is used to embroider the design with whip stitch by counting the threads. It is a very laborious work and takes nearly a month and a half to complete a carpet of 3' x 5'. Tapestry work is popularly done in Srinagar and Anantnag.

Zalakdozi is the hook embroidery, named after a hook resembled a crochet. John Irwin states that, Zalakdozi was probably introduced in Kashmir by Damascus craftmen during sultan Zain-ul-Abidin's rule. Various articles are prepared by hook embroidery and one of them is Namda, a felt carpet. It is an important textiles of Kashmir. Namda is either in white or various colours that is richly embroidered by wool with chain stitch. It is a special work on carpet known as crewel for which chain stitch is the base supplemented with satin and whip stitches. The carpet designs selected for Namda ranged from Persian to French, like Chinar leaf, Shikargah, Theridar, Bulbuldar, Guldar, Badamadar, Kalka and so on.

A variety of articles are made by Zalakdozi, bags, foot wears, curtains, cushion covers, bed spreads, table mats, dress materials etc.

Kashmir embroidery perhaps is the most popular commercial embroidery not only because it has retained its rich heritage but also has made necessary adoption according to the likes, choice and demand of the market. The Directorate of Handicrafts has started a school of design with a view to produce and exhibit new designs. Along with old designs new articles with new design are constantly being introduced. Kashmiri embroidery not only provides employment and livelihood to thousands of people but it depicts the rich century old tradition and heritage of India.

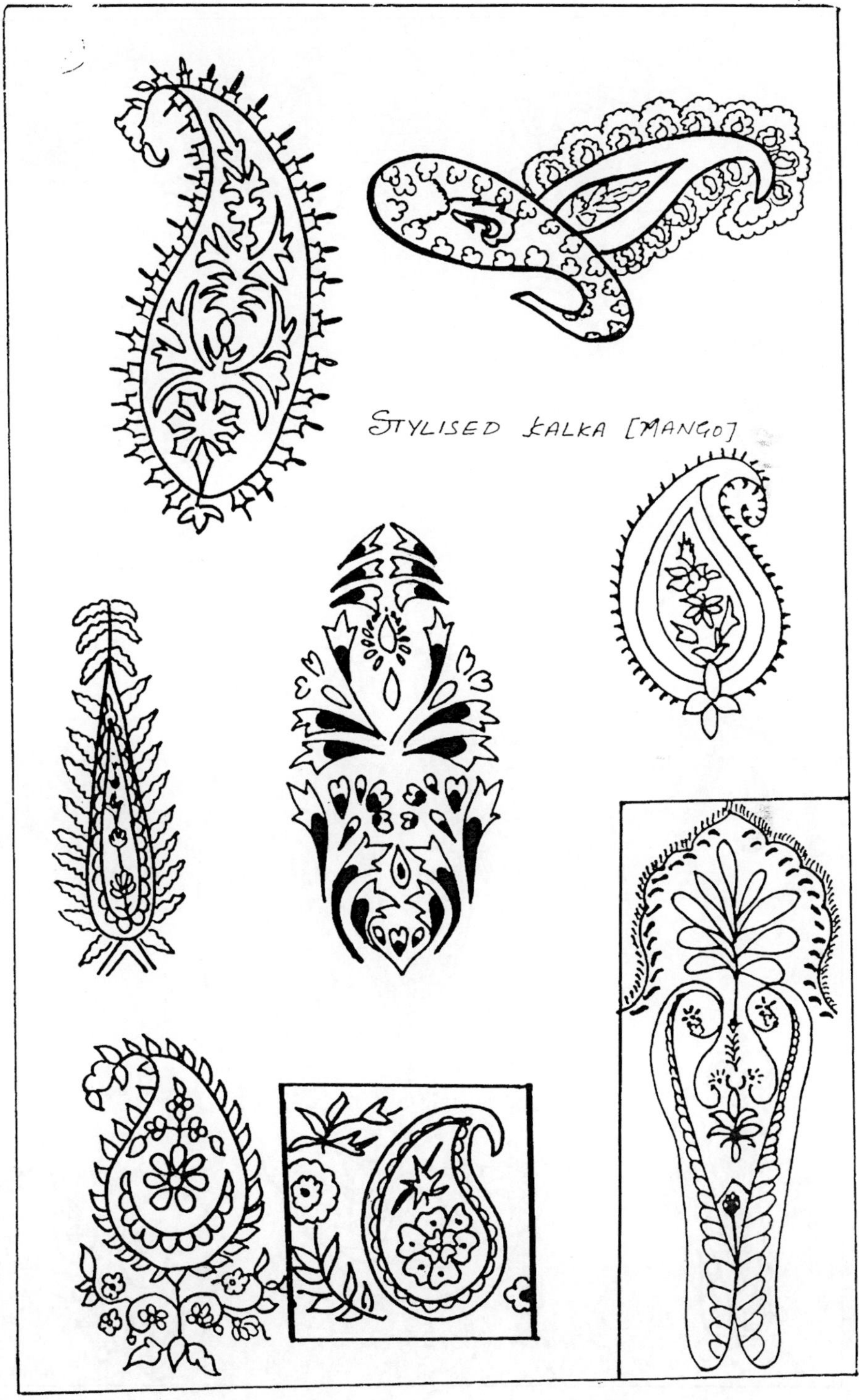
STYLISED KALKA [MANGO]

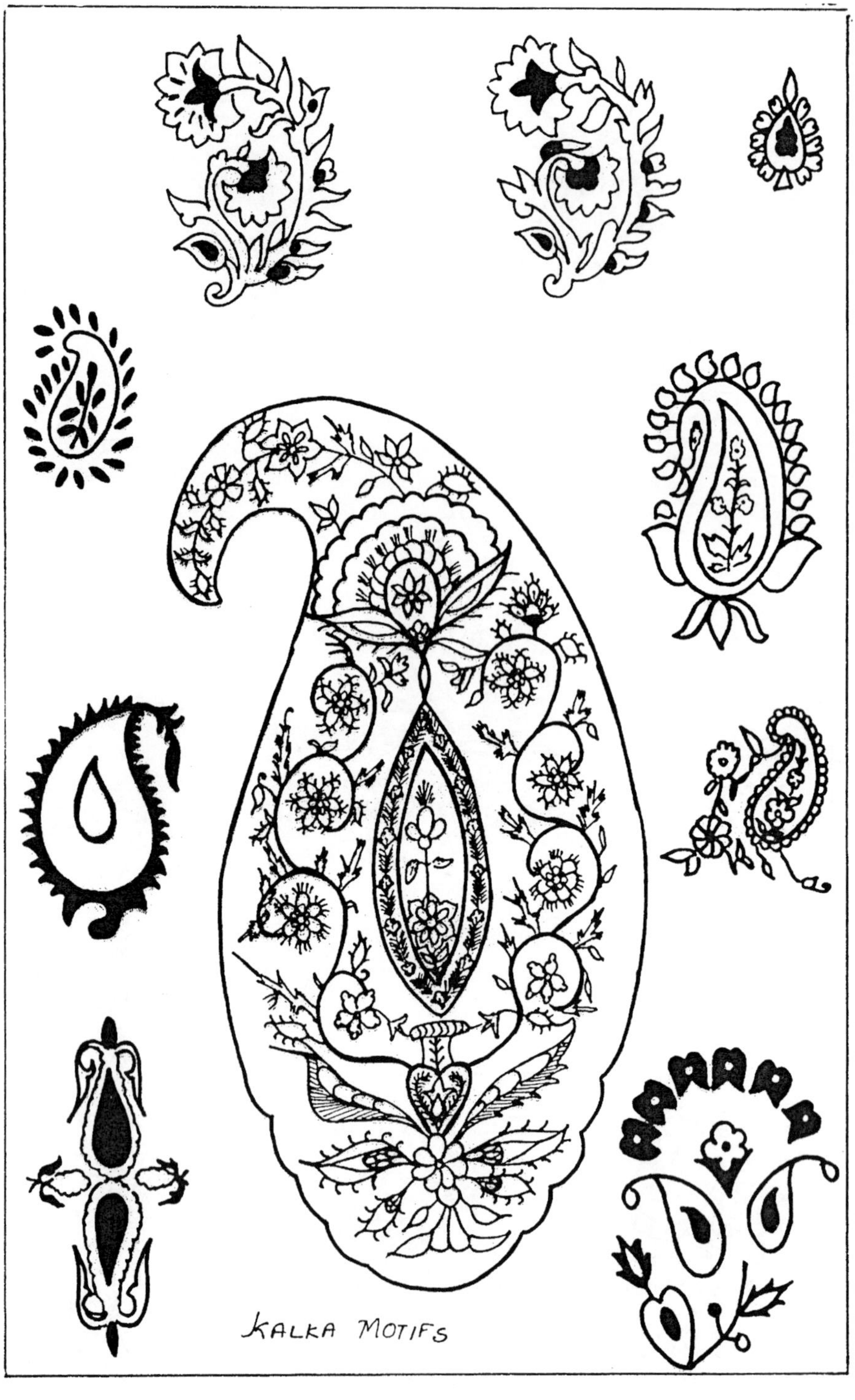
KALKA MOTIFS

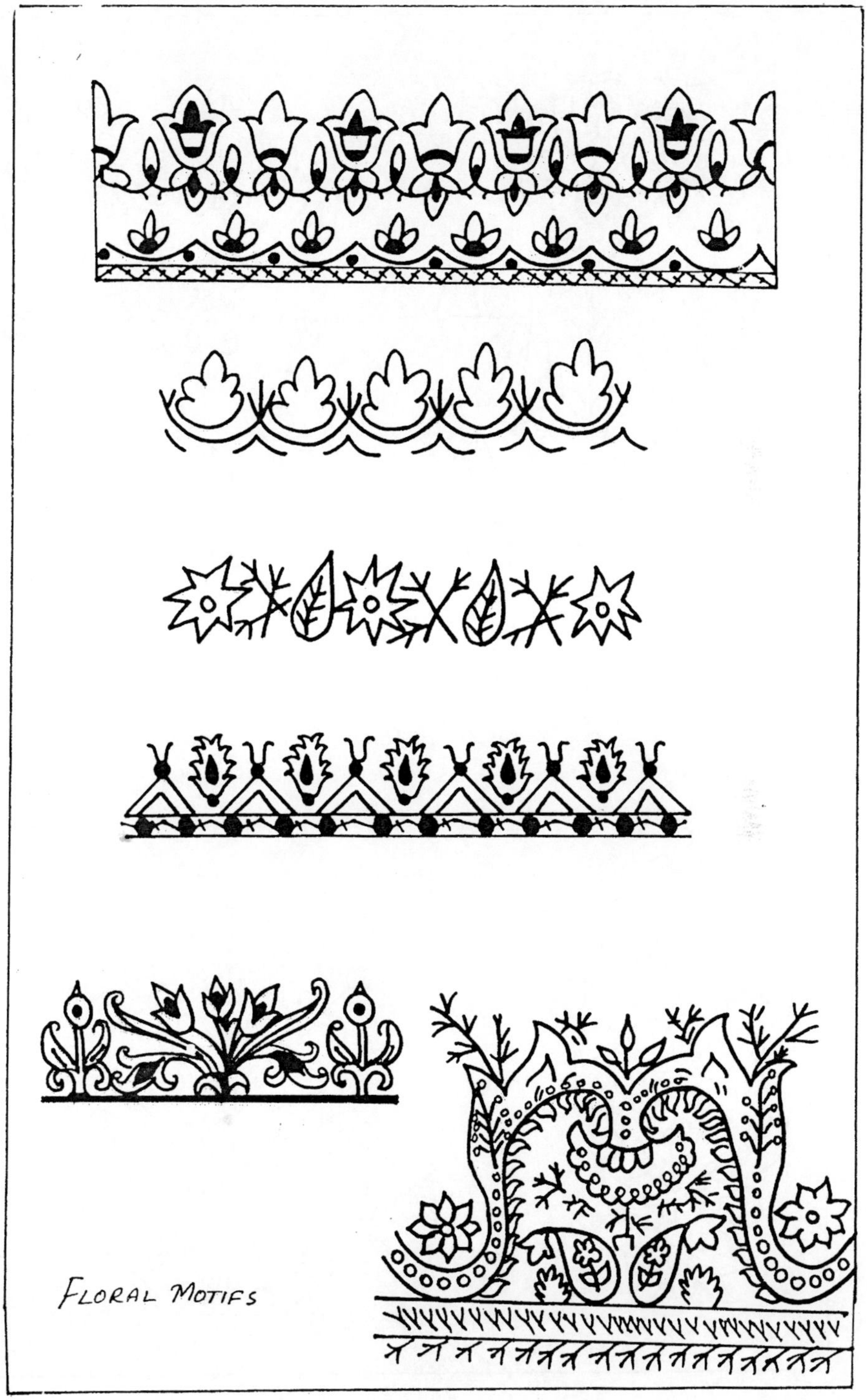

FLORAL MOTIFS

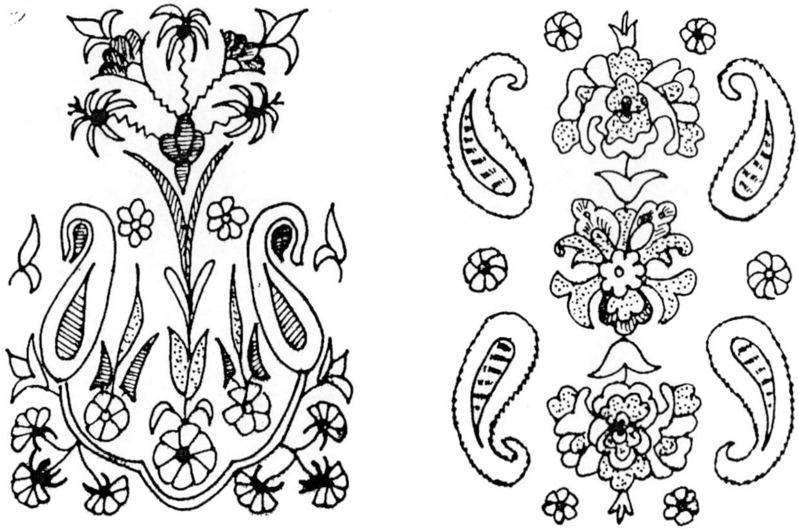

STYLISED KALKA AND FLORAL DESIGN

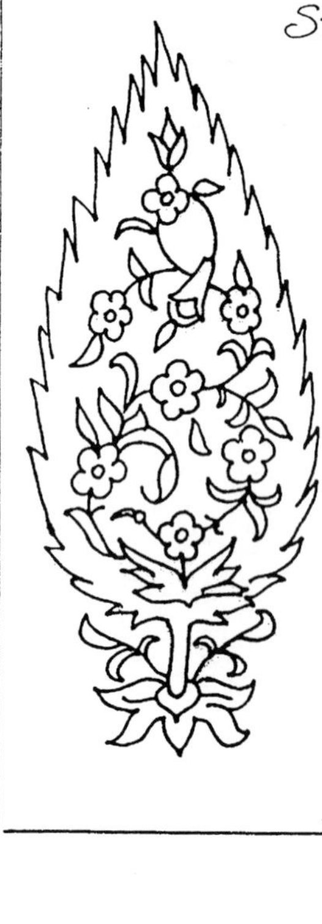

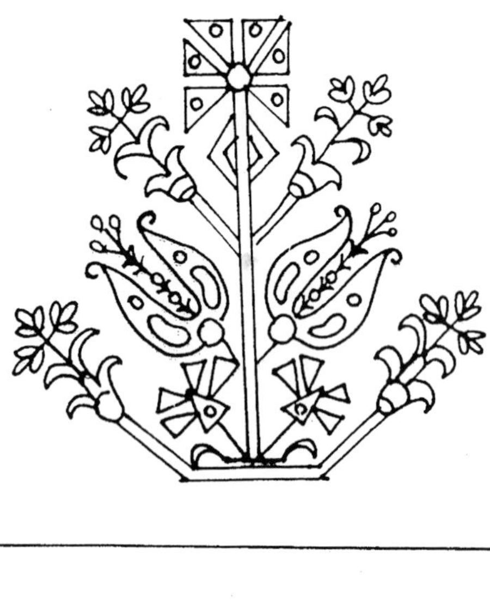

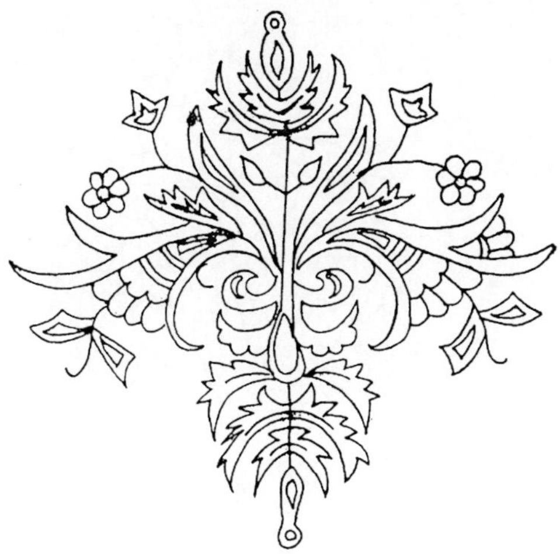

STYLISED CHINAR LEAF

CENTRAL MOTIF OF ZALAKDOZI NAMDA

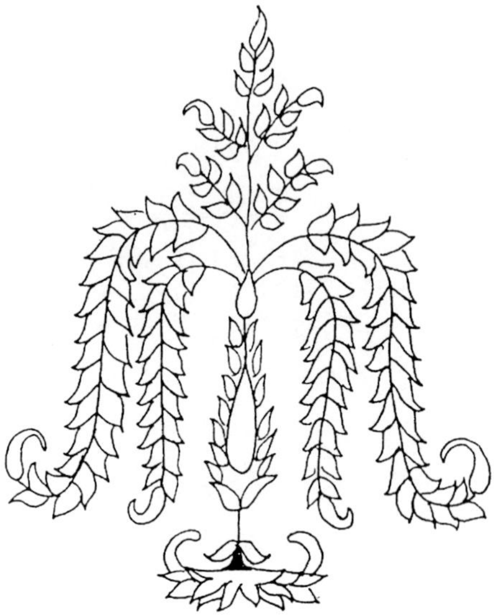

STYLISED CONE MOTIF

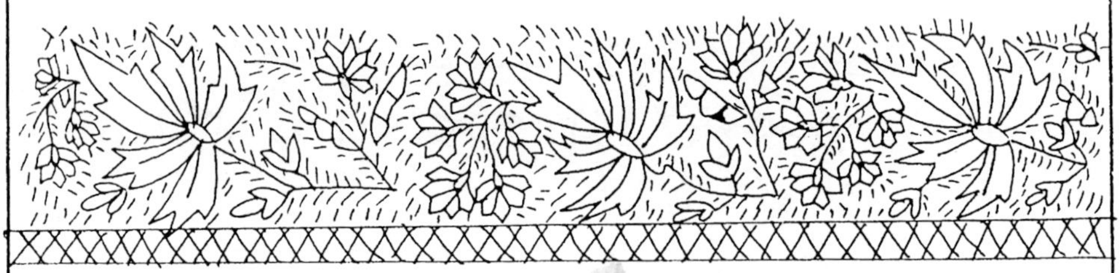

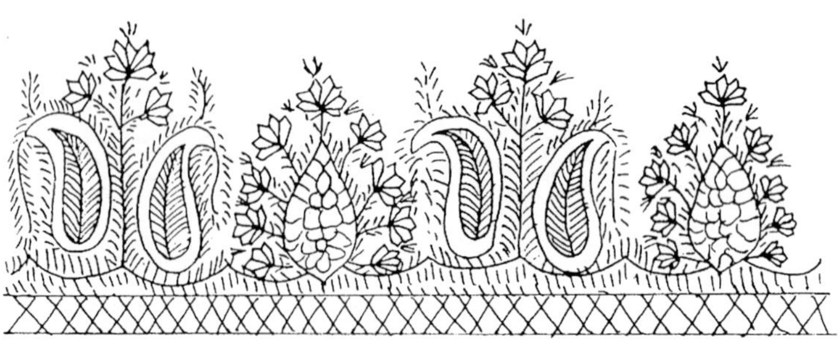

BORDER DESIGN OF CHINAR LEAF AND KALKA

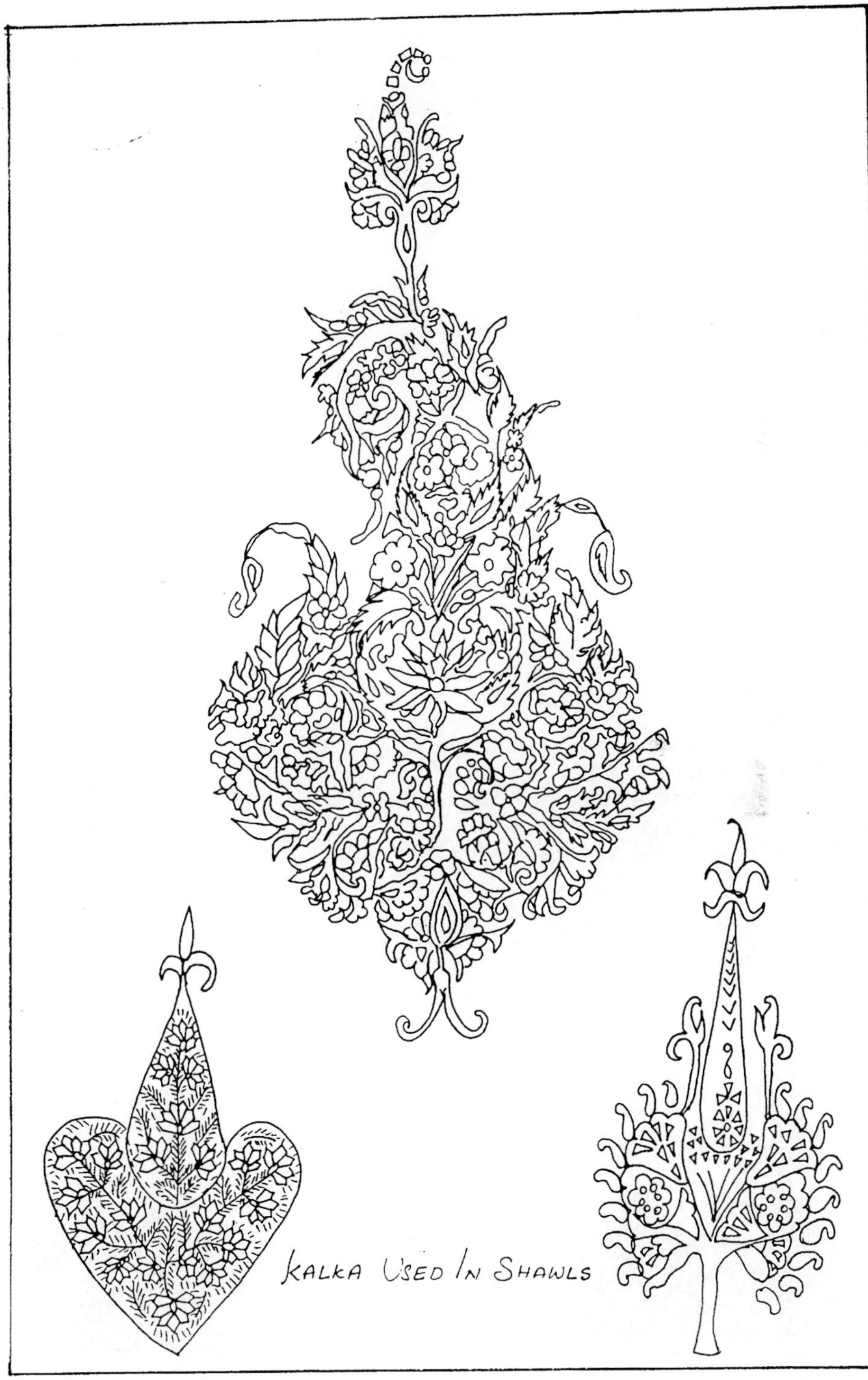
KALKA USED IN SHAWLS

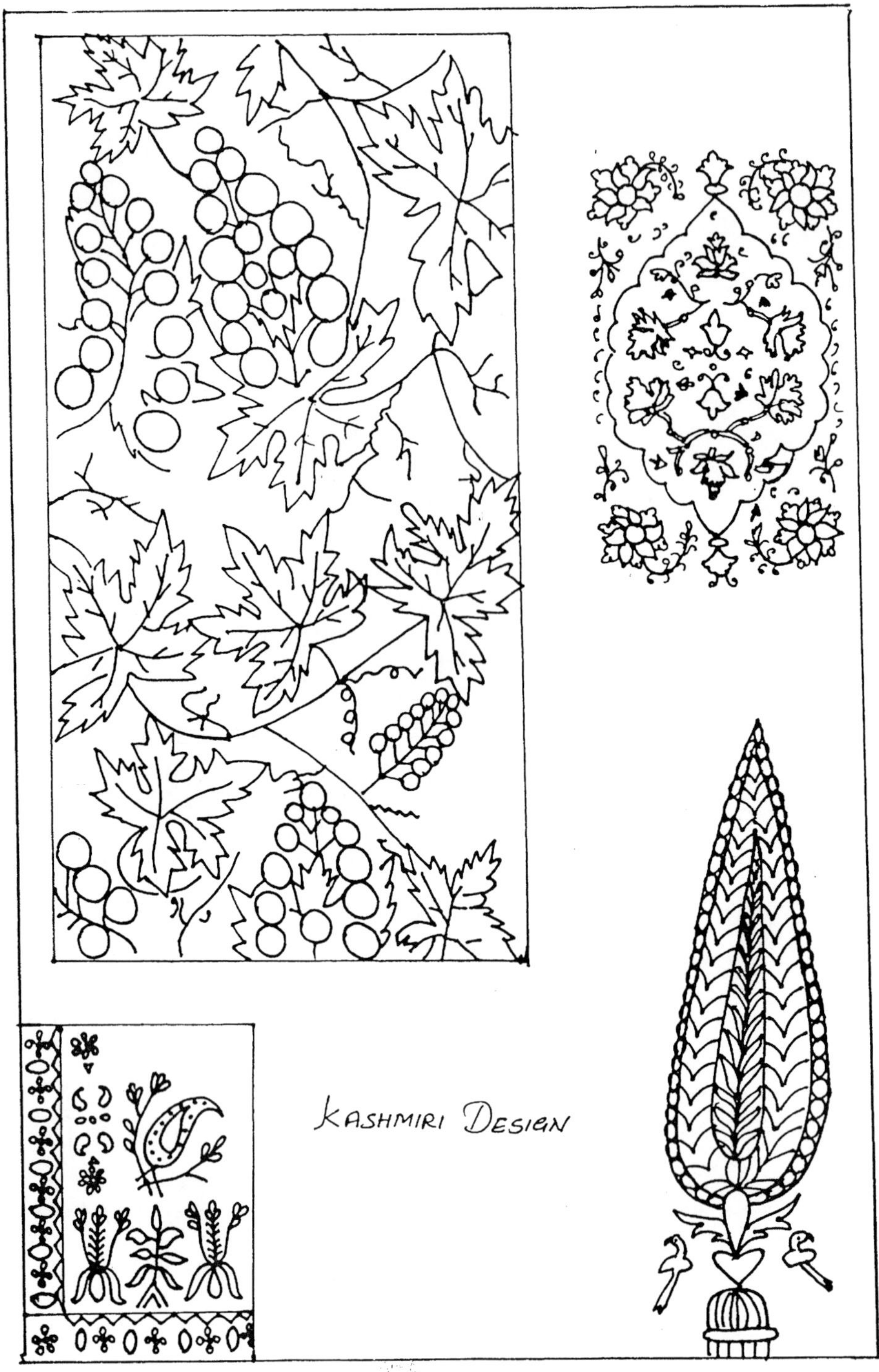

KASHMIRI DESIGN

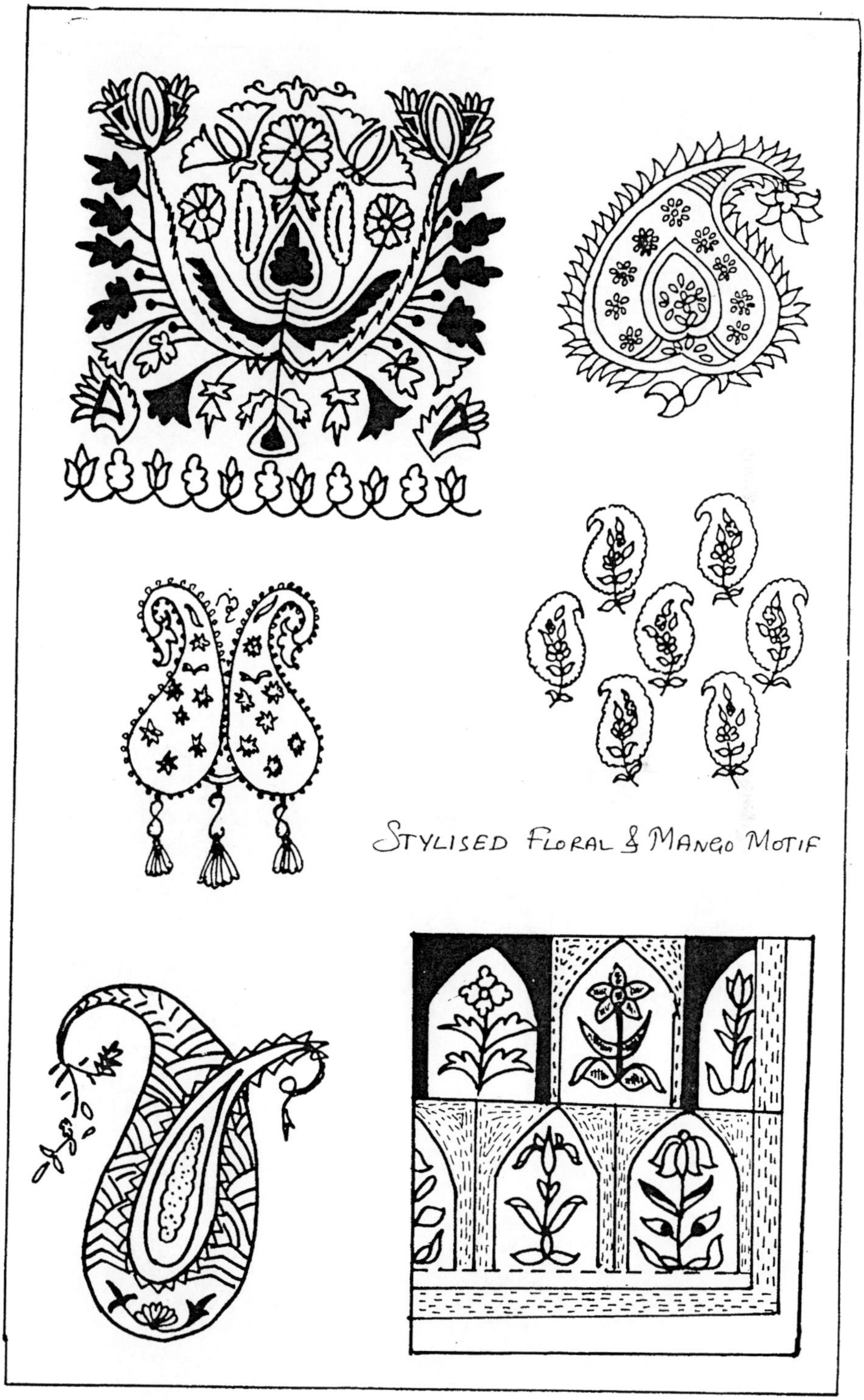
STYLISED FLORAL & MANGO MOTIF

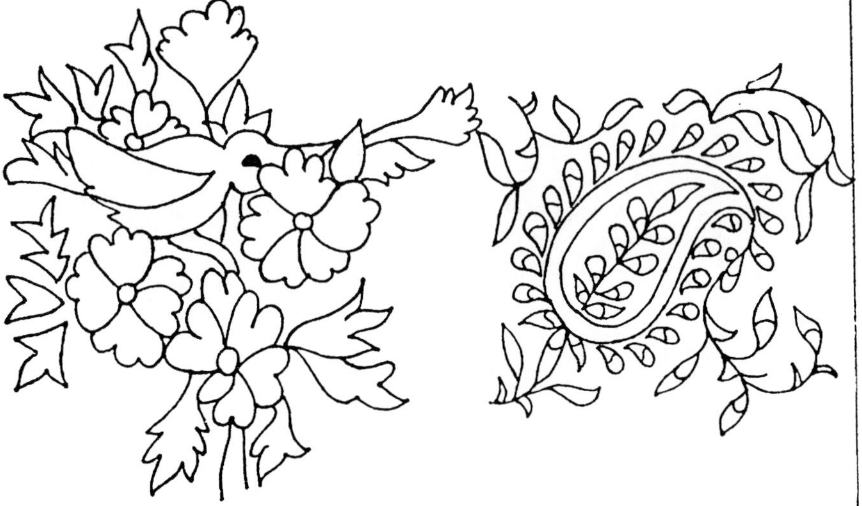

FLORAL, KALKA AND BIRD MOTIFS

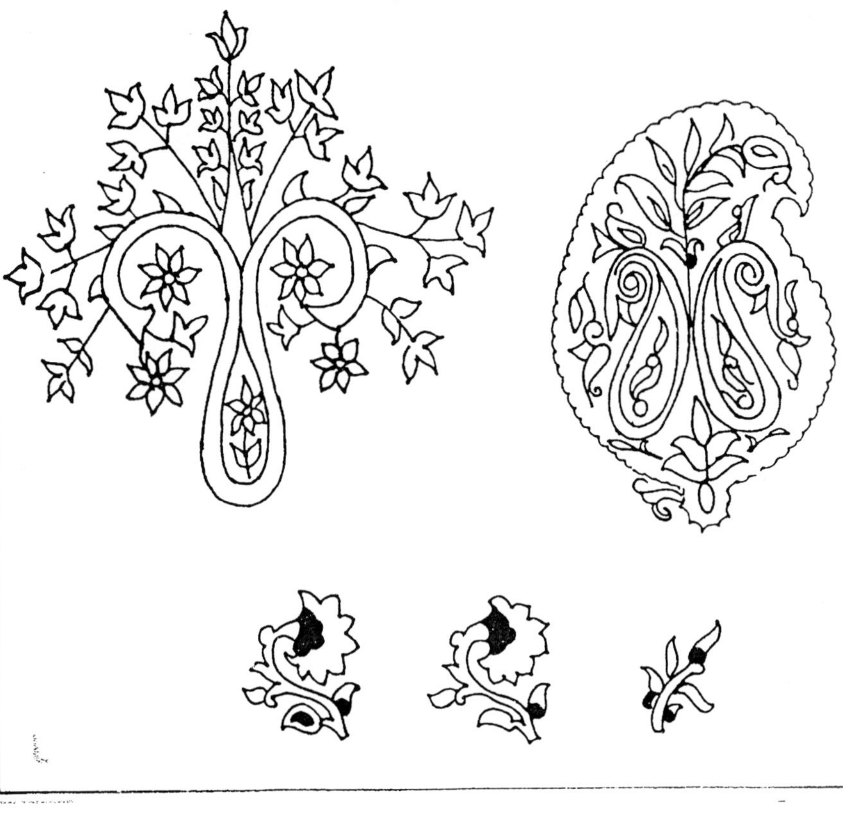

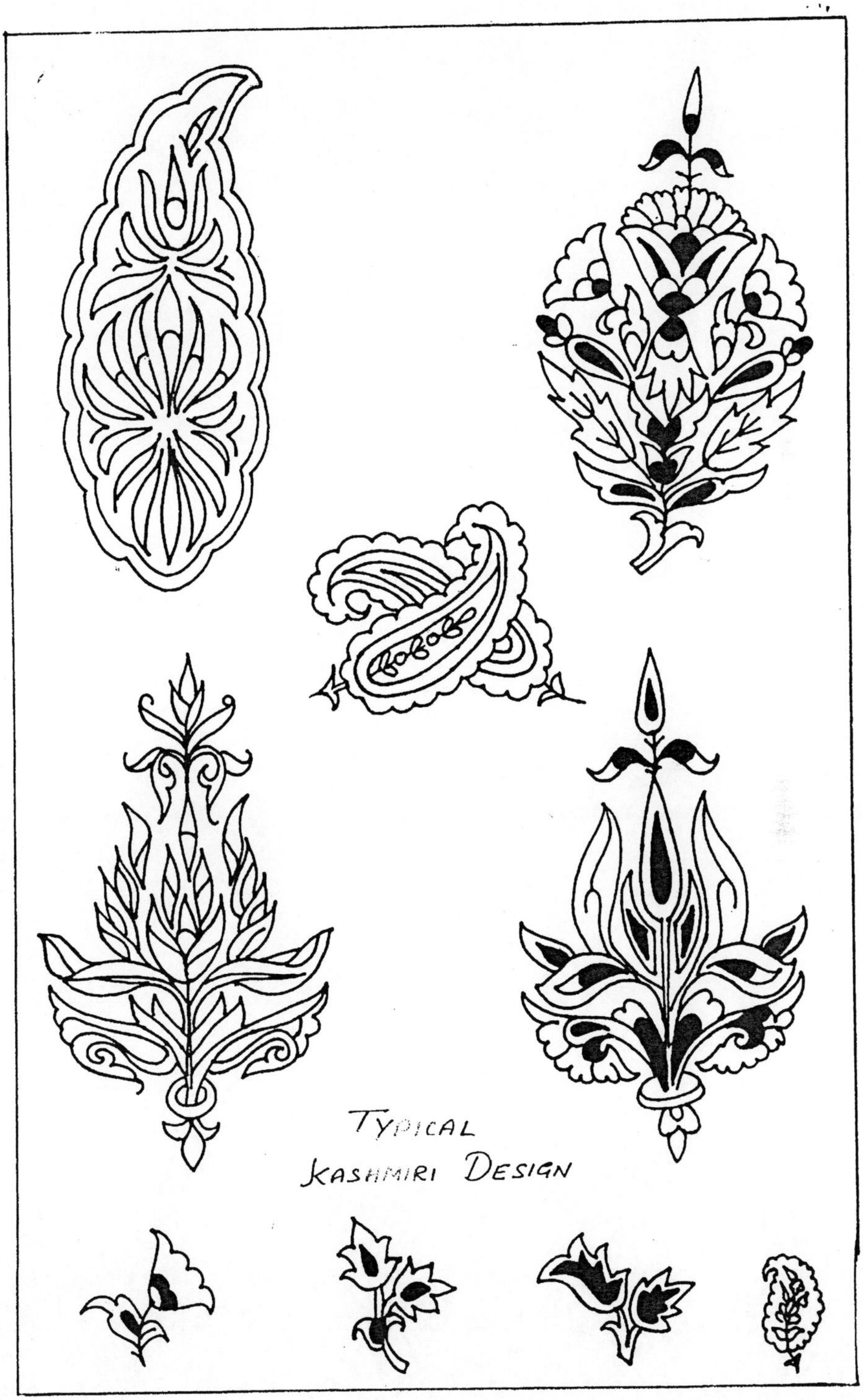
TYPICAL
KASHMIRI DESIGN

CHAPTER 7
EMBROIDERY OF MANIPUR

Manipur is a 'Land of gems', surrounded by hills, vallies and lakes. The inhabitants of Manipur are expertised in weaving, varieties of beautiful and intricate weaves and are also skilled in music and dance. The Manipur women are also famous in their unique style of embroidery. However, the varieties of stitches in the needle work are relatively limited in number. The tribal people employed a bamboo needle to work all along the warp threads.

The embroidery is done mostly on their traditional wear and each tribal groups specialises in its own particular style of designing.

The border of 'phaneyk', the lungi or sarong worn by the women, is usually decorated and adorned by embroidery. Women in Manipur, do weave their phaneyk, in a combination of dark coloured stripes against light ground or a simple dark coloured plain fabric witnout any stripes or the whole phaneyk is covered with series of stripes in three different colours with a black coloured border only on one side.

The motifs for the embroidery are taken from nature; flowers, birds, animals, geometrical forms and circles are effectively used with charming multi coloured combinations. The motif commonly used is a circular design 'Akoybi', an all over pattern. Each circle is joined to the other, with each circle being further broken into other patterns. Smt. Kamaladevi Chattopadhyay relates this design to a mythological tale "one of the husband of Goddesses killed a snake named Pakhamba but later he tried to atone for his sin by copying its scaly patterns of skin to perpetuate them as a source of designs in the field of Taxtiles". Some even believe that the circular motifs are the inspiration of swirls of water, lotus and other objects associated with lake. The colours used in akoybi are two shades of red with little of black and white.

The phaneyk is dark but is matched with red, phem or chocolate colours. The embroidery is so finely and evenly worked along the warp threads, many times to a stranger, it seems like woven decoration. Another simple pattern 'tindogbi', the motifs appear like a silk larva sitting on a castor leaf and feeding it. It is an out come of inspiration by silk work rearing.

'Hijaya Mayek' is another well known all over pattern embroidered in white and black to emphasise the running lines and circular movements. According to Jasleen Dhamija a famous carpenter was carving a boat and accidentally a long piece of wood while chipping fell on the lawn nearby. The carpenter presented this piece of wood to the king and was highly impressed by the natural flowing lines on the piece. The king later suggested to incorporate these flowing lines in the embroidery of Phaneyk. However, now a days this design is associated with costumes of older people and elderly women. This embroidery is done with tiny satin stitches, done very close to each other.

A special shawl worn by the warriors during war times was also embroidered by the women at home, known as 'Zamphie'. Only the people, honoured by the king were permitted to wear this special shawl. The richly embroidered cloth used by the emperor is termed as 'Ningthoupee'. The ministry in the court of the King were supposed to wear a long coat with distinctive embroidery called as 'Saijounba'. The ministry in the court used turbans as their head coverings, always associated with tiny embroidered flags and this flag used as means to identify the rank of the courtier. Such embroidered flag are known as 'Phiranamba'.

Applique work is also another specially of Manipur. The elegant motifs of red colour were appliqued on the yellow borders of the dance costume. 'Kumi', the skirts. Mirrors and sequences were stitched with rich red silk floss. Delicate applique of white on white is done on turbans. Some of the presentation for the bride like curtains, cushions and other linen were decorated with applique work. The abhla work probably migrated from Dwaraka by Vaishnavas, as mirror work is found mainly in Gujarat.

'Sami lami phee', the wild animal warrior cloth is a black shawl with bold embroidery also called as Angami Naga shawl. Nagas are basically hunters and used to hunt many wild beasts. As a symbol of pride, they used to stitch the leaves cut into the shapes of wild animals. Later the Manipuries started incorporating these animal motifs into woven patterns. The whole shawl is divided into horizontal penels and the animals were distributed within these panels. Some commonly found animals are elephant, camel, sheep, cock, butterflies etc.

Now a days this embroidery is done on cushion covers, wall hanging, bed spreads, table cloth, apart from chaddar.

AKOYBI DESIGN

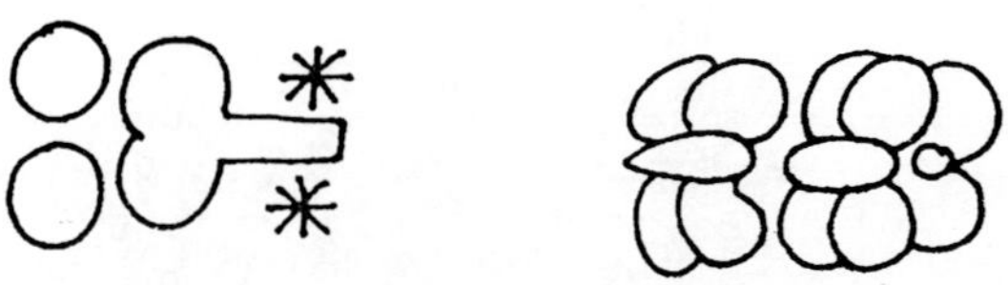

BUTTER FLY

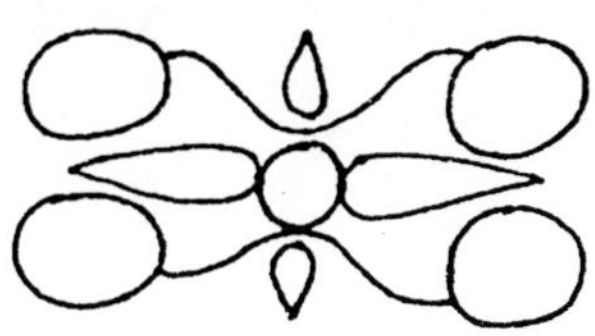

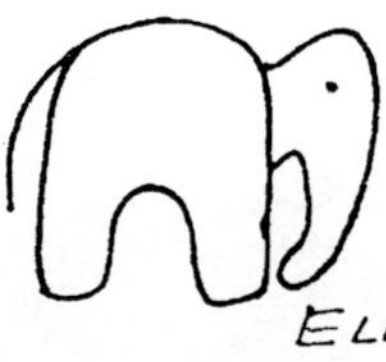

ELEPHANT

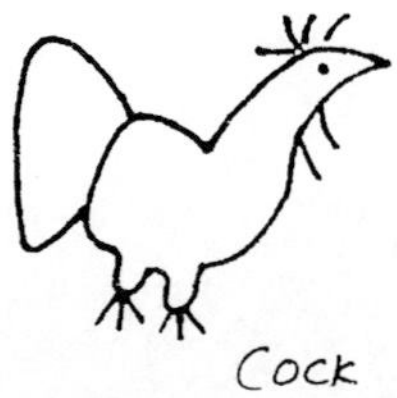

COCK

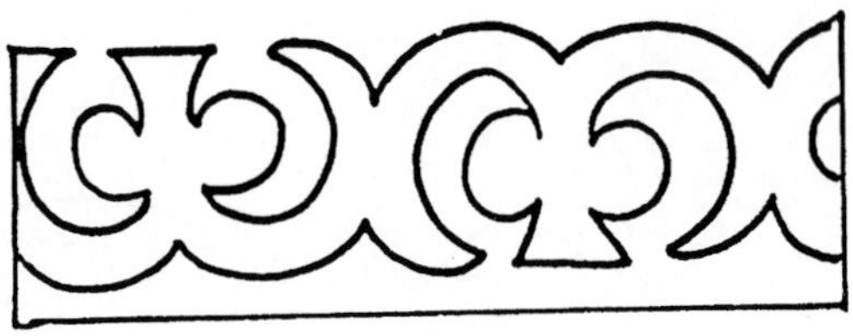

HIJAY MAYEK

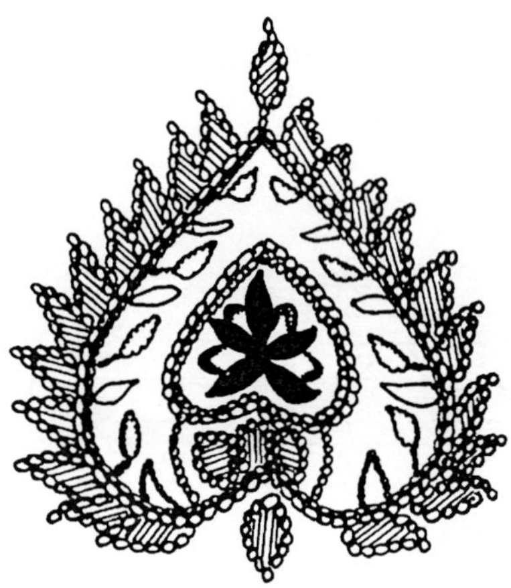

CHAPTER 8
APPLIQUE CRAFT OF ORISSA

Orissa a relatively smaller state situated in eastern part of our country. The world famous traditional craft of this state is Applique craft, a French term explaining about the technology of applying patches of colourful fabric pieces on the base. The raw edges of these patches are finished with a definite mode of stitchery work. The main difference between applique craft and patchwork, is, in the latter case small fabric pieces are joined together to form a relatively larger piece and in some cases the patch work is done to cover up or repair a damaged fabric. Applique craft is pride of Orissa mainly carried out in and around Puri district, and Pipli is the main center in the district. The art is also flourishing in Paralakimidi and Khallikote of Ganjam and Baudh districts respectively. Very often applique is combined with embroidery and is more prevalent in Ganjam district. The legent states that a villager from Butapali came to Puri on pilgrimage to Jagannath Temple, took shelter and rested at Pipli. During his stay he learnt the art of applique of Pipli and carried the technology to Butapali along with him. Probably, this is how the craft has commenced at Butapali recently and is practiced only in his family, surprisingly.

The applique art entirely differs from other techniques of decorative arts like, printing and painting, wherein the former many times produces three dimensional effect too and is unique by itself.

It is a home scale craft or a family craft where all the family members are been involved in preparing bold and brightly coloured surface enrichments which is totally different from the tradition crafts such as embroideries, Kalamkari of Andhra Pradesh, block or screen printing effects.

Applique work is a stitchery craft, basically rooted from the professional tailors, called 'Darji' as early as 1054 A.D. who are commonly identified by the surnames Mahapatra and Maharana. Malley says, Pipli, the main center of applique art today, was once upon a time had rice and textiles as their main trade though the majority of the population come from Darji caste who used to prepare small cloth bags used to keep money, the Batavas, and embroidered quilts, the Sujnis on small scale. A progressive craftsman, Hatta Maharana of Pipli, well versed in applique, mentioned that his kith and kins, residing in Puri are working on Chandua (Canopy), Chhatli, tarasa, used during festivals connected to Lord Jagannath and Raja of Puri i.e. it is said probably the Darji of Puri might have migrated from Pipli who are the pioneers of applique art. However, it is realised that the Maharajas of Puri, specially appointed the artists, called 'Sebaks' (Sevaks) to prepare the articles used during festivals and other religious functions. On the other hand, apart from sebaks the Darjis were also requested to supply the requirement of tailored articles for Lord Jagannath for festivals. It is evident from this background that the applique craft of Puri is mainly connected with religious festivals and procession and hence, prepared canopies, umbrellas, door curtains, hand bags, banners, coverings of dummy horses and cows and at present as per the demand certain household textiles like bedspread, cushion and table covers, garden umbrellas, sea-shore umbrellas, lamp shades, sari borders are also prepared. Many times applique is combined with embroidery and is adopted on leather goods too.

The colour scheme basically consisted of bold hues like black, red, yellow and green, though in contemporary pieces bright shades of blue and turquoise-blue were being used.

The Sebaks used to get remuneration for the articles they made for 'Seba Puja' of Jagannath temple, as 'Bhoga' (eatables offered to the deity) or in the form of money. Working as Sebaks is profession of a couple of families and the craft is transferred from generation to generation as hereditary. The well versed, skilled, artistic craftsmen, usually the elderly member of the family is been employed to prepare the articles for deity. 'Sardar' is the head of Sebaks whose work may be assigned to another elderly, skilled, artisan if he fails to perform his duties due to negligence. Sardar being a responsible and hardworking individual gets additional Bhoga.

The Sebaks prepare Canopy, Trasa (banner), Chatti (a sort of Umbrella) used outside the temple during the festivals and processions. Few other articles like Magadha topi (Made of cloth with fine applique) used by Kamsa in Kamsavadha drama, dice board, prepared by patch work of black and white cloth pieces used during Kumar Purnima festival. Trasas are named according to the colour of the base material. Garuda Trasa and Gobinda Trasa have yellow and black background respectively. These trasas are carried on the head during the occasions of festivals and processions. Besides temples, the Oriya Maths (Monastic house, monks house) are also decorated with banners and canopies, who use trasas, Chanduas and Chatti during the festivals. However, the deteriorating financial position of few Maths lead to the fall in the demand of these articles. Darji community still exists in some districts of Orissa, do meet during the fare, every year, held at Kedargouri in Bhuvaneshwar and discuss their problems.

The general rule for selection of base material (cotton) is that, it should have enough strength to hold the light weight applique pieces. In olden days, before the inception of cloth mills, the coarse variety of hand-spun, hand-woven Khaddar was used as ground fabric, on which thick felt and velvet clothes were appliqued. At present the khaddar has been replaced by mill made, strong and refined quality long cloths, Markin and Salu are used. Markin, relatively coarser, unbleached, plain woven cotton cloth and Salu though has the same background is comparatively finer and lighter. Both the materials are used as base and fills. Embroidery work is also seen, in which case fish and frogs are the motifs. Sometimes specially designed motifs do have mirrors in them.

Selection of the design is the first step involved followed by cutting the motifs from the selected applique material. However, specially prepared motifs are made separately. These motifs are then placed on the base cloth in predetermined layout and sequency. The raw edges of the cut motifs are neatly and evenly turned in and sewn on to the base or sometimes embroidered without turning the raw edges. The base is a dark, bold and brightly coloured material on which motifs of other colours including white is also appliqued.

The layout of the motifs varied according to the size and articles to be prepared since the shape varies for each article. Canopy is a square piece, umbrella is circular, trasa is some what circular, having a small pointed part of the circumference as neck. The motifs are encircled with number of borders, inside and outside, many times it even reaches the edge of the ground fabric. For example the square canopy may have either square or circular central motif, which later is bound by several borders of different widths.

The size of applique piece varies from one metre to a very small size of 1.5 cms. The small pieces are for fine decorations and borders whereas the large pieces of geometrical pieces are used as central motifs for canopies and so on. The natural and stylized motifs in the design through medium size, either reduced or enlarged according to the size of the piece. Sometimes the figured motifs are padded to bring about embossed effect and make them more naturalistic.

The craft of Orissa is mainly connected with religious festivals and processions, the motifs picked up are from actual life, modified stylized forms, nature, animal and plant kingdom, and ofcourse geometrical as per the shape of the article. The commonly used motifs are, lotus, peacock, gander, duck, elephant, swan, parrot, fish, lion, betel leaf, bela leaf, creeper, tree (gachha), sun (surya), moon (chandra) and rahu (the demon that swallows the sun and the moon during eclipses). The main stitches adopted for applique craft are, the simple running stitch, the Bakhia, used either to attach the specially made (not the simple cut our figures) motifs permanently on the base or to keep the patches in position temporarily on the base, till they are finally sewn. Bakhia, the small running stitches, picked up several at a time at each insertion of the needle; Taropa, a simple hemming, slip or invisible stitch, used to sew the applique pieces on the main ground cloth; Ganthi, the blanket or button hole stitch used to embroider the motifs; chikana, the chain stitch predominantly used in applique work, not only decorative but functional too; Button hole stitch used to attach the small mirror; Ruching stitch used for gathering up of a cloth strip to make an applique motif.

With passage of time, few modification have been brought about in the applique art like, use of refined mill made cotton cloth, bleached or unbleached instead of coarse, khaddar; the stereotype monotonous effects of applique has been broken by use of embroidered motifs; velvet cloth for applique is no more in practice, apart from flat applique, padded and embossed effect is obtained, the craft at present has been extended to produce house hold articles such as bed spreads, cushion covers and so on. It has been observed that, there is gradual decline in the number of Darjis engaged in applique work, at present. Many have taken up other professions including agriculture as their main occupation to have better livelihood. The Rajas, Maths and temple authorities had encouraged and patronised the craft. But the craft met a great set back due to gradual decline in the financial position of temples and maths and merging of Indian feudatory states. However, the Government is trying very hard to revive and uplift the dying craft of Orissa and searching the outlets to market the products. Though the internal market is limited, an effort is made to take an entry in the International market, by improving and sophisticating the products. The Government has also encouraged the artisans to work in cooperation by establishing cooperative societies.

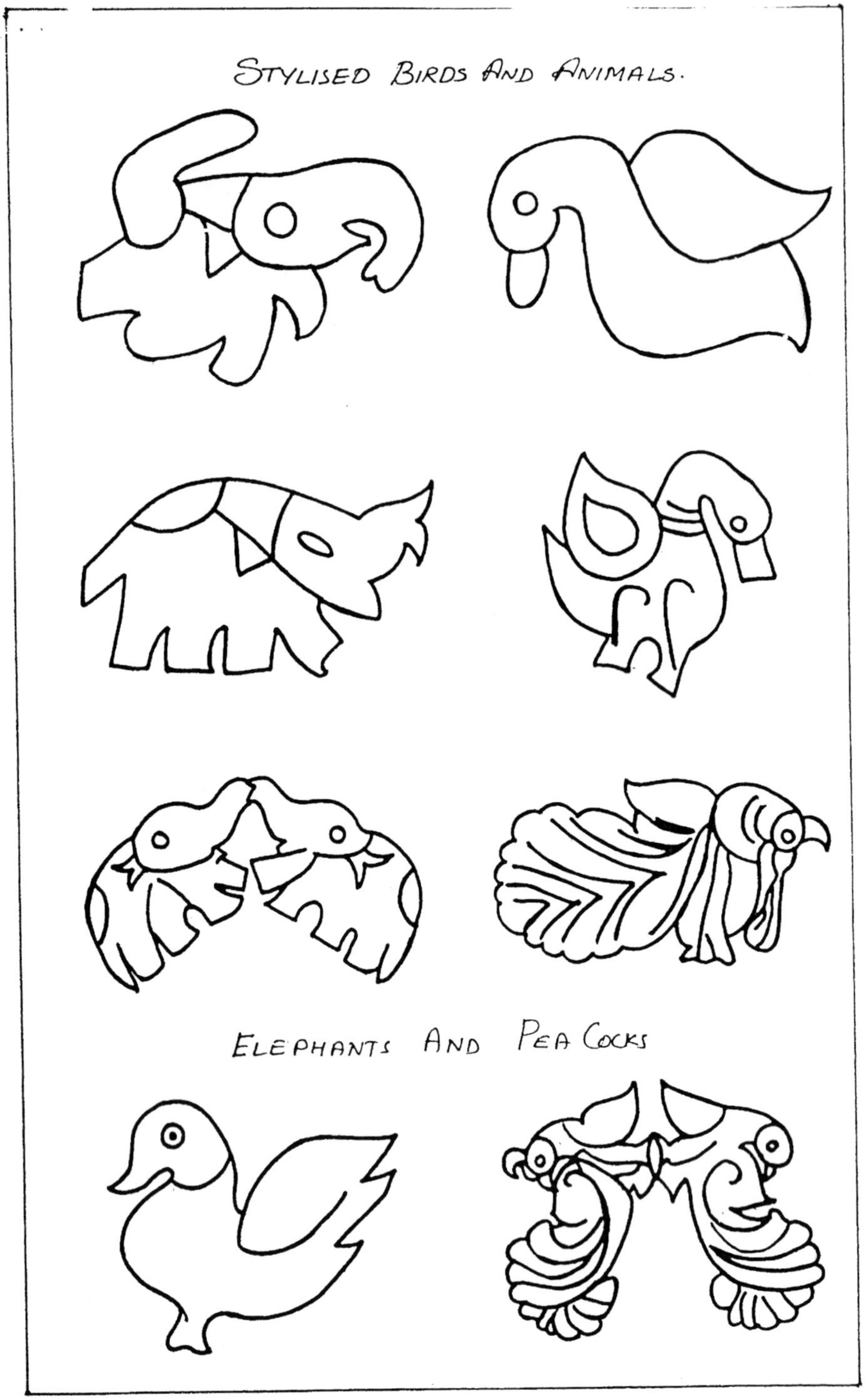
STYLISED BIRDS AND ANIMALS.
ELEPHANTS AND PEA COCKS

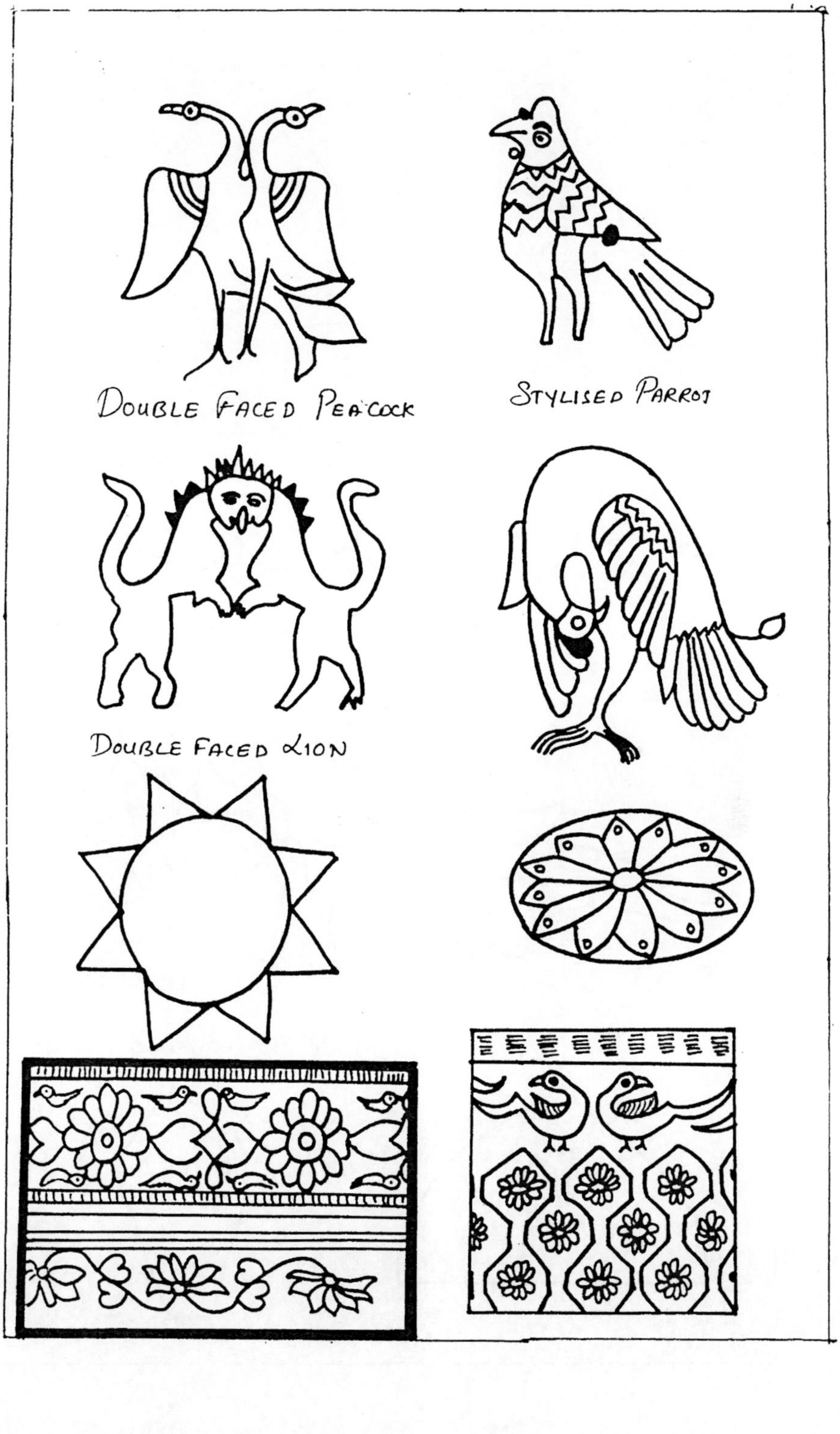
DOUBLE FACED PEACOCK
STYLISED PARROT
DOUBLE FACED LION

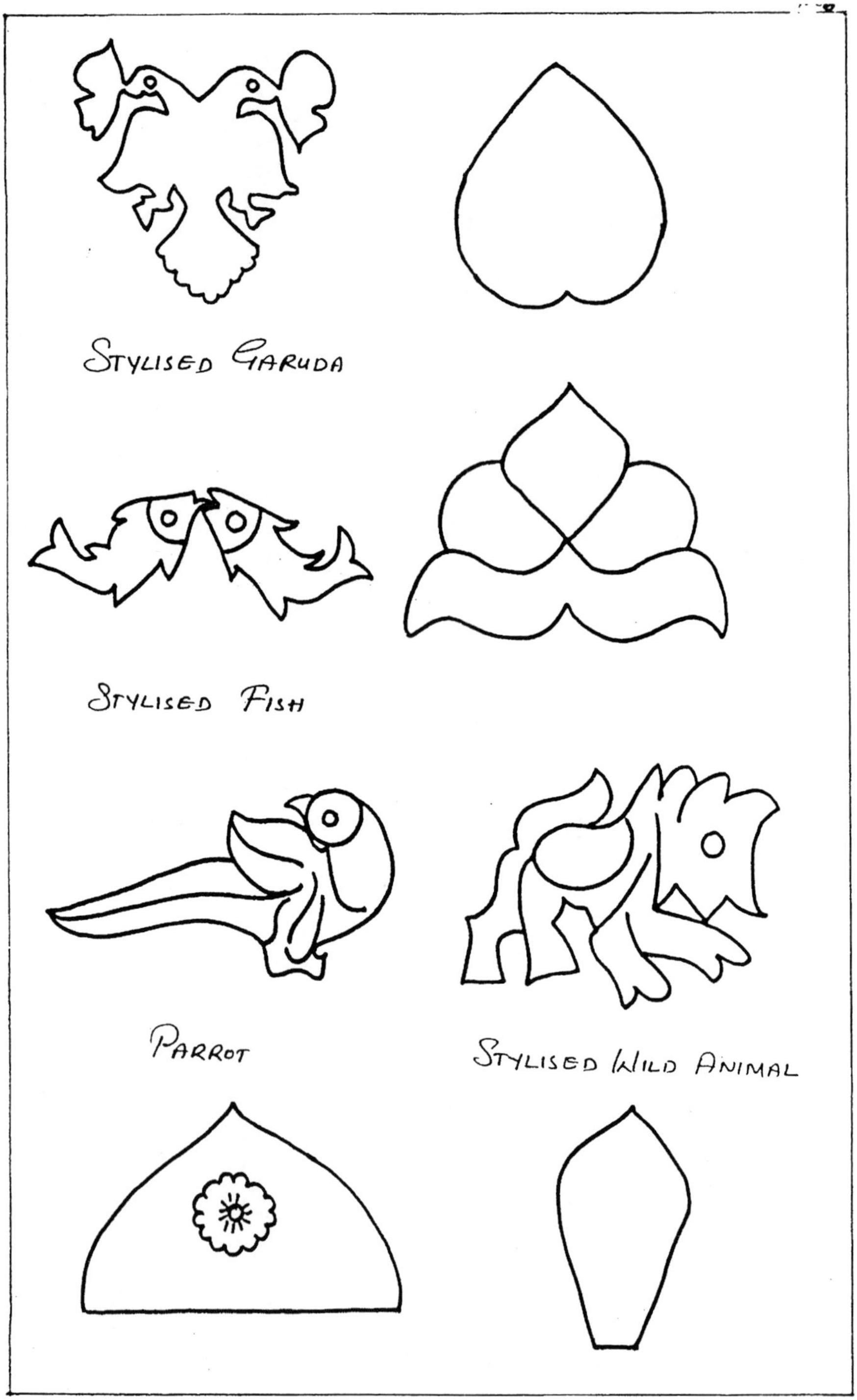
STYLISED GARUDA
STYLISED FISH
PARROT
STYLISED WILD ANIMAL

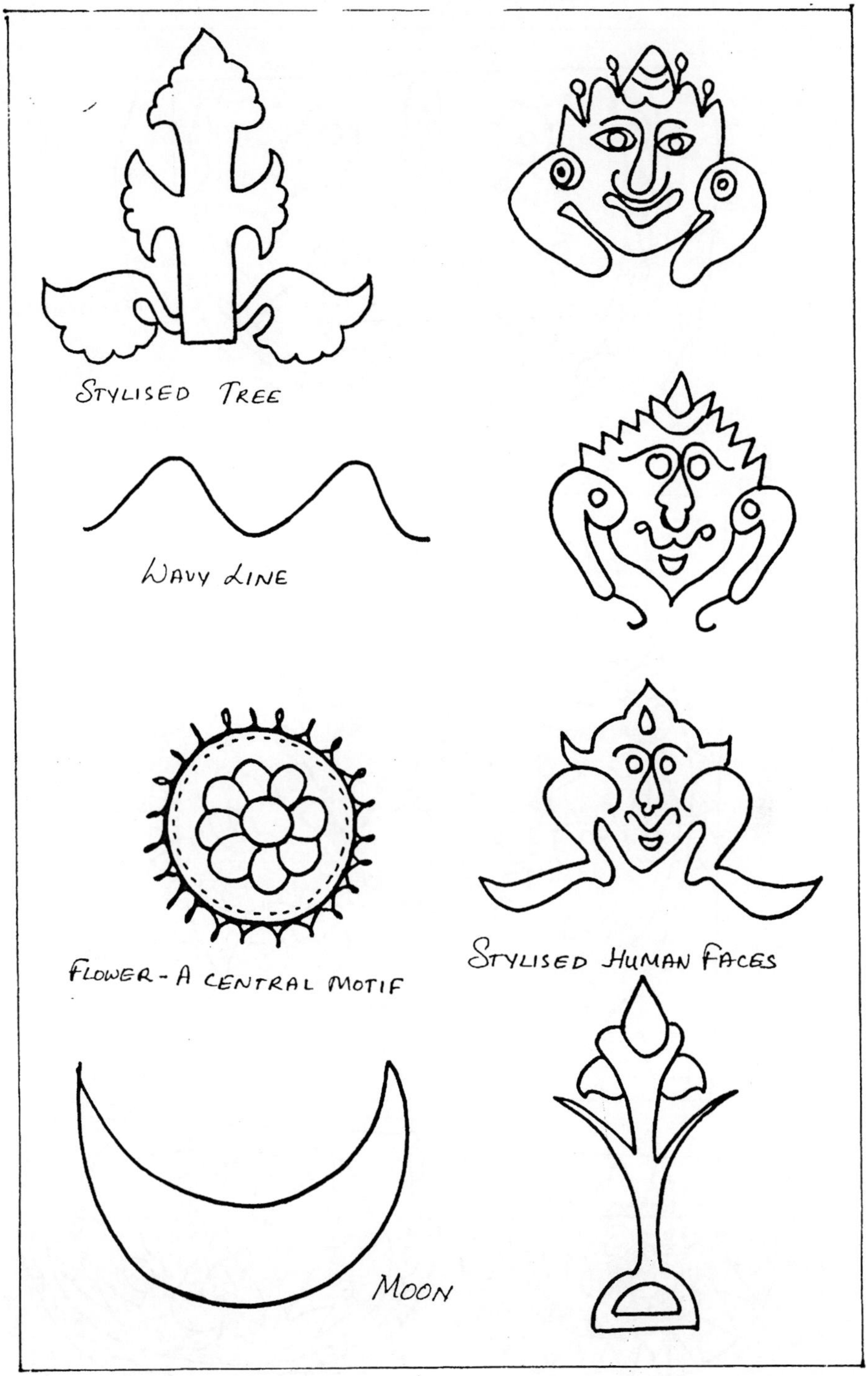
STYLISED TREE
WAVY LINE
FLOWER - A CENTRAL MOTIF
STYLISED HUMAN FACES
MOON

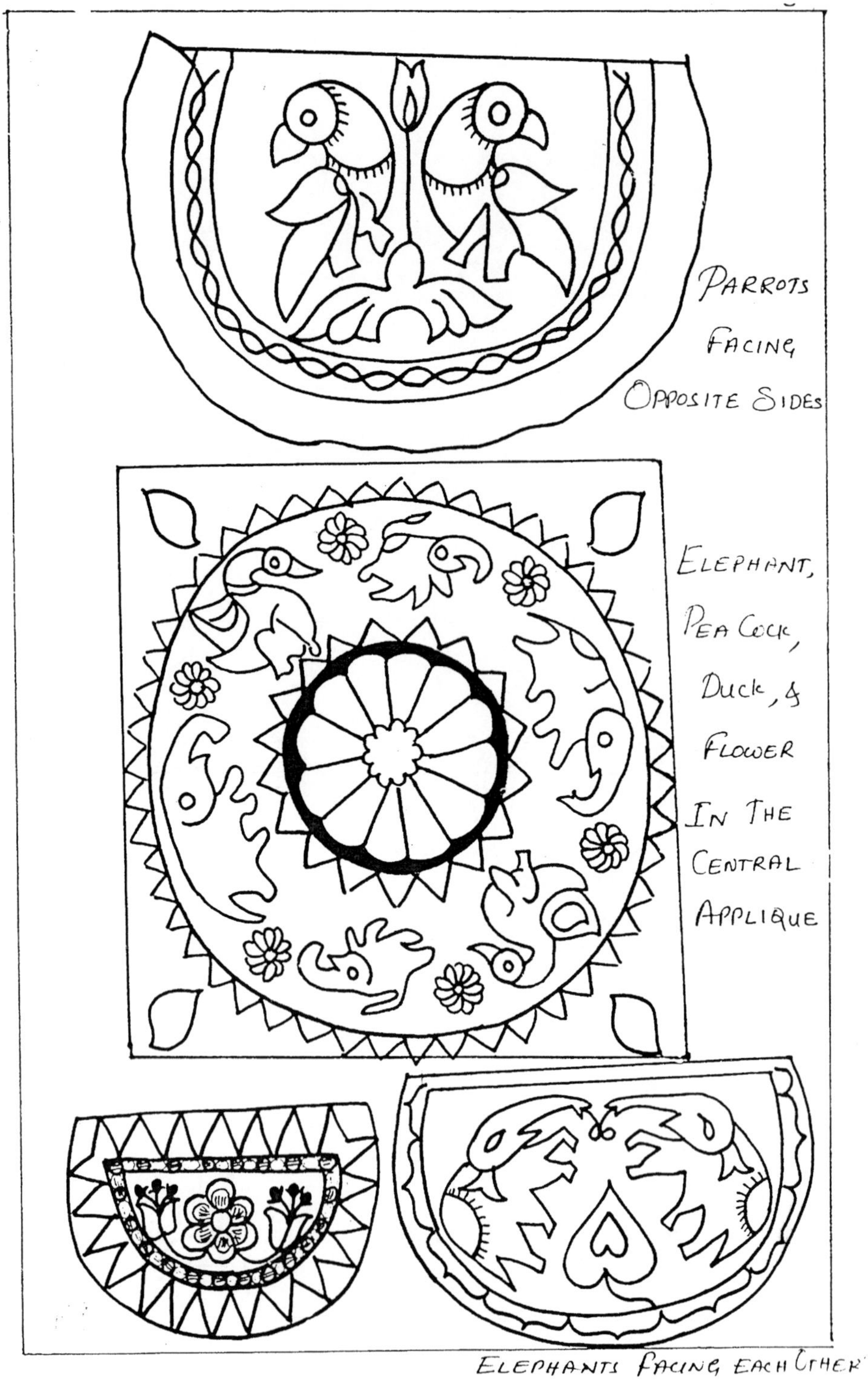
PARROTS FACING OPPOSITE SIDES
ELEPHANT, PEA COCK, DUCK, & FLOWER IN THE CENTRAL APPLIQUE
ELEPHANTS FACING EACH OTHER

CHAPTER 9
PHULKARI OF PUNJAB

Punjab the term has been made up of two words 'Punj' means five and 'Aab' means water, which discloses five rivers were flowing in this state before independence (1947). In ancient Indian history Punjab was referred as 'Sapat Sindhu' meaning seven rivers, sixth being Sindh in north-west and seventh being Saraswati in south-east. The land of this region is very rich and fertile covered with Kashmir hills, Himachal Pradesh, Haryana and Rajasthan in north, north-east, south and south-west respectively. It is in Punjab where famous Indo Aryan civilization took birth, cultivated and spread to other parts of the country. The main occupation of this brave population is agriculture. Punjabis have a boisterous like style which is apparently expressed in their folk tradition. Their traditional dances Bangra and Gidha express their rhythmic life style and a similar exuberance is reflected in their art and crafts such as phulkari and chope.

Phulkari is analysed as 'Phul', flower and 'kari', work i.e. floral work or flowering. It is a special , traditional hand work mainly found in Gurgaon, Hissar, Rohtak, Kurnal and Delhi. However, in West Punjab this embroidery is famous as 'Bagh', means garden, in which the entire surface of the shawl is decorated with floral designs.

The exact history and origin of this traditional art is not fully known, due to lack of evidences and documentations. However, it is said that, an earliest mention on Phulkari was made in the famous love story of Heer-Ranjha written by Waris Shah (1725-1790), Heer has many costume included phulkari articles too. From this it is quite obvious that, phulkari an article customarily presented to the girl during her wedding. Bhana Bhatt mentioned in 'Harshacharita' around seventeenth century that, some folk were embroidering flowers and foliages on the wrong side of the cloth where the technique and stitches were similar to the ones used in Bagh and Phulkari. On this basis Jasleen Dhamija expressed that a similar embroidery was prevalent in different parts of India, but did survive only in Punjab, while similar motifs are seen in the traditional art of Bihar and Rajasthan. Some opined that this embroidery migrated from Persian art, where an embroidery form called 'Gulkari' having similar literal meaning, 'Gul' means flowers and 'kari' the work, Which did resemble Phulkari, There is another theory which discloses that the Jat tribe of East Punjab, basically peasants, migrated from central Asia, are the pioneers of this craft. This theory was strongly supported by Flora Ann Steele, in her famous paper on phulkari work. She also mentioned that people carried out phulkari with cotton thread in olden days and with passage of time silk floss was introduced and now it is prepared with vivid, luxurious colour combinations.

The earliest available articles of embroidery were Rumal, the kerchief, embroidered somewhere during fifteenth century by the sister of Sikh Guru, Guru Nanak which was similar to Chamba rumal, Shamla a ceremonial costume of fifth Sikh Guru. This reference indicates that phulkari must have been originated during the fifteenth or sixteenth centuries.

Phulkari is an integral part of the life of Punjabi girl. In any simple or elaborate functions, festivals, get-together functions, one or the other type of phulkari or Bagh is invariably used. It is said to be auspicious, a symbol of happiness, prosperity and 'suhag' of a married woman. However, it is considered as a great treasure. The rough and coarse base material of phulkari symbolizes hard and tough yet colourful life of Punjabi women, the rich and glossy work with pat portrays her dreams and aspirations. It can also be added here that, phulkari adds delicacy, elegance and grace to the heavy personality of Punjabi women. Therefore, phulkari is a part and parcel of Punjabi girls trousseau the maternal mother, grand mother take special pains, care, interest, attention and pride in embroidering 'chope'. However the girl also had to work on it from her early age. It depicts her skill, art and hard work that adds to her eligibility as bride. It takes years to complete such shawls used during wedding ceremonies. They are also a symbol of love, affection and faith.

Chaddar, Bagh and Chope are the three types of embroidery which are grouped according to the craftsmanship. 'Chaddar', the shawl, the veil having surface decoration is used by the bride during the 'Phera' ceremony i.e., when she takes seven rounds of the holy fire, known as Suber. It is always a red coloured Khaddar having five flowers centrally arranged and other four motifs in each corner of the shawl. 'Bagh' having over all inter connected designs and were geometrically conventionalized. 'Chop' is little longer than the usual shawl, where only the edges along the selvedge were embroidered with golden yellow coloured silk floss against red coloured khaddar.

Hand spun and hand woven khaddar is the base material for phulkari women, specially young unmarried girls, after completing their household work, used to get-together in place and engaged in group spinning (Trinjan), knitting, crocheting and embroidering. There are three types of hand woven fabrics, khaddar being a loosely spun and coarsely woven fabric and the other Chaunsa khaddar, woven with fine yarn, on which Baghs were embroidered. The third type material, the Halwan, light weight finely woven fabric popular in Hazara and Rawalpindi districts of west Punjab are exclusively used for phulkari. However the most popular fabric on which phulkari done was the inexpensive, durable and easily locally available khaddar. White khaddar used to be dyed indigenously by local dyers using natural vegetable colours.

Soft, glossy, untwisted silk thread is employed for the stitchery, which is basically supplied from Kashmir, Afghanistan and Bengal. However, the best quality, pat comes from China. To complete a phulkari work it requires around 50 to 100 grams of silk thread whereas Bagh can be completed by utilizing double the amount of floss. Apart from silk, cotton thread, the Bandi is also sometimes used on white cotton material. However, woollen yarn is employed for handwork in some parts of Punjab. The colours predominantly used red, orange, green, white, golden yellow and deep blue.

The design of phulkari are seldom traced but have been worked by counting both warp and weft threads. However, to overcome the faulty designs the area or boundaries of the design is demarked with a row of running stitch using green pat.

The darning stitch is the basic unit of phulkari and the workmanship of both Bagh and Phulkari are graded according to its length and density of the stitches. The usual length ranges from half to one fourth of an inch. Every thread in the ground fabric is picked up from the obverse side and is done so finely that hardly any background material would be visible. The untwisted silk floss covers the background completely thus, provides the body. However, the needle craft consists of mainly long and short darning stitches, worked on the wrong side of the khaddar. Though the work is simple in appearance, requires long practice a year or so and good eye sight to master this technique. The symmetry of the motif will be visible deliberately on missing any single thread. For outlining the borders and marking the areas, stem, chain and herring bone stitches are used. Double running and satin stitches are also employed. However, the edging is done by buttonhole. Earlier this khaddar was woven in narrow width and hence two to three such widths used to be joined from wrong sides to get a size of two and a half yards long and one and three quarter yards of width. The joints of the base fabrics were expertly covered with herringbone stitch. The colour of the base khaddar is red, blue, black, rust, maddar brown and white.

The Punjabi women are genius in creating motifs though there is limitation of using darning stitch only wrapway and weftway. The newly created intricate and complicated designs were highly stylized, but were never copied, referred or traced from any books. They are the creation of the versatile Punjabi ladies. The motifs comprised of, the things used in day today life, articles precious to them, which are valued and considered sacred and aspired but all had geometrical base.

Geometrical, all over designs are commonly used for Baghs. Basic geometrical shapes, like triangle, square, rectangular, vertical and horizontal lines are intelligently incorporated to produce complicated patterns, further appropriate application of colours help to produce highly stylized motifs such as parrot, lotus or rolling pin and so on. As the word phulkari itself suggests a large variety of flowers like lotus, cotton and sunflower; among fruits, orange pomegranate, muskmelon, pear, mango, dates are common, few vegetables like brinjal, chili, cauliflower, bitter gourd, pumpkin, maize cob are also used. Varieties of both domestic and royal animals such as cow, buffalo, goat, cat, rat, donkey, rabbit, pig, frog, tortoise, camel, horse and elephant; domestic village birds like hen, chicken, sparrow, pigeon, crow and owl; few household articles like various types of utensils, rolling pin, brass urn, pitcher; domestic activities like churning curds, pounding wheat or corn, spinning a cone and so on.

TYPES OF BAGH

Bagh is a latter innovation has conventionalized geometrical motifs all over. The whole back ground is embroidered usually with two shades of pat like golden yellow and white, orange and yellow or green and crimson. However, Baghs have been given different names on the basis of their utility and motifs embroidered.

RESHMI SHEESHA (SILKAN MIRROR)

Embroidery is done in white floss giving an impact or image exactly like a mirror, done on a dark background. The motifs consist of different types of geometrical diaper motifs, a very fine and delicate work.

GHUNGHAT BAGH (VEIL TO COVER THE FACE)

A three cornered shawl used by the bride to cover the head and it is customary to draw the veil on the face (ghunghat) in presence of elderly people. Embroidery is done on the triangular patch which covers the face. A similar Bagh in east Punjab is called as Sarpallu, which has still an elaborate embroidery. Both Ghunghat and Sarpallu Baghs have red background on which golden yellow and multi coloured motifs will be worked out.

VARI DA BAGH

'Vari refers to the clothes and jewellery articles presented to the bride from groom's side and Bagh is an elaborately embroidered article made by the grandmother of the groom, almost taking four years to complete, forms an important items of the vari. The red ground fabric is covered with tiny lozenges, usually embroidered with yellow colour. This bagh is the speciality of west Punjab, now in Pakistan.

VELANIAN DA BAGH

The name had been given on the basis of the traditional motif, the 'Rolling pin' the domestic kitchen device, quite a popular motif. The pattern has rows of rolling pins distinguished through various colour combinations. Sometimes the rows of rolling pins are insert with consecutive rows of zig-zag lines or small circular lozenges, producing an image or shape of rolling pin.

BAWAN BAGH (BAGH WITH FIFTY-TWO MOTIFS)

As the name suggests (Bawan) the bagh has fifty two different geometrical designs placed equidistantly all along the body of the bagh. The body is divided into small squares and are demarked with intricate geometrical border. Each square has a unique motif in bright colour, depicting the mastery over the craft. Only women folk are expert in this art, which is gradually becoming rare and slowly extinct because of its elaborately.

SURAJ MUKHI BAGH (FACE OF SUN)

The Bagh is covered with geometrical designs, built up with lozenges. Each composite lozenge has three small lozenges arranged diagonally. Each of these three lozenges have another smaller lozenge in the center, emphasized with dark out line. The outer most and larger lozenge is out lined with double running stitch. The geometrical designs in the border may be worked with either darn or double running stitch. Suraj Mukhi Bagh is popular in eastern Punjab.

Various other Baghs are named according to the motif employed for stitchery such as, Kakri Bagh (cucumber motif), Karelian da Bagh (bitter gourd motif), Mirchi Bagh (Chili Motif), Anaran da Bagh (Pomegranate motif), Dhaniya Bagh (coriander motif), Gulkerian da Bagh (holly hock motif), Motia Bagh (jasmin motif), Genda Bagh (marigold motif), Guttan da Bagh (Kite motif), Jahazan da Bagh (Aeroplane motif), Zanjir da Bagh (Zig-zag line motif), Bungle da Bagh (bungalow motif), Kanglan da Bagh (comb motif), Rumalan da Bagh (Kerchief motif), Chandrama Bagh (moon motif), etc.

The Bagh are also named according to the number of colours used in the embroidery viz. Dwiranga (two-colours), Pancharanga (five colours), Sataranga (seven colours), Navaranga (nine colours) and so on.

The famous Mughal gardens are also named for the Bagh such as Char Bagh, Shalimar Bagh, Chaurasia Bagh, Dhoop-Chhaon and so on. Tota Bagh and Mor Bagh were the names given for the Baghs having predominantly parrot and peacock motifs respectively.

TYPES OF PHULKARIS

Though the craftsmanship is one and the same, the embroidery of Punjab, they are distinguished for better understanding on the basis of types of motifs used, colour of the base material, stitches employed, area or part of the base material embroidered and their utility.

CHOPE

A precious red coloured phulkari, prepared and presented by the maternal grandmother of the bride at her wedding function. The triangular designs are embroidered with golden yellow pat by double running stitch, which appears identical on either sides of the cloth. However, a small Nazar buti is embroidered in one corner of the chope to keep off the evil eye.

Chope is always emphasised on the border, having large triangular or pyramid shapes having their basis parallel to the selvage. The gap between two such triangles is fitted with another triangle in opposite direction. Each triangle is further designed into some sort of geometrical that too bird motifs. The body of the chope, many times remains uncovered but rarely is been filled with small triangles spreadout wide apart. This manual workmanship is so fine, delicate, intricate and neat that, it is very difficult to identify the right side of the chope. The chope is draped around the bride at the time of 'Chura Charana', a ceremony when the bride wears red ivory bangles presented by her maternal uncle.

SUBHAR

Another rich, gorgeous, red coloured phulkari worn by the bride, during her wedding, at the time of 'Pheras', taking rounds around the holy fire. Though the colour of the base material and floss is same as that of chope, the area embroidered varied. Subhar has a central and four corner motifs where the center has a group of five motifs and similar ones repeated at the corner.

TIL PATRA

It means sprinkled sesame seeds, scarcely embroidered. Small tiny embroidered dots in the body, of an inferior and inexpensive khaddar is usually presented to the maids during wedding or any other such traditional auspicious occasions.

NILAK

As the name suggests, it is a phulkari of blue colour. The farm women use this khaddar on which embroidery is done with yellow and crimson pat though glaring but exhibits attractive contrast colour combinations. Sometimes Nilak is also worked on black khaddar. The motifs commonly embroidered are the articles used at household like, comb, fan, umbrella or rumal and flowers.

SHISHEDAR PHULKARI

Number of diaper designs along with mirror are inserted on either red or brown background. These were the speciality of south-eastern Punjab, but now in Haryana state. However, it is gradually becoming rare and extinct.

DARSHANA DWAR OR DARWAZA

This phulkari is a presentation, the Bhet, to some of the religious institutions offered during certain ceremonial functions. It is a design worked on a panel, which is draped over the entrance gate from where people take the Darshan (see), of their deity.

THIRMA

A phulkari done on white khaddar is generally termed as Thirma. It is a speciality of Hindu women, an important treasure, was presented by bride's family during her wedding. However, the prosperity, status, standard of living of the bride's family will be sealed on the basis of number of Thirma presented, and in some cases as many as fifty one pieces were presented, an affluence of the girl's family.

The designs consisted either floral or geometrical by using red, green, blue or purple floss. The two main characteristics of Thirma is, it will have two vertical bands on either sides separated by a row of herringbone stitch with green floss and the pallu being embroidered. This work is popular in Rawalpindi, Peshawar, Hazara of Punjab district now come under the jurisdiction of Pakistan.

SAINCHI PHULKARI

It is the folk embroidery of Malwa region of Punjab, depicts the true rural life where, the motifs are being traced, outlined before embroidering. The motifs depict the various activities of rural life, different household articles, daily chores of a housewife and other such incidents i.e. the various agricultural operations like, ploughing, harvesting, a water carrier, smoking hukka, guests drinking sharbat, wrestlers practicing wrestling, hawker carrying his articles; domestic chores like, pounding, grinding, churning, spinning, weaving and so on. In other words the whole life of the villagers is exhibited colourfully through Sainchi Phulkari. The plain red or black khaddar used as veil or wrapper, for daily wear, is known as 'Salu or Saloo'.

Other phulkaries named according to the motifs used are, Butiyanwali (floral buds), Char or Aath Kaliyan (four or eight buds), Amban di (mango slice), Pakhian di (fans), Kangiyan di (combs), Chattariyan di (Umbrella), Moran di (peacock) and so on.

NAZAR BUTI

Its main purpose is to drag off the evil eye. In order to achieve this, a small corner or portion of the design is retained unembroidered, indicating that the work is yet to be completed. Similarly, few motifs of the main design or a small buti in a corner worked a distinct dark shade of blue, black or purple, which as such is not been used except to denote Nazar Buti. There is another way of expressing Nazar Buti where, a part of the design instead filling completely, simply outlined. The women being orthodox and religious minded, some commence their craft with a small religious symbol in one corner of phulkari praying for its speedy and successful completion.

Though, phulkari depicts the traditional embroidery of Punjab has lots of diversity in type and colour of base material, threads, stitches, motifs, area to be embroidered, number of colours used, size of the khaddar, and articles prepared, regionwise, sectorwise as well as religionwise.

Phulkari, has not remained as a domestic art but on commercial scale entered the international markets of European countries and U.S.A. Owing to its demand the manufacturers introduced numerous new designs with variegated colour combination according to the taste of the market. T.N. Mukerji, in his book, Art Manufacturers of India mentions that, the demand for phulkari enhanced ever since it was exhibited in Punjab exhibition during 1881. George Watt mentions surprisingly that, a sample of Phulkari pattern ordered by the European trader was totally different than the Indian style, specially the length of stitch which was about one inch. This kind of demand, taste and workmanship definitely affects the basic concept of traditional Phulkari and in no time leads to deterioration of the quality of the work. The exported goods were not used as auspicious ceremonial articles but mostly taken as household textiles.

On the other hand the social and economical changes in the life style of the Punjabis has lead to rarity of these exquisite embroidery. The group spinning (trinjans) has been transferred to schools and colleges. Girls are now attending the schools, leading to greater extent of social mobility, availability of wide variety of fabrics, modification of traditional stitches into much simpler forms, increased demand, shortage of time to meet the demand and so on, have adversely affected the traditional art of Punjab. At this juncture, a thought to revive this super art is felt to be very essential. Adoption of new type of material similar to khaddar, tracing on block printing the outline of the design, use of viscose rayon floss, have been encouraged. There are many private and Government institutions who undertake the production of phulkari article. It is surprising to know that Rajasthan has also involved in phulkari work.

CHOPE EMBROIDERY

Another traditional embroidery of Punjab, needle work leading to double satin stitch. This existed since three decades, a popular art in western part of Punjab, before independence. Material being coarse khaddar, worked with double satin stitch, designs beings never traced but always memorised. Outline of the design is completed with running stitch using black colour. The stitchery of chope was similar to that of the one used for Bikaner and Jaisalmer embroidery of Rajasthan. The motifs come from either geometrical or stylized floral base, which would facilitate by counting threads. It is surprising to know that, the motifs on chope did not have nomenclature. Household articles like, pillow, cushion, sofa, table covers, bed, spreads and covers were prepared. Apart from Bagh, Phulkari and Chope, gold and silver embroidery flourished in Patiala state of Punjab. However Patiala and Rajpur are the famous commercial centres of hand embroideries at present, who employ cross stitch and satin stitch to fill the motifs , along with pat as well as salma and sitaras.

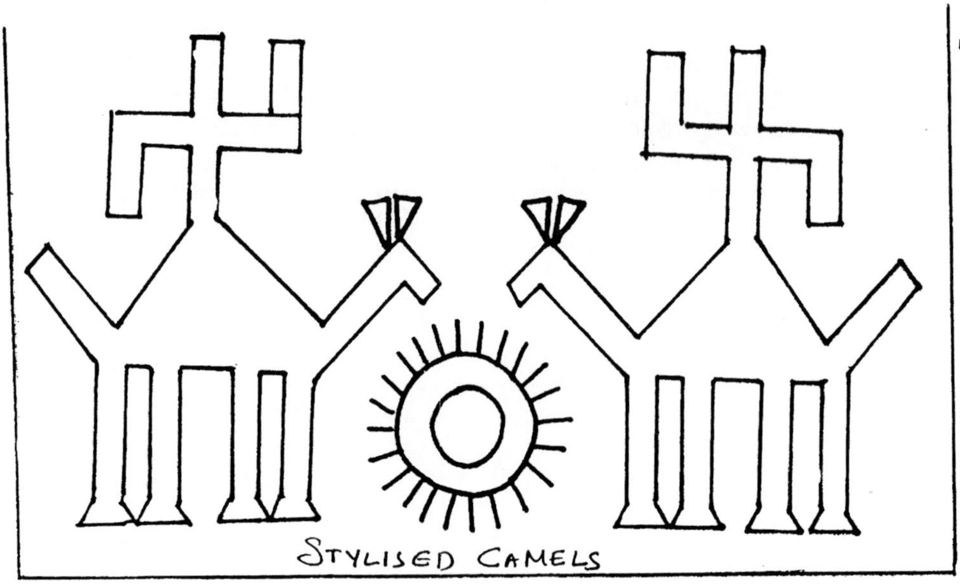
STYLISED CAMELS

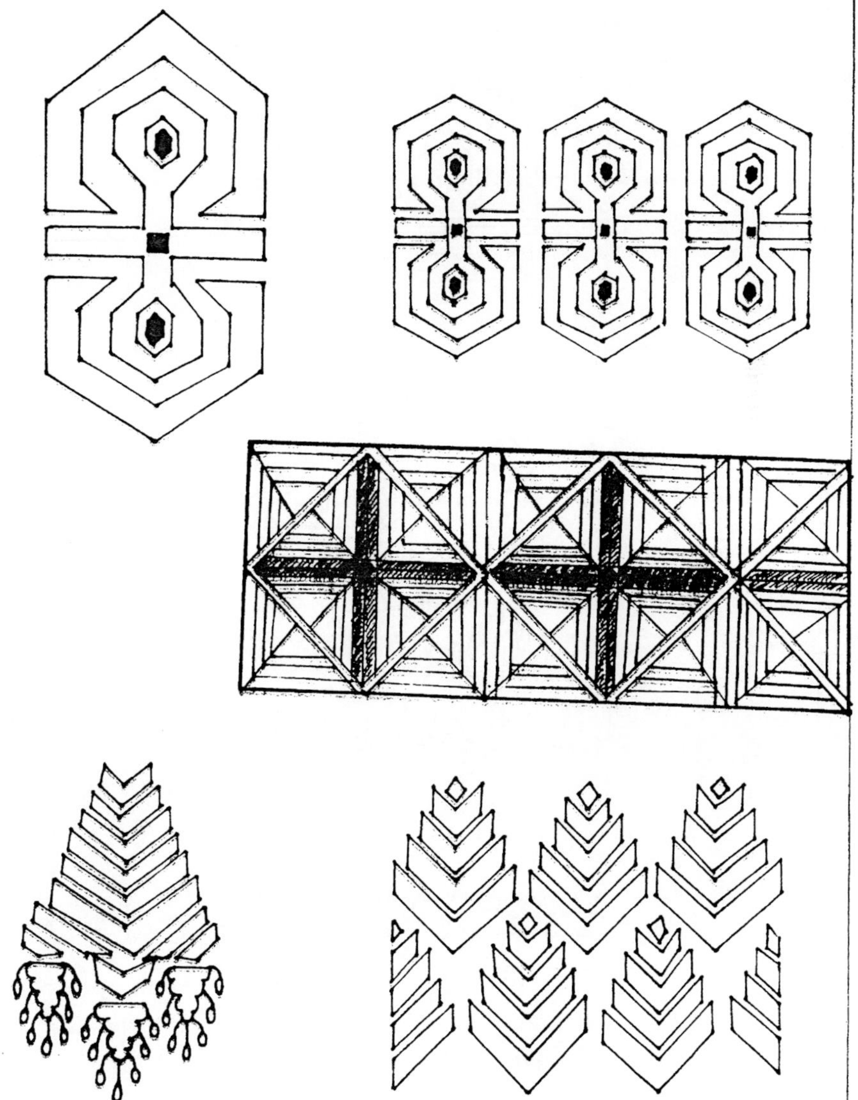

Geometrical Motifs

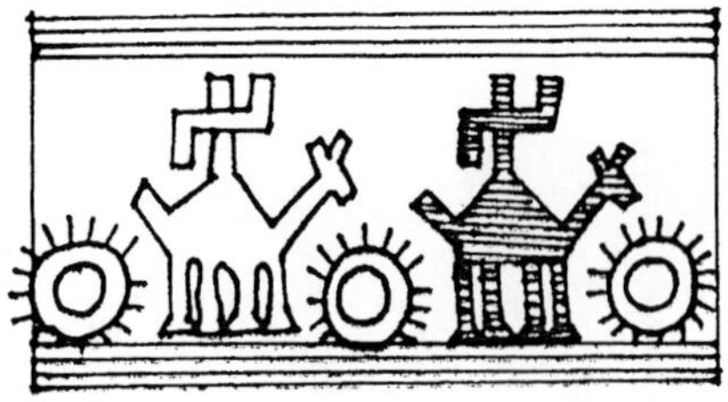

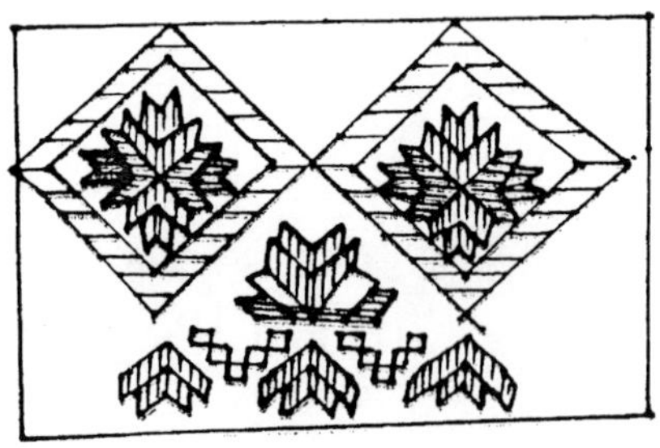

LOTUS - GEOMETRICAL FORM

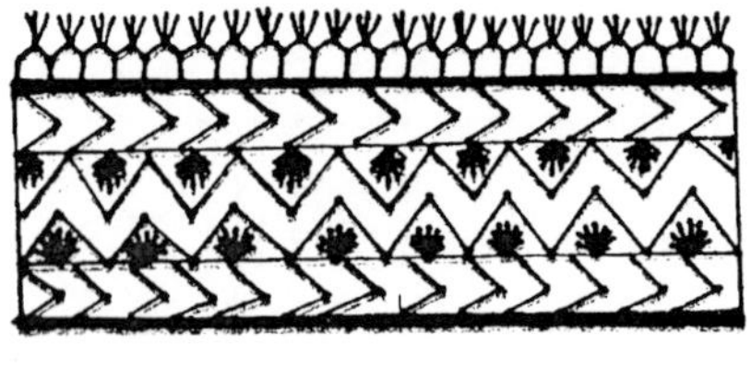

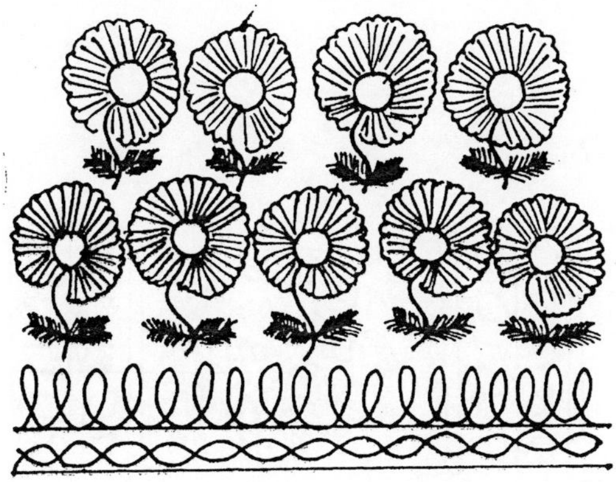

BORDER DESIGN

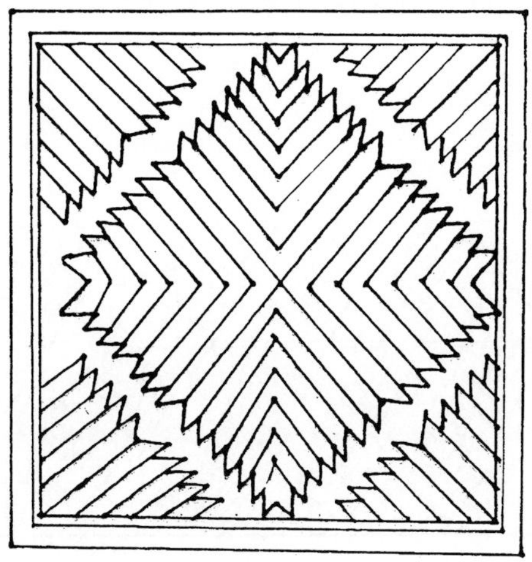

CENTRAL MOTIF

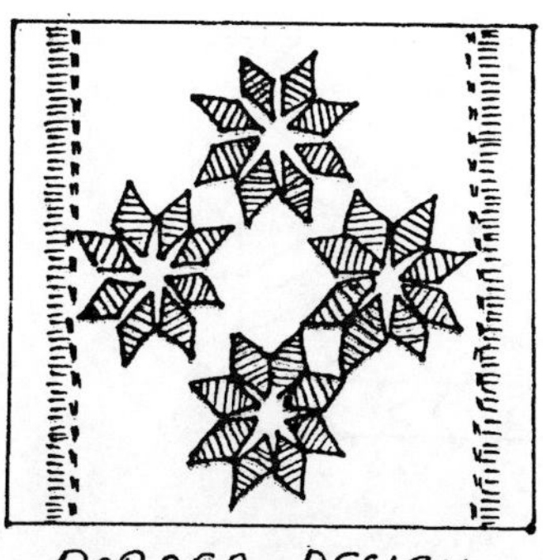

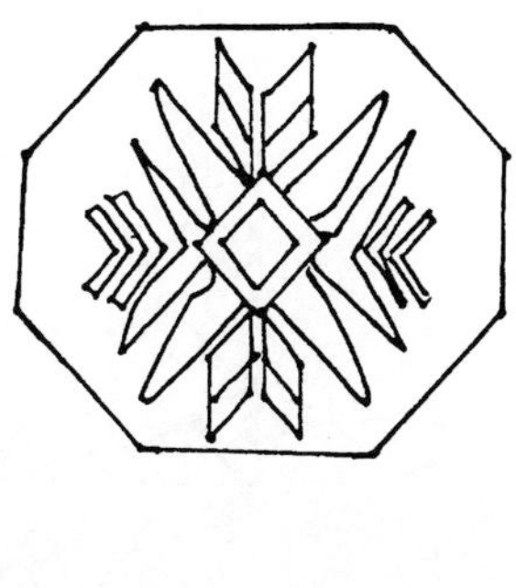

BORDER DESIGN

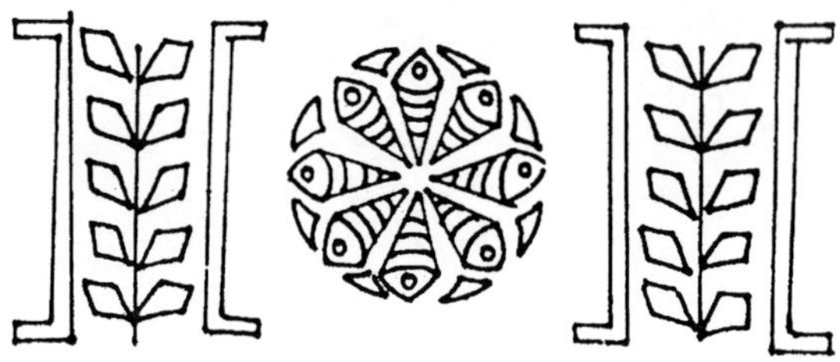

STYLISED TREE & FISH

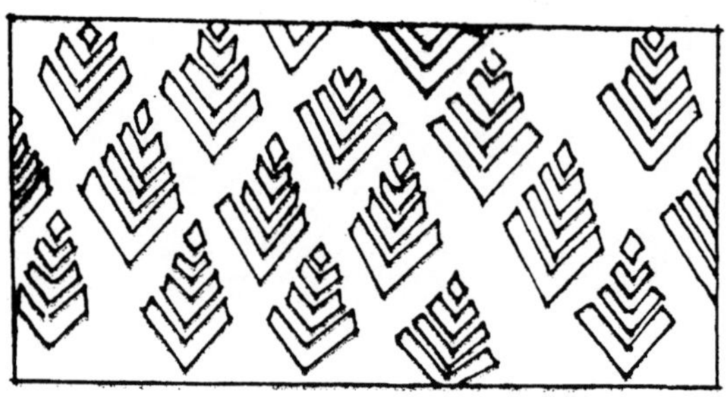

ALLOVER DESIGN

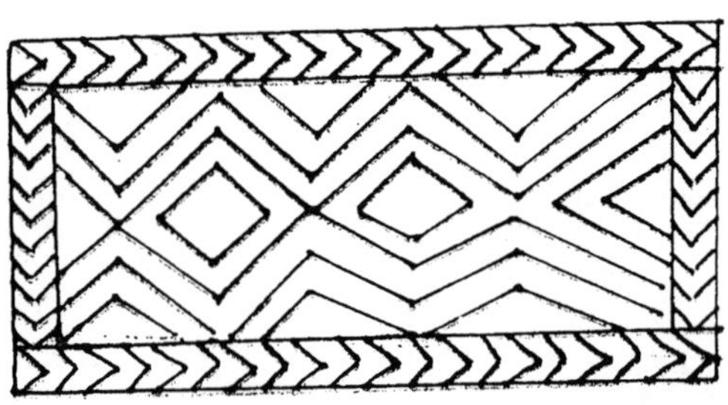

BORDER

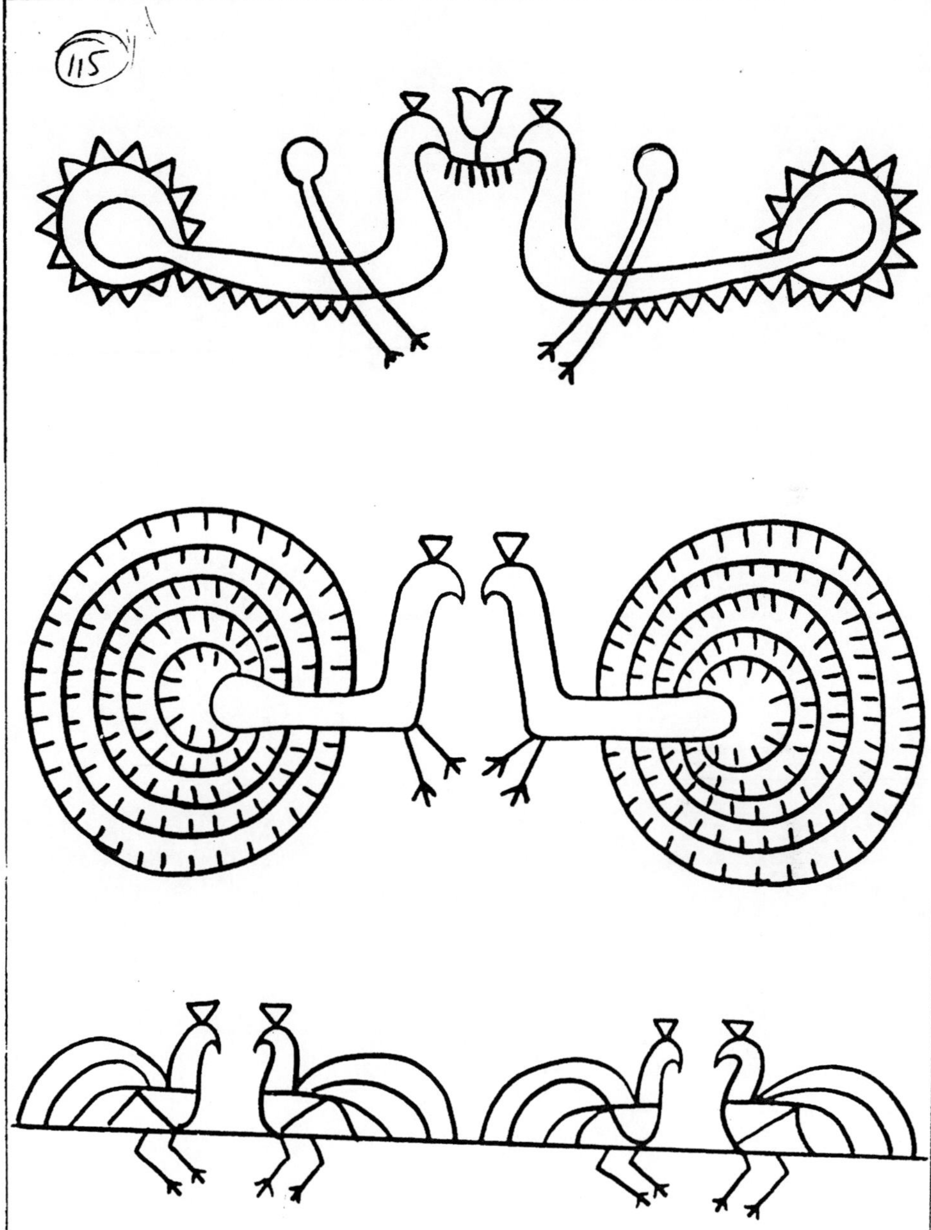

STYLISED BIRDS

CHAPTER 10
EMBROIDERY OF RAJASTHAN

'Rajasthan' the word, derived from 'Rajaputana' which means the dwelling place of heroic princes known for their bravery, situated in the western part of India. Arawali hills that runs from north to south-west divides Rajasthan into two parts where north-east portion is covered with 'Thar' the largest desert consisting of hot, dry and sandy climate. Rajasthan is bordered with Gujarat, Sindh, Punjab and Himalaya. The culture and civilization of Mohenjodaro-Harappa and Indus valley are thrived from Udaipur and Bikaner. The culture of Rajasthan has given birth to several ethnic clans. Few among them are Ahir, Bishnoi, Jat, Mahajan, Marwari (Marwadi), Manghwal, Rajput and Suthar and so on. The socio-cultural history of Rajasthan has influence of neighbouring states and moreover a great deal of similarity in performing customs, social participation and mode of dressing is evident among various clans. Despite of few variations, the motifs, colours, patterns, stitches and above all, the essence of embroidery is similar.

Rajasthan, a colourful state has a rich weather and heritage of varied embroideries, each community practicing in its own style. It is amazing to note that the women folk of remote villages, unexposed to the modern civilization are expertised in preparing articles of great aesthetic value, commonly used at household level. The striking colour combinations, bold geometrical designs are in contrast to the tepid and arid sands of the desert. Perhaps, this is one of the ways through which Rajasthanis add colour to their lives. However, the embroideries of Rajasthan can be grouped as folk, religious and court embroideries.

I. FOLK EMBROIDERIES

A large varieties of folk embroideries are practiced in different districts of Rajasthan and it is impossible to trace the history and origin of this art. A reference on folk embroideries is made in 'Art Manufacturers of India' by T.N. Mukherji and certain collections of embroidery samples from Jaipur and Bikaner were sent to the Indian exhibition. A mention about cross stitch was made by George Watt, which was practiced by Jat women. Folk embroidery is also known as 'Bharat Kaam' which means filling work. The main stitches employed in folk embroideries are - Mochi Bharat, Heer Bharat, Applique work, Jaisalmer Applique work, Bead work and Meo embroidery.

Mochi Bharat

It is also known as chain stitch prevalent in Barmer district a predominant stitch from Kutch of Gujarat. The cobblers, known as Mochies, prepare leather foot wear by chain stitch and expertised in decorating these goods with embroideries, which gradually evolved into the textile decoration. It is believed that this stitch originated in Bhuj (Kutch) and probably spread to the neighbouring states, so also Rajasthan. Mochi Bharat was done on personal articles by Mochi and Menghwal communities of Rajasthan.

Hand-spun and Hand-woven khaddar is the base material, having two varieties, coarser used for heavy ghagras and choli and finer or lighter variety for chunnies (odhanis). The common colours used for the base were blue, red and black. The white khaddar is usually dyed at home with natural, vegetable colours. These days, Mochi Bharat is done on mill made cotton fabric of medium weight and the additional colours for base are white and maroon. Green colour is very rarely used as a base.

Embroidery is done with either cotton or silk, untwisted thread called pat, dyed professionally. Thar, Parkar and Shikarpur districts of Sindh have well established dyeing centers. Bright and vivid colours are administered for the craft and most commonly used ones are yellow, red, white, green and crimson, whereas blue, orange and purple were used in little quantities. The inner part of the design is worked with lighter and outer with darker shade, that being the trend depicts vein like effect.

During early times the design was traced on the material with the help of perforated paper but now this primitive technique has been replaced by the use of wooden blocks, (chipas) prepared by professional carpenters 'Suthar' where the motif is impregnated by block printing technique.

The needle used for Mochi Bharat is called Ari or Katharni, which is very fine awl, having a small notch just above the point to form a hook. Before proceeding for embroidery, the material has to be fixed on frame. The thread is pulled from the wrong side (obverse side) of the material to the right side with the help of Ari, to form loops. The outline of the motif is worked first and filling (bharat) is done later. Sometimes mirrors are also introduced in the center of the motifs which are fixed with button hole stitch.

The main motifs come from bird, animal and floral kingdoms. The most popular and commonly used bird motif is, peacock, our national bird. However, parrot either single or couple and garuda are used in combination with floral motifs. As far as animal motifs are considered elephant and horses are the most common. Elephant carrying palanquine with few human beings is the most popular motif. Lord Ganesh with his steed, rat, horse with a rider and camel carrying Dhola are also among the popular motifs. Flowers occupy an important place in this art. Variety of small flowers, arranged scatteredly known commonly as buttas or butties is executed. Stylized lotus is one of the popular floral motifs. A seven petaled flower with foliages and creeper having small mirror discs in the center is also seen. Guldasta, cluster of floral sprays are used either in the corners or borders of the article. Sometimes these guldastas are surrounded by peacocks. Besides floral, animal and bird motifs human figures are also observed. Figures of dancing ladies in the traditional costume, ghagra and odhani, and men wearing short gathered tops of Saurashtra depicts the influence of Gujarat embroidery. This embroidery is done primarily on ghagras and cholis. But now is done on other household articles like bags, table covers, cushion covers, jacket, caps, bonnets wall hangings and so on.

Heer Bharat

Heer Bharat is nothing but filling the design with thread work. This filling is done either by button hole stitch or long and short (double satin) stitch, which resembles the art of Kutch and Kathiawar on one side and Haryana in the other. According to Jasleen Dhamija the area of Kutch, Sindh, Baluchistan and Jaisalmer have perhaps people from the same stock with a similar traditions and background. The semi-desert conditions, their dependency on cattle which necessitates their leading a more or less semi-nomadic life are common to all of them. It is also true that the Jats, the migratory tribe of central Asia (who came to India) were responsible for developing this embroidery.

This Bharat is done on hand-spun hand-woven as well as mill made light or medium weight cotton and woollen clothes. The base colour is comprised of blue, red and a blend of both, brown. Embroidery is worked with cotton, woollen or untwisted silk floss of various colour combinations white, black, red, green yellow, blue, pink and purple.

The mode of working is very simple, where the stitches are made either in vertical (warp way) or horizontal (weft way) directions. Jat women use long and short stitches for filling, on the contrary the Barmer women use double satin stitch, herring bone, button hole and stem stitch for the same. This resembles the embroidery of Sind and sometimes use in combination of Sindhi Taropa. The long satin stitches resemble phulkari of Punjab. Mirrors of various size and shapes are used in Heer Bharat. Geometrical motifs are predominant, however stylized birds are also seen. Floral and animal motifs of geometrical base are also evident.

Applique Work

Marwari community of Rajasthan is expert in applique art. Rajasthan applique work is similar to the patchwork of Kathiawar the 'Katab'. Applique work did exist in Egypt, where men involved in embroidery work, collect old, bright and bold coloured small cotton fabric pieces, cut into definite shape and proportionate sizes and sewn to a new base material. Since a similar workmanship is existing in Rajasthan, it is believed that there exists influence of Egyptians on patch work to some extent.

Mill made medium weight white cotton cloth forms the base on which patches of various tints, shades, sizes and shapes are arranged in a pictorial pattern later trimmed, slip stitched, whipped sometimes finished with running stitch and button hole. However, this applique art differs from that of Bihar embroidery, where the patches are first stitched to base or ground fabric and later the motifs are cut out and finished. The motifs selected for applique are animal, floral and human figures which are highly stylized. Each art piece depicts an important theme.

Earlier the women of Marwari community decorated household articles by applique work. This article was one of the important items of dowry of the Marwari girl. Now, the art has been commercialised and it is prevalent in Jaipur, Udaipur and Barmer districts, where variety of wall hangings, bed covers, cushion and sofa covers, covers for camels, cows, oxen and canopies are prepared. However it is not done on new dresses perhaps the applique work involves use of fabric from wornout articles.

Jaisalmer Applique Work

The quilts made by patch work well known as 'Ralli' produced in Jaisalmer, which is nothing but the quilt made by sewing several layers of old fabrics, where the upper most layer being made of new white cotton cloth. The main stitch used to hold all the layers together is the simple running or darning stitch. The colours used for patch work are olive green, brown, maroon and black. The technique of patchwork is similar to that of khatwa of Bihar, and the corners with tassels of either cotton or silk and sequins called 'Phuladi' Navali cholis, saddle cloth, bad spreads, cushion covers and purses were decorated by Jaisalmer applique art.

Moti Bharat

It is nothing but a bead work, originated in India, somewhere in the middle of nineteenth century. It was the exclusive art of cobbler then, but later women from other community too become masters in this art. The art became one of the popular documents that depicted the life style, custom, tradition of its creators. Moti Bharat is predominant in Jalor district of Rajasthan.

This art is not worked on a background of fabric, instead the opaque white beads form the base on which the transparent beads are worked by stringing them together in various shapes and forms of birds, animals, human figures and other household devices. The mode of working the Moti Bharat is explained by John Irevin in his Indian embroideries .... as 'work row by row' three beads being taken up at stitch on the row, the stitching of beads moves forward one position, so that as the work progresses, row by row, a closer rhomboid network is formed.

Earlier, blue, green yellow and red coloured beads were commonly used, obtained from Italy and other parts of Europe as well. Now wide range of coloured beads are available locally for the craftmen to make use of.

Stylized human figures, geometrical designs, scenes from daily life, horse and camel riders, elephant with haudha, calf sucking mothers milk, horse with carriage, the famous love legend of Rajasthan Dhola and Maru are the designs repeatedly used. Various articles like, purse, caps, toran chaklas play articles, pattis, cradle decoration, showpieces, play articles for children are prepared by Moti Bharat.

Meo Embroidery

Meos are the cultivators from Alwar and Bharatpur districts of Rajasthan. Their tradition, life style and customs are similar to that of Jats of Haryana and Malwa (Punjab).

The Meo women involved in surface enrichment, similar to phulkari of Punjab. T.N. Mukerji writes in his Art Manufacturers of India as 'Meo sheets and the dresses of Jat women are embroidered with silk in Alwar state. It is practically Phulkari work'.

Fabric used at one time was the Khaddar, hand-spun and hand-woven and the embroidery was done on ghagras and odhanis. The main stitches used are the chain and darning and thread employed is silk floss. The background is worked with darning stitch with golden yellow colour and the motifs are worked in either white or black colours by chain stitch. Green, red and purple colours are sparsely used.

Dancing doll, human figures, highly stylized peacock with its rich multi coloured plumage, are the motifs used. However, those motifs are usually accompanied by zigzag lines, swirlings and flowing lines, and hence differs from phulkari work. As said by Kamladevi Chattopadhyaya "The strange balancing of geometrical forms with circular movements of flowing lines gives it a starting effect as of a horizon broken into geometrical forms, in which is combined a floating tree or a peacock'. Such an effect is not possible in phulkari, because in Meo embroidery along with darn stitch, chain is also used, which is possible to achieve circular, swirling effects. Meo embroidery is done on dresses, foot wears, cloak draped over the oxen and so on.

II . RELIGIOUS EMBROIDERY

Rajasthan is embodied with numerous religious shrines and temples of Jains and Vaishnavas. During religious festivals and ceremonial occasions, it has been the custom to offer gifts to these holy places. And this is how the religious embroidery has taken birth. The custom of giving offerings existed since fifteenth century and the most common ones are Pichhvais, Gaumukhi, Chandravo and so on.

Pichhvai Embroidery

Nathdwara, a place near Udaipur, has Vallabha sampradaya of Vaishnawa clan, an important centre of Pichhvai embroidery. It is said that the richly embroidered cloth Pichhvai (pichwai), originated and grew up around the temple of Srinathji as Krishna was fostered by it.

Most of the designs are obtained from Bhagavatpurana of certain themes like Krishna leela, Gokulavana, Rasmandala and so on, however the Pichhvai depicts Krishna as Srinathji. Pilgrims offer

Pichhvai to their deity which is hung behind the idol, while offering homage and many times the 'Bhaktas' (pilgrims) carried home as treasured souvenir of the deity. Most of the times Pichhvais are hand painted, an imitation of embroidered piece, not prepared traditionally at Nathdwara. Hence, there exists vast difference in the base material, motifs and colour combination.

The traditional Pichhvai is done on coloured cotton, satin or velvet varied season wise, as such summer and winter respectively. The motifs are wide variety picked up from nature; animals like cows, calves, fish; birds like parrot, peacock, garuda; fruits like Kalka; flowers like lotus and above all Hanuman, Ganesh and Sun (Surya). The traditional Pichhvai has Srinathji with his dark blue face surrounded by his playmates, cows under ever green tree. This colourful embroidery always has black outline. Sometimes gold and silver threads are also used to enlighten the structural units of the motif. The pilgrims get Pichhvai ordered, where the devotee himself gives the outline of the design and the actual embroidery is done by Mochis, gold and silver workers. Darker shades like red, green orange and Yellow are commonly made use of.

In few cases Pichhvai are also made of applique work, where the base material is invariably red in colour, a white cord for emphasizing outline and cream, green, yellow and black in needle work.

Pichhvai apart from being used as a hanging or curtain behind the image (idol), simhasan (covering for the throne). Chandarvo and Divalgiri hangings, Gaumukhi the armoured glove and Bajoth, cover for the Paduka (foot) stool of Srinathji.

Jain Embroidery

Jains occupy the main trading population of Rajasthan where Jain temples at Dilwara and Renakpur are very famous. They are highly religious, orthodox, nonconformists, lead a definite mode of life style, who indulge in offering variety of embroidered gifts at various Jain Mandirs, such as torans, door carves, canopies, panels, hangings and so on.

The history of Jain embroidery reflects back to earth in sixteenth century. The calico museum has a small fragment of Jain embroidery for its credit, probably a piece which was embroidered during fifteenth or sixteenth century.

The main base material being satin of blue red or violet in colour sometimes the rich looking soft velvet is also used. Basic stitches comprised of stem, satin and chain and worked with silk floss of blue, green, yellow and white colours, along with little combination of silver thread, to add to the lustre.

The basic concept of Jain philosophy has been picturised on these articles along with floral motifs, the main ones are Mandala, depicts Jain beliefs and shows different parts in heaven where various Gods and Goddesses live; Adivipa a representation of Jain cosmology, which depicts universe; Ashata Mangala or Ashtamangalika implies eight suspicious objects, related to eight Jain Tirthankaras. There was great influence of court embroideries during eighteenth and nineteenth century which is evident in some of the articles where human figures have been dressed similar to the court people.

III. COURT EMBROIDERY

The pioneers of court embroidery are the Mughals who spread this art to the courts of various states, so also in the princy places of Jaipur and Jodhpur of Rajasthan. The embroidery consists of gota, salma and thread work. The museum of Jaipur has the rich pieces of this embroidery decorated with gold and silver work along with gota work.

Gota Work

It is nothing but weaving the borders with gold and silver threads also known as Badla work. This work is very famous in northern India, where gotas are available in several widths and designs and are attached to various part of the costumes. It is done on cholis and the material ranged from coarse cotton to fine jeorgette, voile, chiffon, cambray, satin, mulmul and poplin. Sikar district of Rajasthan is famous for Badla work.

The main stitchery included, back, running or hem stitches exclusively done by women folk, has two distinct styles folk and classic. Folk style has specific motifs such as stylized animal, birds, flowers and also geometrical. The main feature of folk style is the gota, prepared and then cut into definite shape, size and affixed or patched to the main costume, where as in classic style, it is worked by using glossy sitaras, salmas, sequins and sometimes is used along with applique work, described by Kamaladevi Chattopadhyay as "an effect of enameling". The motifs commonly used are animals, birds, flowers and human figures, which later sewn to the ground fabric. The Badla work is done on traditional cholis, ghagras, chunnis, toran, chaklas, panels and so on.

Salma Work

The Mughals, lovers of rich glossy embellishment, have strongly influenced the salma work, the gold and silver thread work, predominantly existing in Jaipur is almost similar to the work done at Bhopal and Lucknow. Among various communities of Rajasthan, Marwaris, Jains and Baniyas have special liking for the gorgeous salma work. There are two types, zardozi, a heavier embroidery, very compactly and elaborately worked and Kamdani relatively lighter work done on fine materials like chiffon, jeorgette etc., worked in smaller areas and hence have more demand than zardozi. The work is done with the help of metallic wires of both gold and silver sitara a small, flat circular disc with a hole in the centre; various colour, shaped and sized pearls; twisted metallic wire like gigai; stiff twisted fine metallic wire, salma; untwisted metallic wire, badla; and sometimes the craft is enriched with the application of precious and semiprecious stones. The colour combination ranged with tints and shades of red and maroon.

The mode of salma work is very interesting. As a first step, the design is traced on the material with the help of oil and ink. The work commences from exterior to interior i.e. the outline of the motif is worked with the twisted metallic wire gigai, followed by filling with twisted circular metallic wire, the salma. For fixing the accessories, back, running, chain, couching stitches are employed. 'Meenakari' the enamel effect is brought about by combining salma work with applique and other hand stitchery, which is an exclusive manual work of menfolk. The motifs comprised of either floral or geometrical and are popular with distinctive names viz; Ganga, Jamuna (blend of gold and silver thread), jamavar (over all elaborate trellised pattern), Jal (trellised pattern), Bel (trellised border). Hazar buttas (fine work with glittering thousands buttis), katao kibel (scalloped trellis border) and so on.

The salma work was though done on household articles in early times, today the work is limited to only traditional costumes of Rajasthan, choli, lehenga and chunnary (odhani). caps, purses and shoes.

Thread Work

Untwisted silk floss pat of green, red, blue, pink are used for hand stitchery, done on white muslin a light weight material, sometimes layered together to give an effect of quilt. The thread work consisted of chain, satin and stem stitches, usually executed on turbans, curtains and bed covers (palangposh).

A special feature of Rajasthan is silk embroidery done on leather goods specially shoes and purses, popular in both rural and urban areas. In case of former the designs used to be bolder and colours being brighter where as in later case it was simple, delicate, sober, floral and foliages with gold and silver work to accentuate certain facets of design. The most popular knuckle pade of leather, lightly colourful, has either landscape or certain scenes of Rajpur paintings like women plucking flowers, birds sailing on the water, birds picking their food, were embroidered.

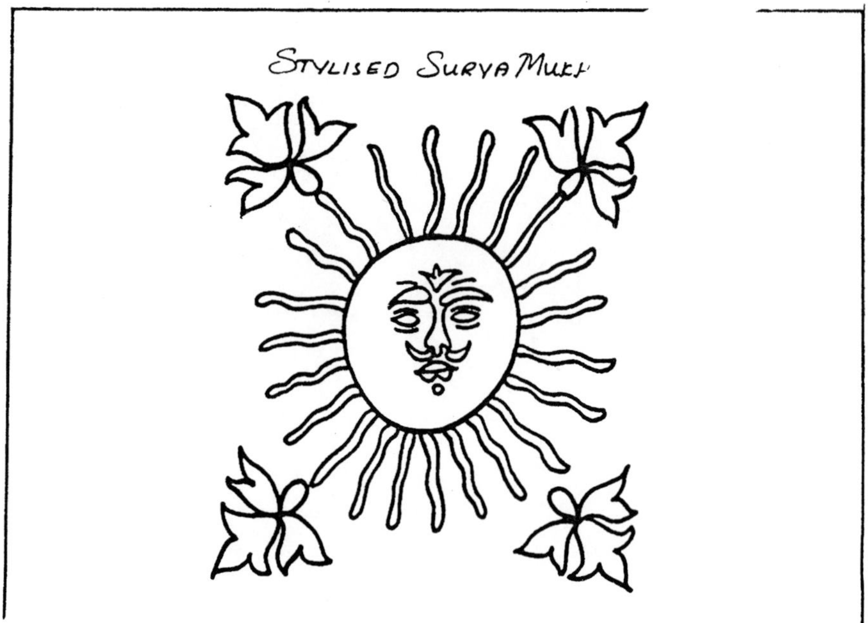
STYLISED SURYA MUKH

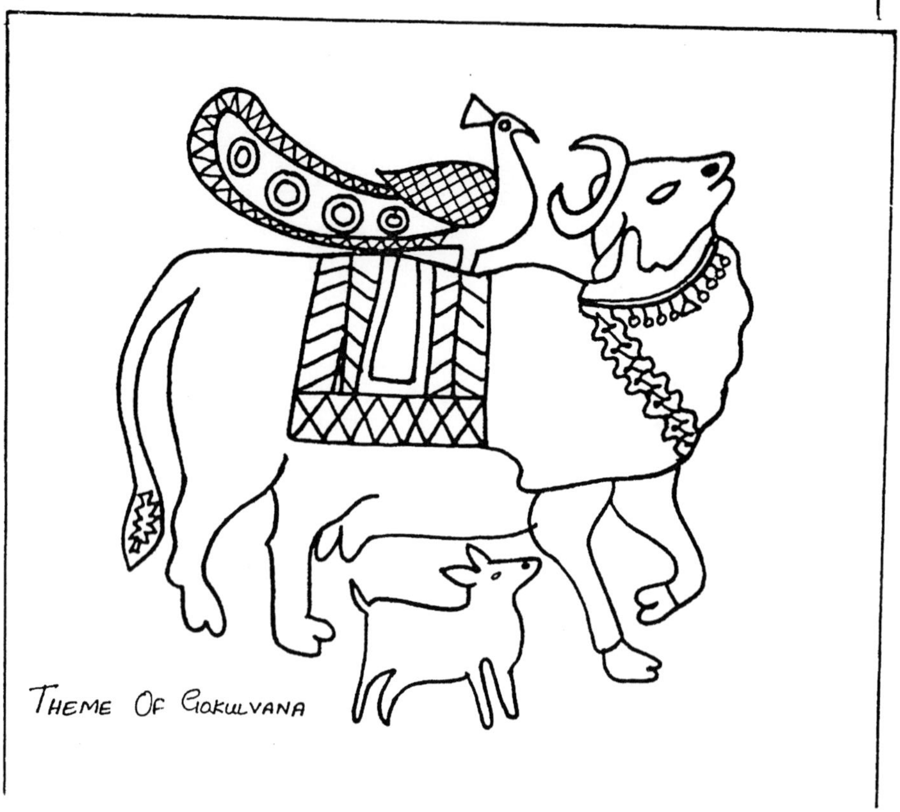
THEME OF GOKULVANA

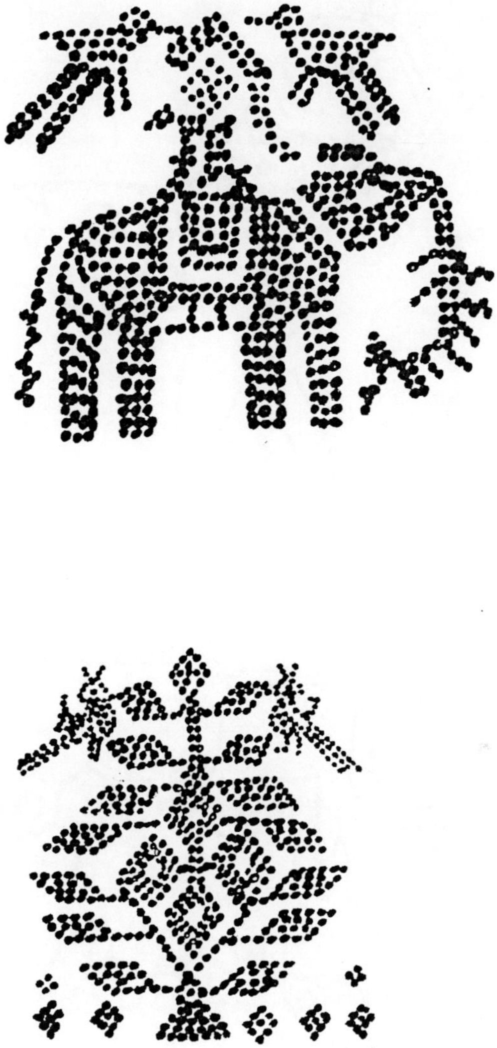

MOTIFS OF MOTI BHARAT

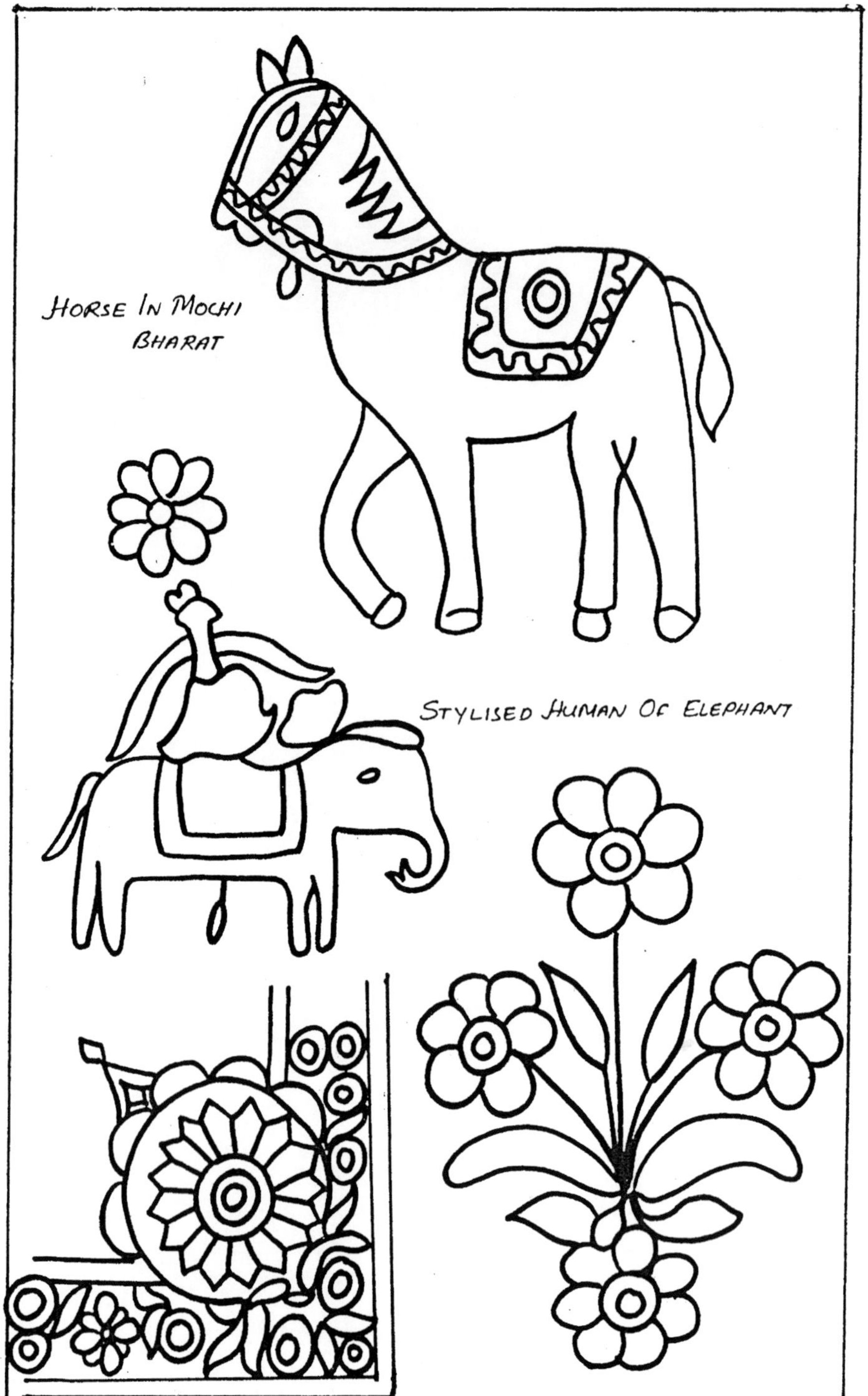
Horse In Mochi
Bharat
Stylised Human Of Elephant

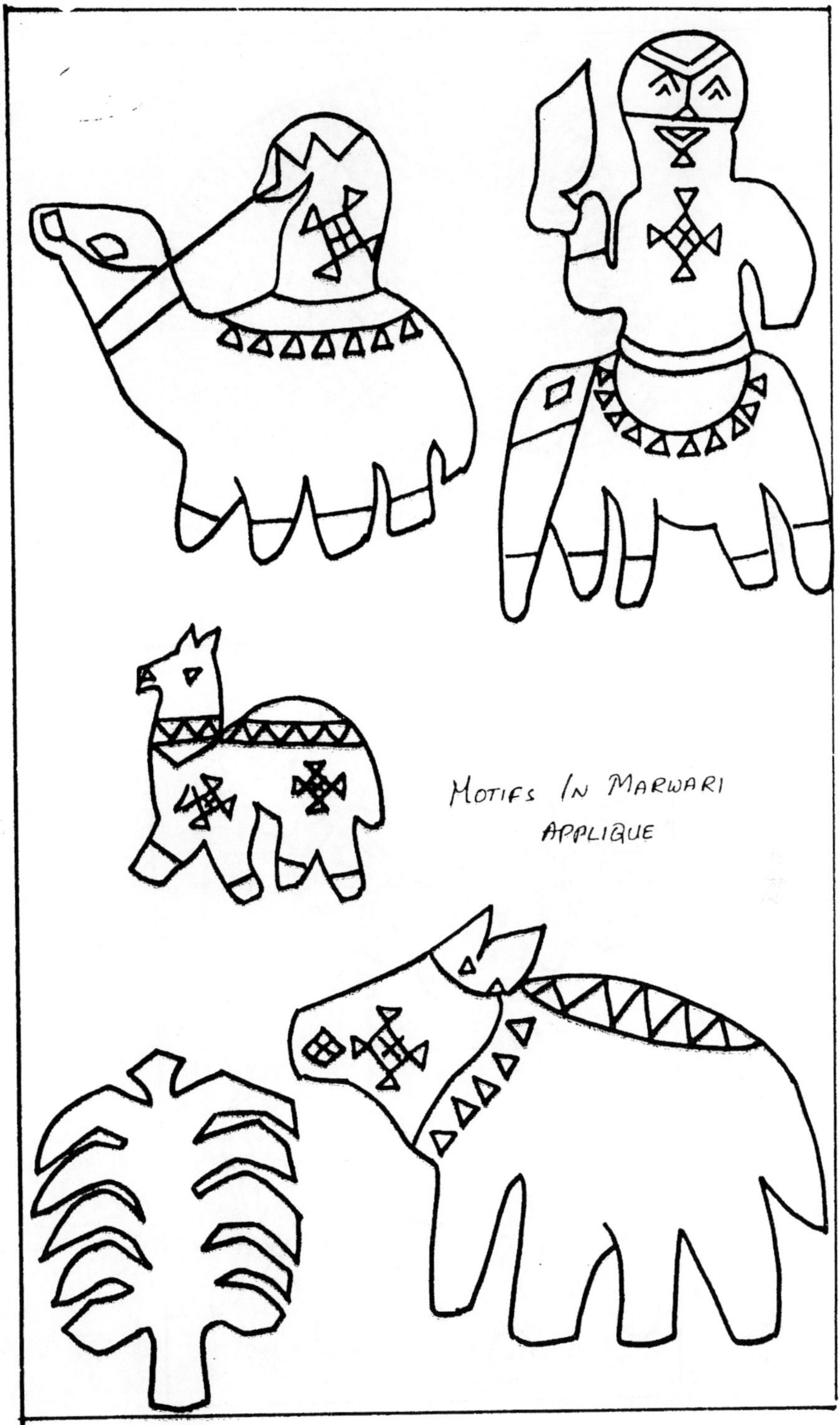
MOTIFS IN MARWARI
APPLIQUE

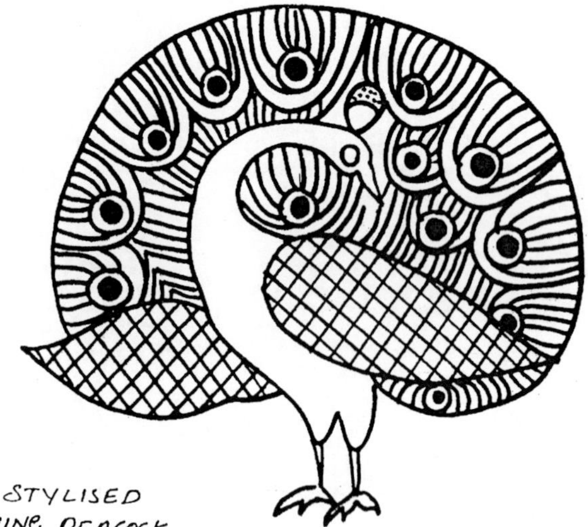

STYLISED
DANCING PEACOCK

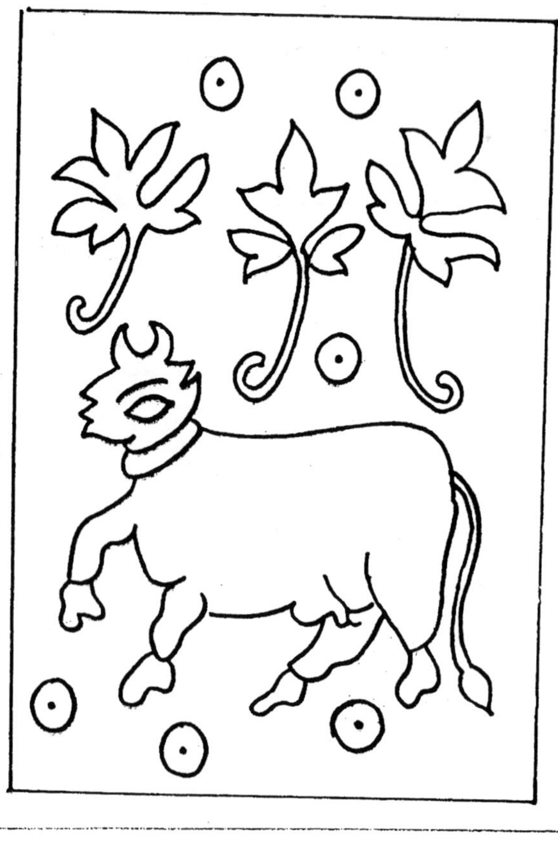

STYLISED
COW

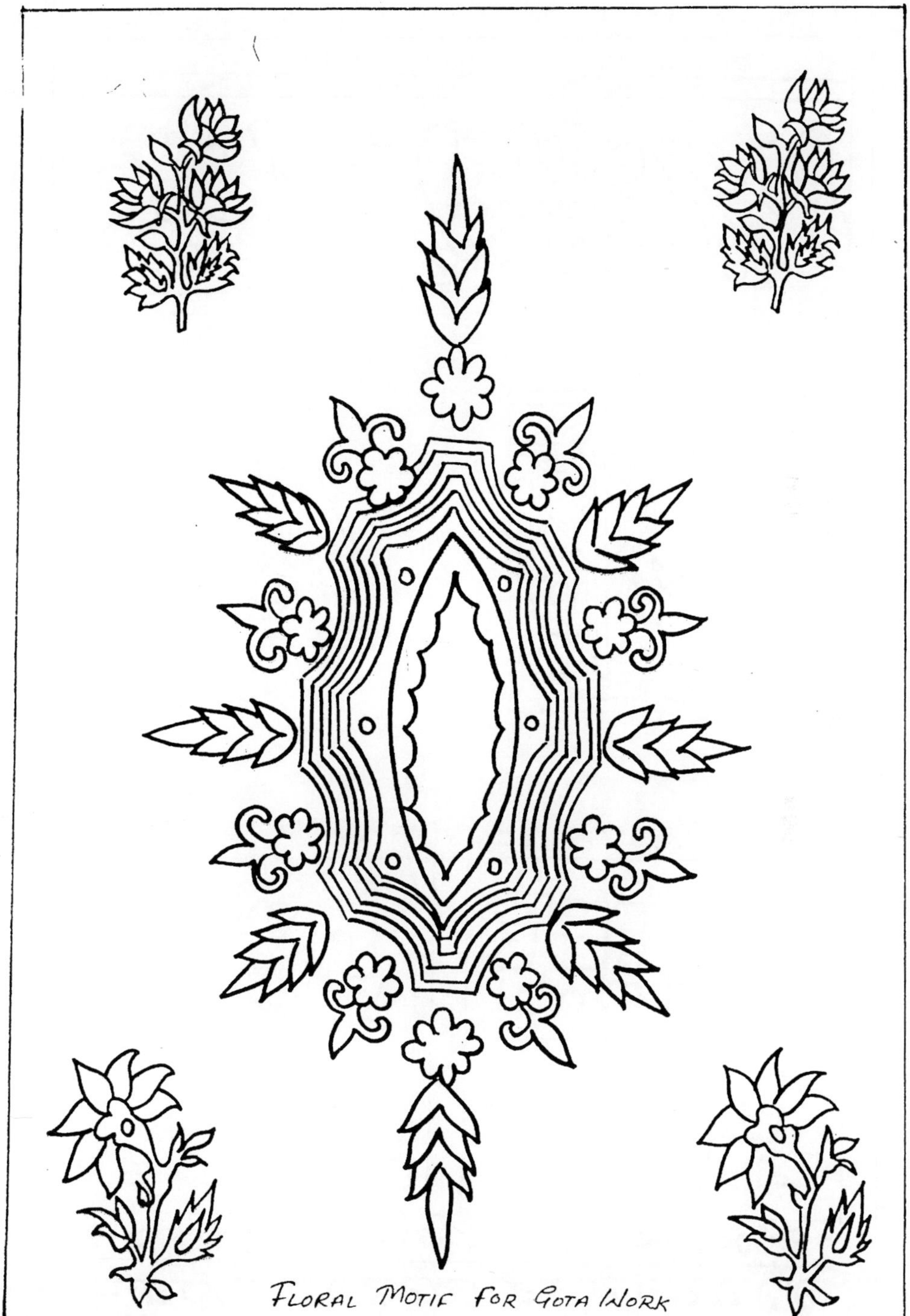

FLORAL MOTIF FOR GOTA WORK

BORDER DESIGN IN MOCHI BHARAT

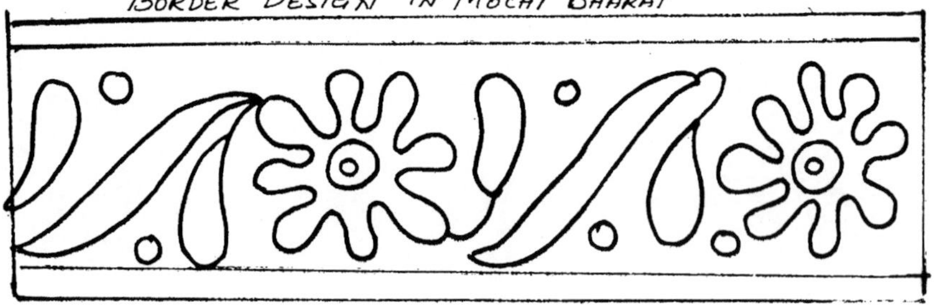

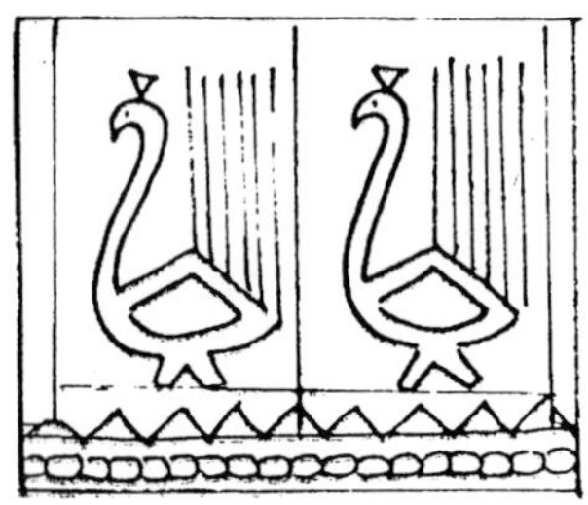

BORDER DESIGN IN MEO-CRAFT

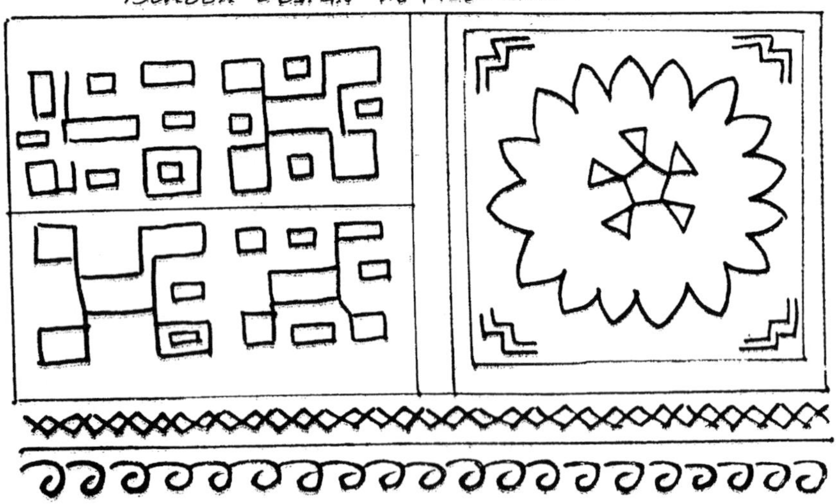

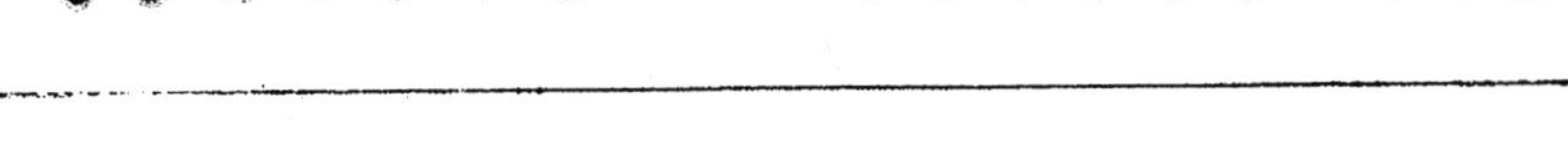

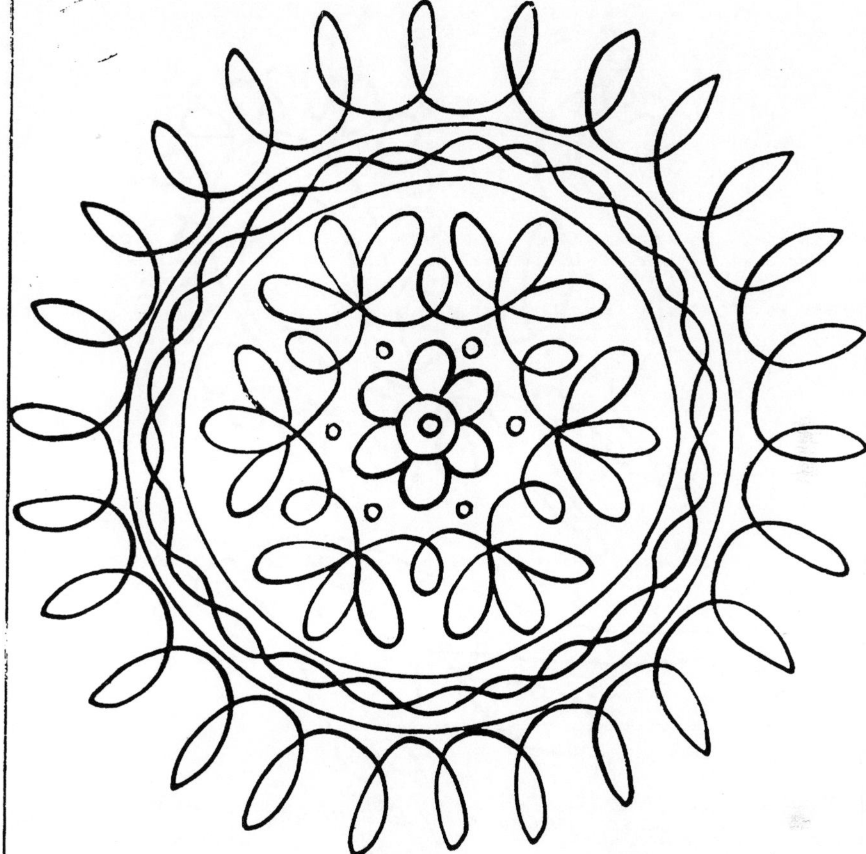

STYLISED LOTUS IN MOCHI BHARAT

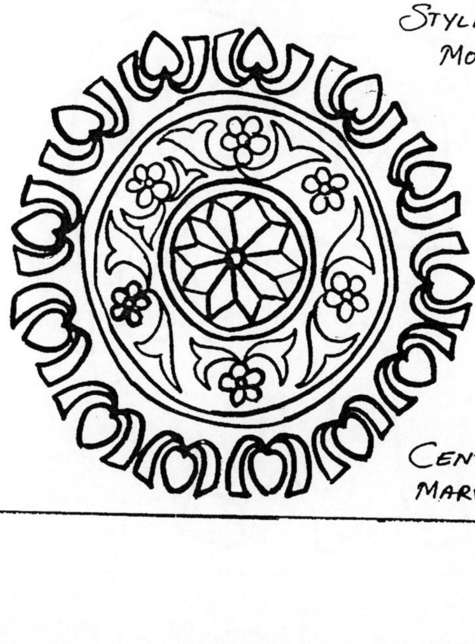

CENTRAL MOTIF IN MARVARI APPLIQUE

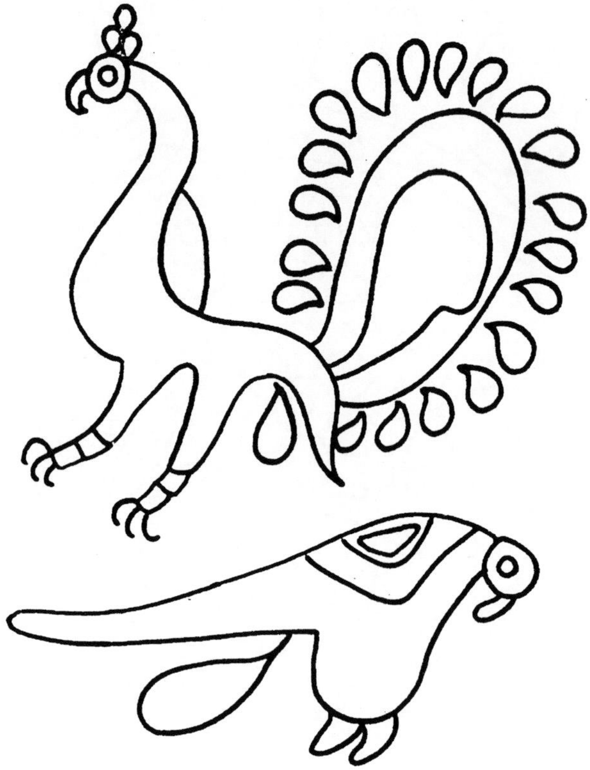

STYLISED PEACOCK AND ELEPHANT

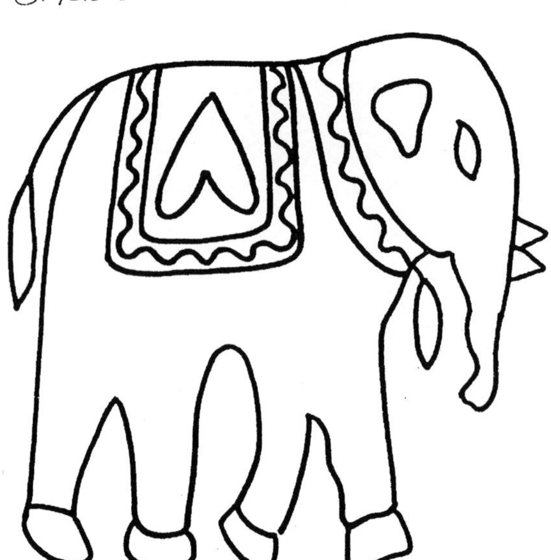

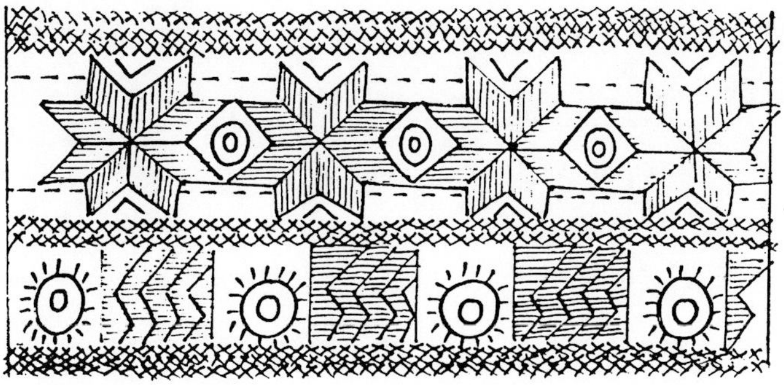

MOTIFS IN HEER BHARAT

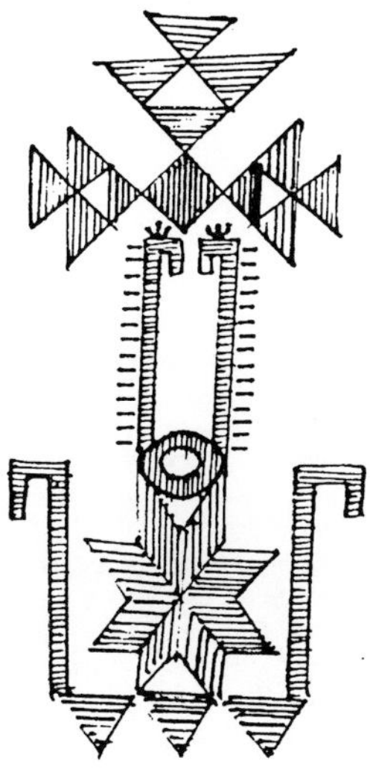

BORDER OF JAISALMAR GHAGRA

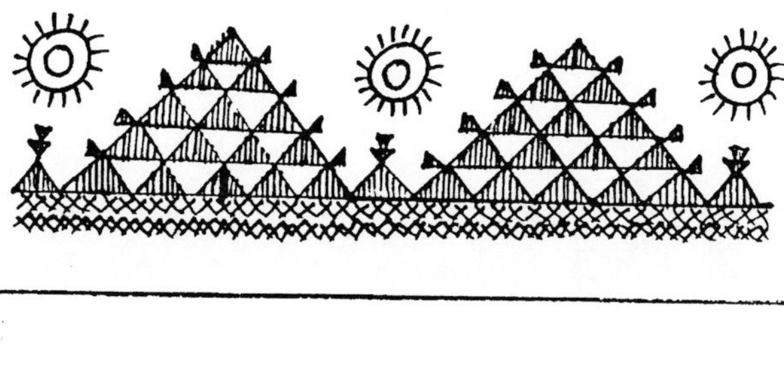

CHAPTER 11

CHIKANKARI OF UTTAR PRADESH

Chikankari is famous as 'shadow work'. It is a very delicate work of Lucknow. There are number of tales narrate about the birth and development of this subtle art.

Jasleen Dhamija explains two stories. A princess of Murshidabad, who was professionally a seamstress and highly skilled in handwork, married to the Nawab of Outh. As a token of love and affection the princess embroidered a beautiful head covering and presented it to her Nawab. The Nawab was extremely pleased with the embroidered cap, worked with fine cotton thread on muslin cloth. The women of Muslim household staying nearby were jealous of princes work. The inmates of harem begaum to produce finer and much delicate work than that of the princess and that's how the great art of chikankari took birth.

A craftman named Faiz Khan practiced chikankari narrated that, a farmer Ustad Mohammad Shair Khan staying near Lucknow offered water to a traveller to quench his thirst and permitted him to rest at his residence. The traveller was very much impressed with the hospitality of Mohammad Shair Khan and inturn taught him the art of chikankari. The chikankars believe that the traveller was sent by Almighty, the Good.

Nurjehan, wife of Jehangir, the Mughal emperor introduced this art, and it was an inspiration of Turkish embroidery. However, the motifs were evolved by herself only.

This embroidery is basically done with white thread on white muslin background. Hence, it is famous also as 'White embroidery'. On narrow strips of cloth, this embroidery gives fine and delicate lacy effect. However, this white fabric is gently beautified by its sheer excellence of ornamentation.

Chikankari though done on the white muslin background now is done on fine cotton material like, voile, two × two, cambray, mulmul, organdie, chiffon, jeorgettes, nets and other similar sheer fabrics.

The motifs are traced prior to embroidery. The designs are prepared and transferred on the wooden block. With the help of engraved wooden blocks, the designs are impregnated on the material with washable colour, by simple stamping technique.

Chikankari is something like unity in diversity i.e., it includes some simple stitches like satin, back, stem, button hole and herringbone stitch, giving a clustorious effect which is simple, gentle and subtle.

There are two styles of chikankari work, flat style and knotted embossed effect. 'Bukhia' is nothing but satin stitch, which is done on the wrong side of the material and the design is delicately outlined with tiny running stitches from the right side. This sort of embroidery gives an opaque effect. The effect of fine muslin background produces a shadow appearance. The simplified bukhia is herringbone stitch. The stitches that cover the back of the cloth is herringbone style gives a shadow effect, from the right side.

'Jali work' gives an effect of open mesh or net like appearance. Sometimes it looks like drawn thread work or lace like. This effect is produced by pushing apart the warp and weft yarns with the help of needle, forming into tiny holes and are later tightened to give the cloth firmness and appearance of a net.

A similar effect like 'bukhia' is produced by minute applique work called 'Katao' or 'Khatawa'. It is a flat style of chikankari, where same fabric as that of background, is used for the intricate kind of applique work. The fabric is cut into fine rounded leaves and stitched on the background, thereby producing a flat effect. The designs are mainly floral.

'Murri' is a knotted style of chikankari, worked in the centre of flowers, giving an embossed effect. It is nothing but french knot, who resembles the rice grain in shape.

'Phanda' is another type of chikan. It resembles millet and gives a raised effect as it falls under the knotted style. This stitch is used to fill the petals, leaves, calyx etc.

'Taipachi' is a simple running (darning) stitch, used to fill the straight or curved lines in the floral design. It is mainly used to give the outlines for the design. It is a flat style.

The motifs employed are mostly flowers, foliages, creepers, flowering streams, fruits like mango, almond, birds like peacock and parrot, i.e., the motifs have been picked up from the surrounding nature.

Chikan work was done on sari borders, pallow with tiny buttas in the body of the sari, blouses, kurtas, cuffs, collars, jubbas, handkerchiefs, caps, table cloth, table mats, cushions, curtains and other household linen.

Lucknow is also been known far another type of embroidery, much different from chikankari. It is done by gold and silver called 'Badla work'. The flat metal thread is used for badla embroidery, serves as needle itself. The metal thread is passed in and out the material and pressed in the material according to the motifs, gives a gorgeous effect, fairy like appearance. The other kind of gold and silver embroidery is called 'Tilla work', where the twisted threads are stitched according to the shape of motifs, in patterns of great intricacy. The whole surface is covered with gold and silver thread like a brocade. The Kinkhab work is done on heavy velvets are used as elephants back cloth, couch covers and bolsters.

Now a days chikankari is almost commercialised where the both men and women have their contribution. The chikan work has gained the foreign market and therefore the articles are produced on commercial scale according to the demand.

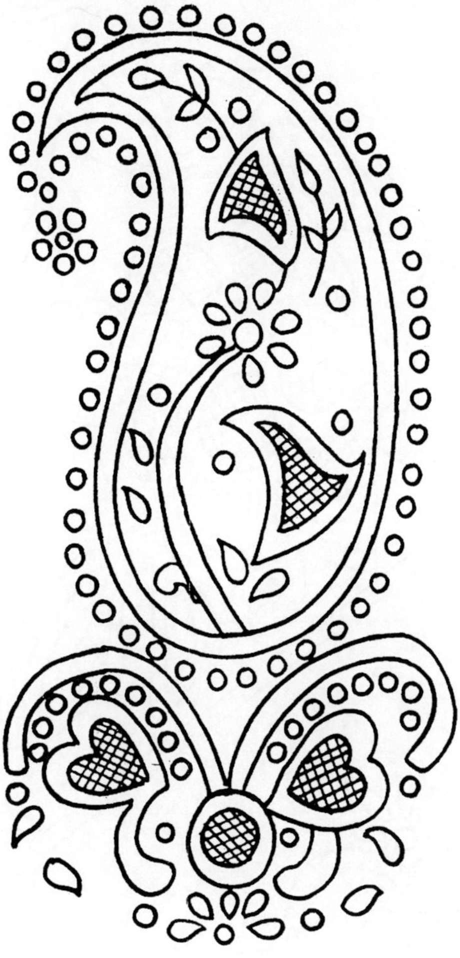

KALKA [KAIRI] MOTIF

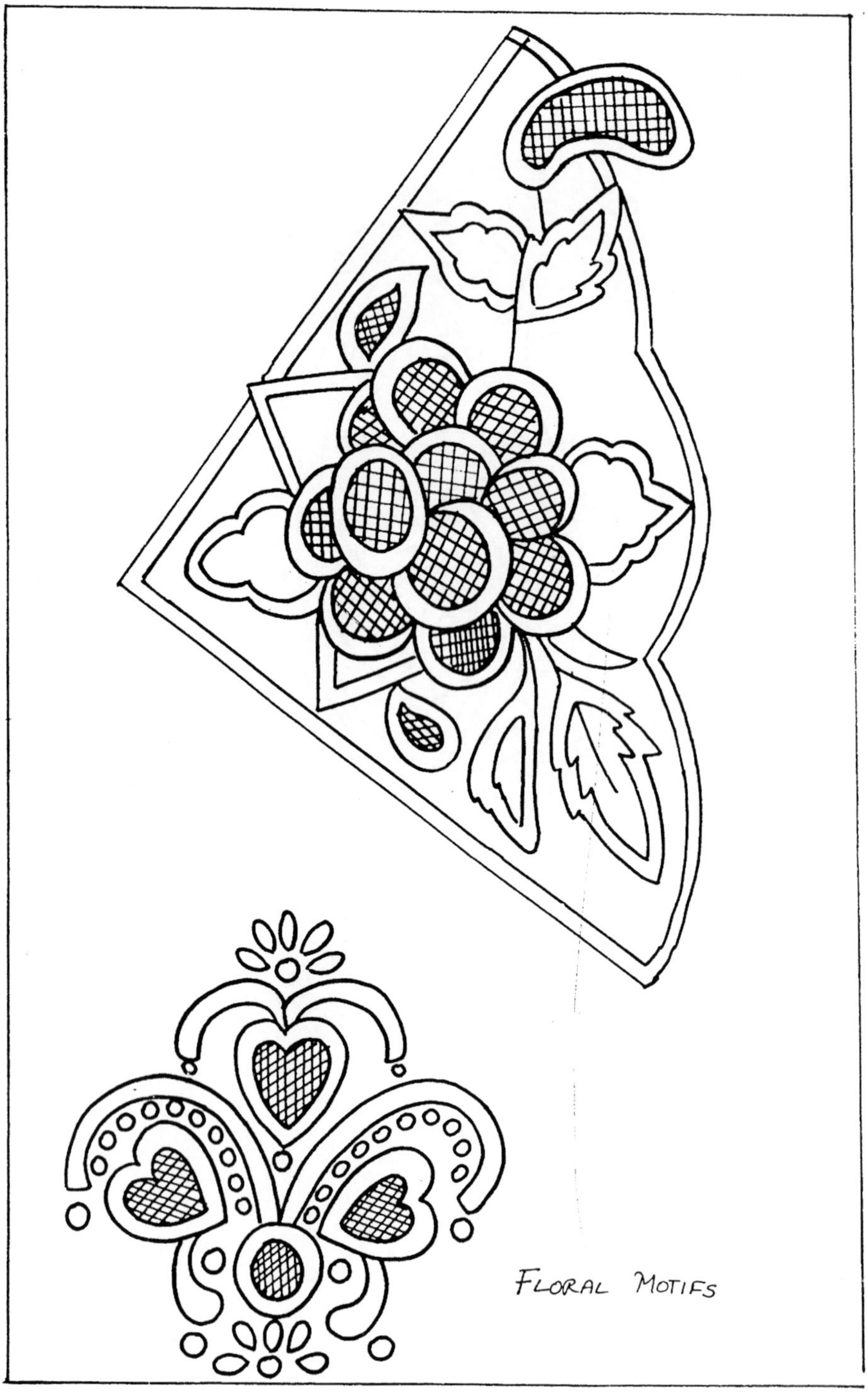
FLORAL MOTIFS

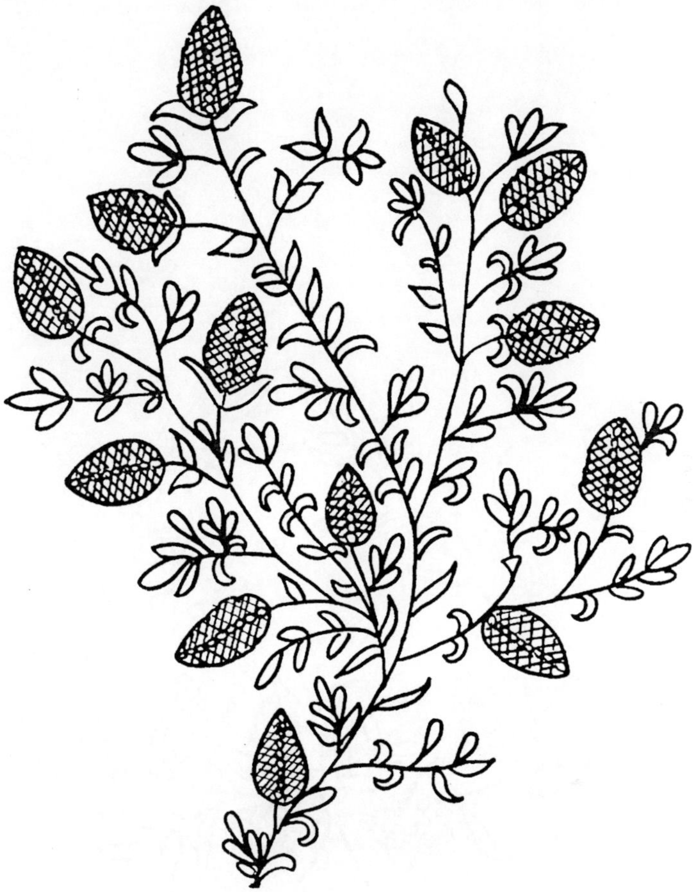

BUDS, FLORAL, FRUIDS AND FOLIAGES

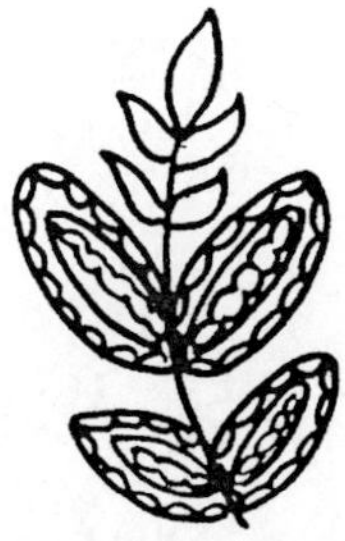

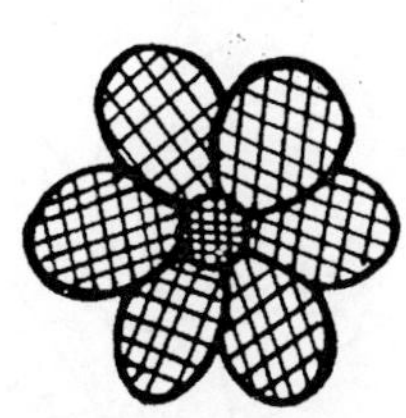

GRAPE MOTIF

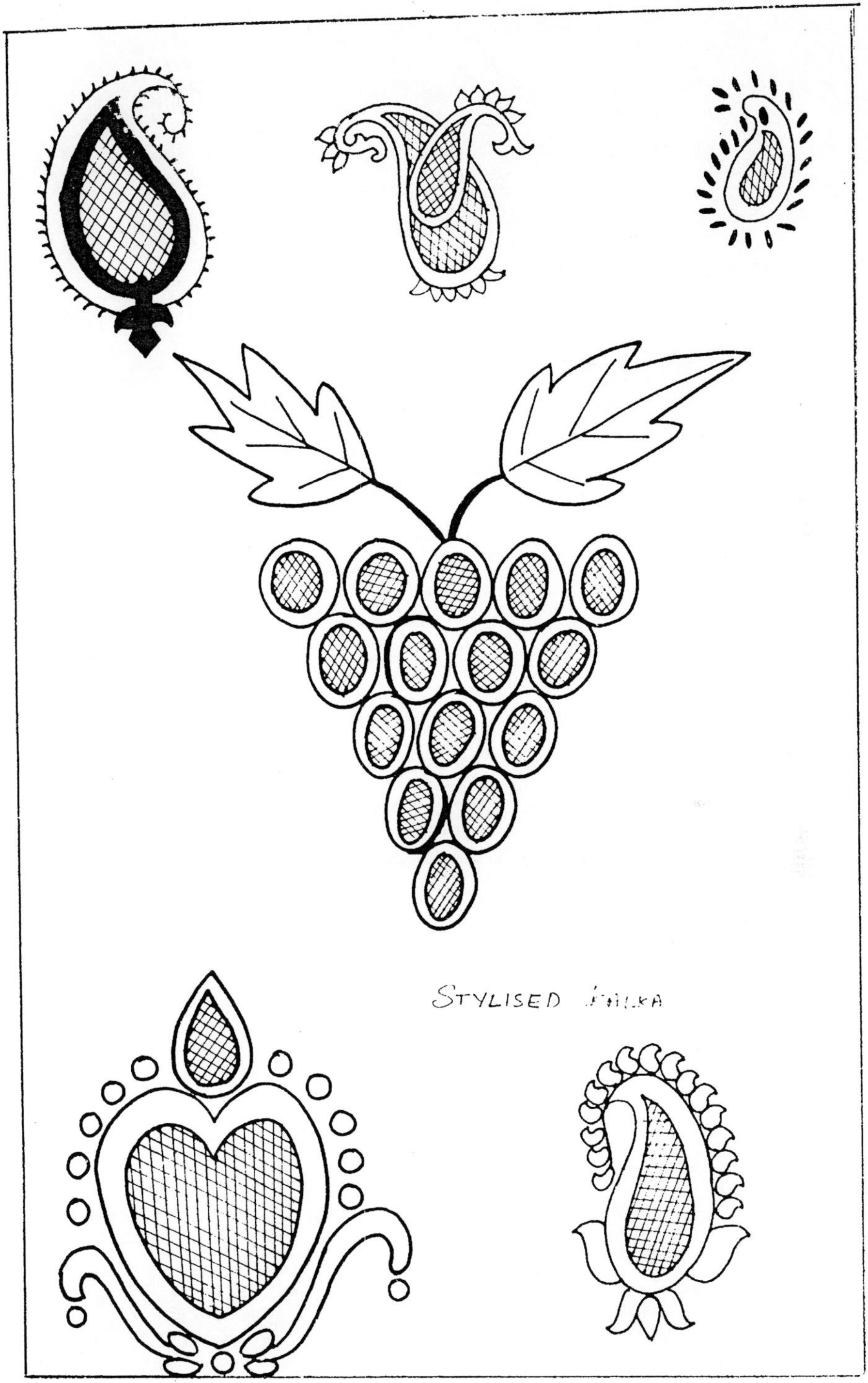
STYLISED

CHAPTER 12
METAL EMBROIDERY

Metal falls in the kingdom of textiles fibers, man-made of which gold and silver were most abundantly used in the field of textile embellishment in ancient times. Gold and silver threads were lavishly used in the manufacture of saris, precisely in the border and pallav region and to enrich the surfaces by embroidering both costumes and the associated accessories. The embroidery done with metal wires is called Kalabuttu or Jari (zari) work, class by itself, has its origin at France i.e. the romance of gold lace manufacture traces back to France, as the birth place. Among the outstanding, famous and gorgeous embroideries, probably metal embroidery seems to be the earliest and the most ancient. Even in the Vedas and Epics references have been made on gold and silver embroidery. This fine work was skillfully done on the fine, light weight and the most durable muslin cloth, one of the world famous traditional textiles of India. A mention was made by Magasthenes that the 'kings wore robes stitched in fine muslin with beautiful embroidery in gold and silver'. Later with the evolution of textile fibers, the Kalabuttu work was extended on silks and satins to produce magnificent brocades. However, these brocades were exclusively of sultans, nobles and other royal families. The skill and delicacy of Indian weaver and embroiderer has overtaken even the finest products of Persia, China and Europe.

A legend explains that Vasco-da-gama, a Portuguese invader had worn a gold embroidered muslin robe and tied a gold embroidered silk turban and used to rest his head on cushion finely embroidered with metal wire.

Originally, the real gold lace being imported to this country from France known as 'French gold lace'. Later this industry spread to other parts of the world and in India, it was mainly concentrated at Surat in Gujarat and Banaras in Uttar Pradesh. Even todays requirement for gold lace in greater percent is met from Surat. Earlier, it started as a small scale cottage industry, gradually the manufacture spread to southern parts, Bangalore (Karnataka) and Kanchipuram (Tamil Nadu).

The manufacturing of real zari threads was a very large industry once upon a time, has declined due to the manufacture of synthetic imitative material but despite of the high cost in the raw material, the quality and the standard of the gold lace is same as ever.

The process of preparing metal lace is very elaborate and is a highly skilled job.

VARIETIES OF GOLD LACES

There are three types of gold laces namely Pure gold, Half fine gold and Imitation gold lace. As the title suggests, pure gold is the most expensive followed by half fine and the least is imitation gold lace. Due to the never ending rise in cost of the raw material, the price of real gold lace is gradually increasing par with the cost of raw material. On the other hand half fine jari looks like pure gold lace and hence been flooding in the market is relatively inexpensive. For a layman it is very difficult to distinguish pure gold and half fine gold, which is possible only by burning test. i.e. on burning pure gold zari the residue will be gold and silver where for half fine gold it is copper and a very low percent of gold. On the contrary it is mere ash for imitation zari.

COMPOSITION OF GOLD LACE

Pure gold lace has inner core as degummed twisted cultivated mulberry silk, over which is wound silver lametta and is later electroplated with pure gold solution. Half fine gold lace has the inner core as degummed twisted mulberry silk, on which wound a thin copper lametta and then electroplated with pure gold. The inner core for imitation gold lace is twisted rayon over which artificial gold colour powder is superimposed to obtain the lustrous appearance. However, this lace gets blacken after some use. It is mostly used on rayon fabrics where quality is no criteria except cost.

There is another inexpensive cheap jari that has entered the market, famous as plastic jari. It is nothing but small thin plastic strips that are superimposed in gold colour or as per the requirement and are identified in the trade as Rexor, Lurex etc.

The process of manufacturing gold thread is an elaborate process. The silver bars are first reduced into different sizes of thin bars, the pasa and finally drawn into thin wires, the tarkashi, which later flattened, the badla and made into lametta. The uniform quality and diameter silk is dyed in yellow colour first and later wound with silver lametta. The final step is gilding where the silver lametta after spinning over the silk core is cleaned and electroplated with thin film of pure gold called kalabattu. The ready kalabattu is sold in the market either in the skein or bobbin form and the unit weight is Marc which weighs 250 gm for eight skeins.

Jari is widely used in weaving as well as in embroidery. Two main devices used to hold the material to be embroidered are Karchob, a rectangular wooden frame supported on two tripods and the other is Thapa, a wooden leg, enhance the speed and efficiency of the embroidery. The embroidery carried on Karchob are of two styles - Zardozi (zardoza) a heavier work and Kamdani, the lighter work.

Zardozi is an elaborate work usually done on coats, household textiles like cushions, curtains, animal trappings, canopies, shoes, chapels, jackets, purses and so on. The ground material for zardozi is heavy silk, velvet or satin which can hold the weight of the dence embroidery. Apart from zari, badla (thin metal strip), gijai (a thin stiff wire), sitara (a small piece appearing like a star), salma, sea-pearls are also used. The wire is twisted into the required position with the left hand is sewn on the material with right hand.

Kamdani is done on relatively light weight material small in size such as veils, scarves, caps, bonnets etc. The embroidery is done with double strand beginning with a knot. This knot also gives a beautiful glittering effect, when a small dot of overlapping satin stitches are made on it. Thousand buttis is an example of the same.

Another ancient style of badla work is called as Makaish. Badla itself is pointed and pierced through the material, cut and pressed. Usually it produced small dotted designs, however, wide variety of elaborate designs can be made by using badla. Gota-kinari, a work mainly practiced in Jaipur where fine shapes of birds, animals, human figures are cut (gota) and sewn on to the material to create a variety of texture.

Rajasthan produces a special type of leather shoes called mofdis on which heavy metal embroidery is done, a most popular foot wear in the region.

Gold and silver embroidery is practiced all over India and main ones are Delhi; Agra, Lucknow in Uttar Pradesh; Ajmer in Rajasthan, Bhopal in Madhya Pradesh, Bombay in Maharashtra, Hyderabad in Andhra Pradesh; Madras city; Kathiawar and Surat of Gujarat.

The main stitches employed in metal embroidery are chain, darning, satin, stem and couching. In Surat, this work is famous either as Badlani or Reshmi-Bharat-Kam. B.A. Gupta describes the Karchobi, a composite unit of pancha kala i.e., Kasab-tiki, use of silver and gold thread and spangles (tiki), Jhik-tiki, use of twisted metal thread and spangles, Chalak-tiki use of zig-zag thread and spangles, Jhik-chalak, use of twisted wire (jhik) and zig-zag thread (chalak), Bharat-Karachi, use of a card board to provide a raised body for the design, the material being used as padding.

The metal embroidery is regionally famous in various parts of the world and articles prepared are also unique by themselves. Bhopal is specialised in making small fancy bags, purses, Lucknow is known for both Zardozi and Kamdani, Surat for Karchobi work, Delhi for chappals and shoes and Agra for evening bags.

In the present days, this metal work is abundantly done on saris and cholis. According to Kamaladevi Chattopadhyay "there are various types of zari threads. The thicker Kalabattu is braided gold thread used in the border, while thinner thread for making lace for batwas (purses), neck strings, tassels etc. The spirally twisted gold thread is called Tirora, used for the curvatures in the design. The dull zari is called Kora and lustrous, the Chikana. The design is traced by using a wooden block or paper stencil."

CHAPTER 13

SIMPLE EMBROIDERY STITCHES

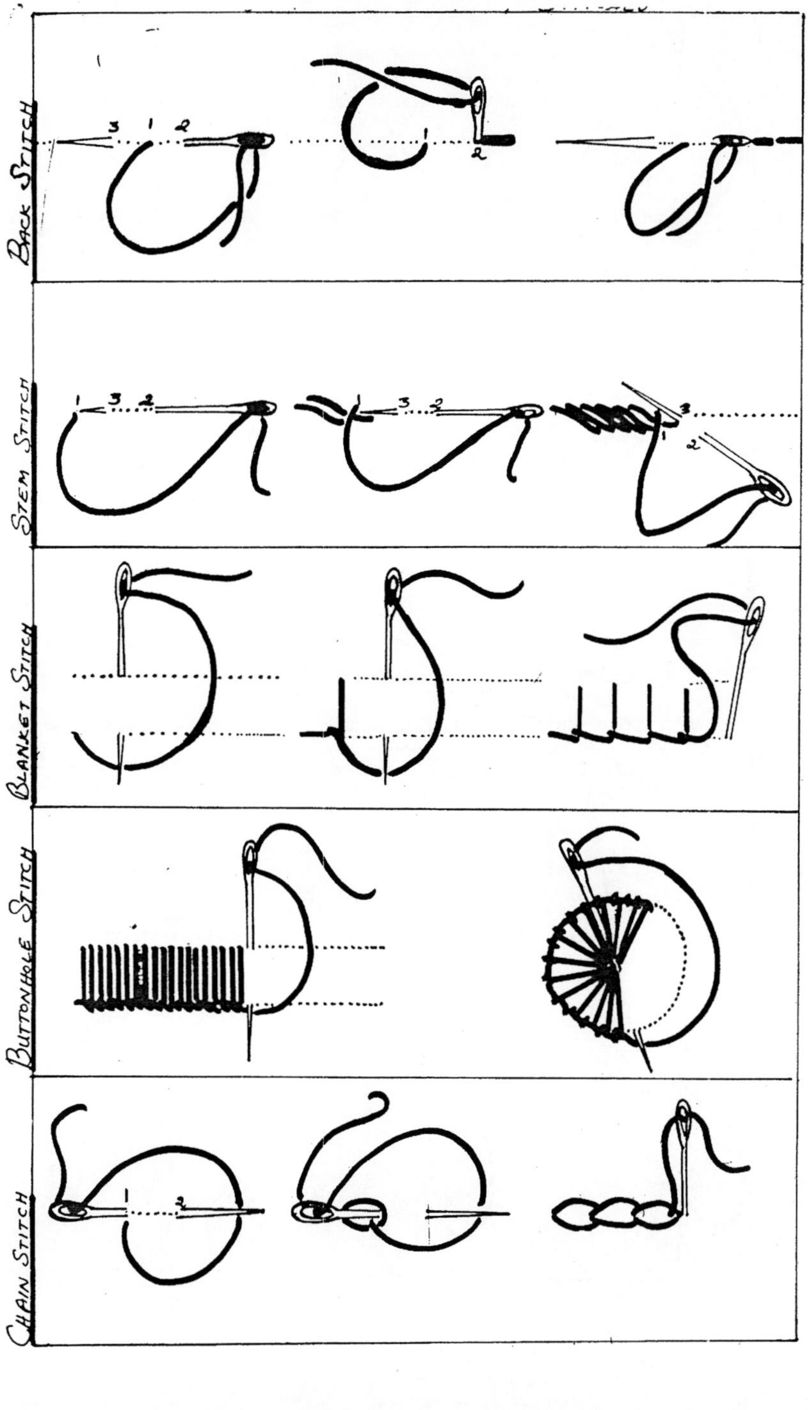

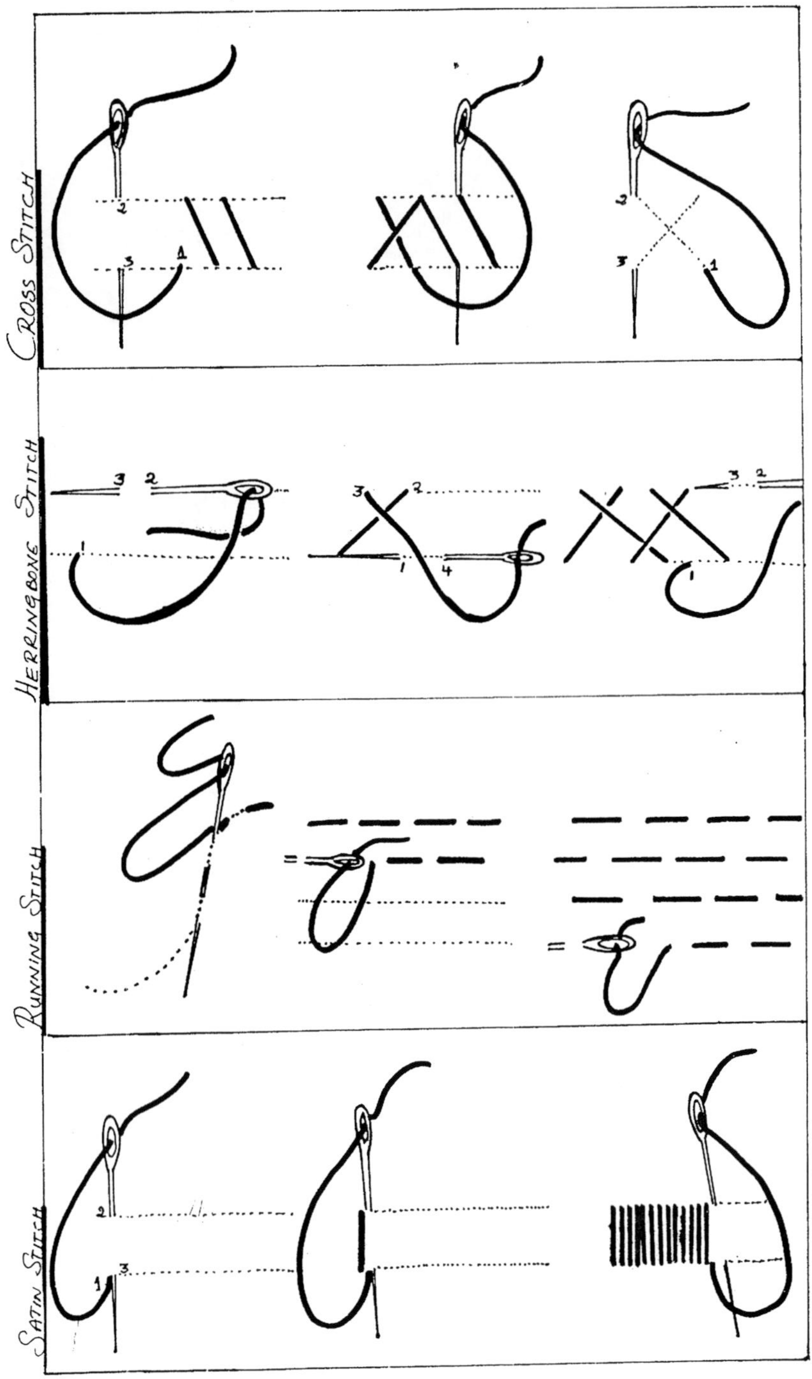
Cross Stitch
Herringbone Stitch
Running Stitch
Satin Stitch

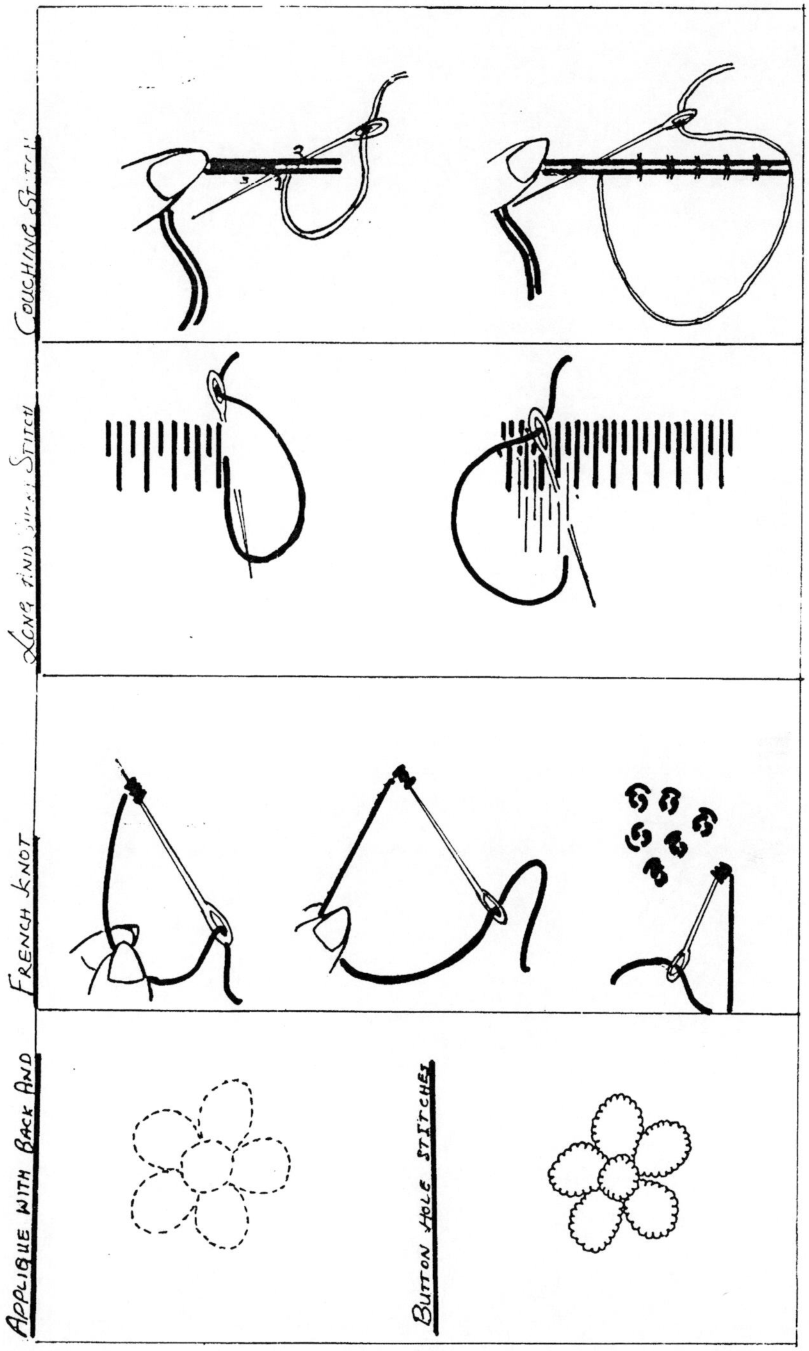
French Knot
Applique with Back and
Button Hole Stitches

Bibliography

1. Bhavnani Enakshi, Decorative designs and Craft-Manship of India, D.B. Taraporewala Sons & Co. Pvt. Ltd., Bombay, 1968.
2. Bhavnani Enakshi, Folk and Tribal Designs of India, Taraporewala Sons & Co. Priavte Ltd. Bombay, 1974.
3. Chattopadhyay Kamâladevi, Handicrafts of India, Indian Council of Cultrual Relations, New Delhi, 1975.
4. Chattopadhyay Kamaladevi, Indian Embroidery, Wiley Eastern Ltd., New Delhi, 1977.
5. Dhamija Jasleen, Living Tradition of Iran's craft, Vikas Publishing House Pvt. Ltd., 1979.
6. Dongerkery Kamala S., Romance of Indian Embroidery, Thaker & Co. Ltd., Bombay.
7. Encyclopedia of Textiles.
8. Joshi Indira Kashuti of Karnatak Popular Prakashan Bombay, 1963.
9. Kannan V.A. Gold Lace Jari, The Indian Textile Journal, Vol. XCIV, No. 8, May, 1984.
10. Kerloskar Ahilya, Karnatáka Kashida, Part I, II and III, Pushpa Bakre, Pune, 1987.
11. Mehta Rustom J., Master Pieces of India Textiles, D.B. Taraporewala Sons & Co. Pvt. Ltd, Bombay, 1970.
12. Neelam Grewal, The Needle Lore, Ajanta Publications, New Delhi, 1988.
13. Pandit Savitri, Indian Embroidery its variegated charms, Pandit Savitro, Baroda, 1976.

INDEX

E

F

G

H

I

J

K

L

M

N

U

V

W

Z